T0276375

My Dear Far-Nearness

By the Same Author

The Essential Henri Nouwen
Henri Nouwen: Writings
Rebecca: A Father's Journey from Grief to Gratitude

MY DEAR FAR-NEARNESS

The Holy Trinity as Spiritual Practice

Robert A. Jonas

ORBIS BOOKS

Maryknoll, New York 10545

Founded in 1970, Orbis Books endeavors to publish works that enlighten the mind, nourish the spirit, and challenge the conscience. The publishing arm of the Maryknoll Fathers and Brothers, Orbis seeks to explore the global dimensions of the Christian faith and mission, to invite dialogue with diverse cultures and religious traditions, and to serve the cause of reconciliation and peace. The books published reflect the views of their authors and do not represent the official position of the Maryknoll Society. To learn more about Orbis Books, please visit our website at www.orbisbooks.com.

Manufactured in the United States of America.
Manuscript editing and typesetting by Joan Weber Laflamme.

Library of Congress Cataloging-in-Publication Data

Names: Jonas, Robert A., author.
Title: My dear far-nearness : the holy trinity as spiritual practice / Robert A. Jonas.
Description: Maryknoll, New York : Orbis Books, [2022] | Includes bibliographical references and index. | Summary: "Reimagining the Trinity to be grasped inside us as three important dimensions of spiritual awareness"— Provided by publisher.
Identifiers: LCCN 2021052777 (print) | LCCN 2021052778 (ebook) | ISBN 9781626984639 (trade paperback) | ISBN 9781608339266 (epub)
Subjects: LCSH: Holy Spirit. | Spirituality—Catholic Church. | Spiritual life—Catholic Church.
Classification: LCC BT121.3 .J65 2022 (print) | LCC BT121.3 (ebook) | DDC 231/.3—dc23/eng/20211118
LC record available at https://lccn.loc.gov/2021052777
LC ebook record available at https://lccn.loc.gov/2021052778

The sixth stage [of the Soul] is glorious, for the aperture of the sweet, which the gentle Far-Nearness gives, is nothing other than a glimpse which God wills the Soul to have of her Glory, which will be hers forever.

—MARGUERITE PORETE,
THE MIRROR OF SIMPLE SOULS

The Mirror of Simple Souls, written in old French around 1290, describes Marguerite's experience of unity with the Divine. Merging Creator and created was deemed heretical, and she was ordered to cease circulating the book and her ideas. She defied the order, was found guilty of heretical depravity by the Inquisitor, and burned at the stake in Paris in 1310.

Contents

Part Three
Practicing the Persons

Preface

I approach speaking about the Holy Trinity with excitement and trepidation. The doctrine that names God as Father, Son, and Holy Spirit conveys a vision of reality that to many seems old-fashioned and abstract. Nevertheless, when explored from a contemplative perspective, I believe that this view of God offers a magnificent and empowering view of ourselves as persons on a planet that is endangered and gasping for the fresh air of a new, more sustainable world. I believe that this ancient teaching of God as One-and-Three is deeply relevant to our daily lives. What's more, its wisdom has a crucial role to play as we face today's social and ecological crises. When deeply understood, this doctrine can help all of us—whether we are Christian or not—to grow in spiritual maturity. In this book I present the Holy Trinity as a mirror in which we can see ourselves as we really are.

Drawing on my experience as a seminary graduate and a trained psychologist who has led interfaith contemplative groups for three decades, I reflect on the Trinity from three directions: as a person who meditates and prays, as a student of theology, and as someone who understands that the Holy Trinity offers us deep insight into Jesus's consciousness—and our own. Many Christians do not know what the Holy Trinity means for them personally. For many it is merely an outdated dogma. Given this contemporary avoidance, I approach this topic rather like an archaeologist coming upon an ancient ceremonial landscape. I carefully sift through layers of human consciousness and theological history, searching for timeless truths that might help us navigate our twenty-first-century challenges. In the process these questions arise: If God is a Trinity, how does this affect us personally? How might Jesus of Nazareth's awareness be like ours? How can a person *live* the Trinity? My emphasis will be on spiritual practices that follow from the doctrine and bring us to a creative and joyful awakening.

As I write, climate change, economic inequity, and a coronavirus are devastating the lives and livelihoods of people all over the world. It is a time of anguish and uncertainty, and, for those not totally overtaken by hunger, poverty, and disease, it is also a time for reflecting on who we are and what kind of world we want to create. What familiar institutions will—and should—survive the multiple crises we now face? Huge scientific and technological changes are coming, many of them driven by artificial intelligence, bio-engineering, and nanotechnology.

This book will not address directly the political, financial, technological, and social transformations needed at this perilous moment in history. Instead, my focus is to provide a pathway for a transformation in consciousness that can guide and sustain our common efforts to create a more just, safe, and habitable world. I propose a fresh interpretation of the Holy Trinity as a lens through which we can see ourselves in our natural splendor. This new perspective awakens our hidden powers of spiritual awareness, powers that direct and propel our actions. When we don't know who we really are, and act from fear and confusion, we carry out actions that, in their unintended consequences, make things worse. This book unveils spiritual practices that follow from what the ancients described as the "Persons" of the Trinity, practices that will help us to be more awake, responsive, and creative with ourselves and others. As we mature in following these practices, a trinitarian consciousness will blossom in us, one that mirrors that of Jesus Christ.

Although I have studied closely with Christian monks and ministers, scholars, and philosophers, I have also been mentored by teachers of Vipassana, Tibetan, and Zen Buddhism, Sufism, and Judaism, as well as by humanists and psychotherapists. All these encounters have deepened and broadened my experience of what it means to be a Christian and have awakened me to the divinely given treasure of awareness itself, a treasure that Christians have ignored for too long. From this broad perspective I offer the Holy Trinity as a window through which we see aspects of ourselves that have been overshadowed by the daily demands of survival, by worry and fear—a way to view life that integrates spiritual wisdom, psychological insight, and our hope for a more compassionate and sustainable world. I believe that beneath our differences of language, geography, religion, and culture, we all have the capacity to cultivate love, peace, joy, and creative self-expression. I invite readers of all faith traditions and those who consider themselves atheist or agnostic to join me.

Introduction

The trinitarian God of Father, Son, and Holy Spirit can seem speculative, and too patriarchal for twenty-first-century Christians. According to a February 2019 poll by the PEW Research Center, eight out of ten adults in the United States know that the doctrine of the Trinity holds that there is one God in three Persons—Father, Son, and Holy Spirit.[1] But most people have only a vague idea of what this means. Without reflection and instruction, we probably think of the Persons as anthropomorphic characters or mythical beings in a magical world outside of us. However, in this book (and in my life) I regard the Holy Trinity as a symbol of a transcendent Presence that is *within us and outside of us*, intimately connecting inner and outer, above and below, heaven and earth. It may be relatively easy to recite the Nicene Creed as a *belief* in the Trinity, but it is more challenging and more rewarding to enter the Trinity as if it were an inner cathedral, with stairs that bring us downward into our personal depths and stairs that bring us upward into the boundless reaches of the Divine. Read from a contemplative perspective, the Nicene Creed is written like a code that must be deciphered, a code that, when broken open, reveals a map of our spiritual awareness.

The great councils of the fourth and fifth centuries that proclaimed God as Trinity were careful not to imply that God is composed of three separate gods who exist in a heaven at another plane of reality. Rather, in my reading of the historic creeds, the three Persons are centers of subjectivity that circulate within one another, each capable of awareness and volition. Creator, Son (or Child) of God,

---

[1] PEW Research Center, "What Americans Know about Religion," July 23, 2019.

and Holy Spirit each has a distinct role to play in our enlightenment and salvation.

Creator is limitless, vast, and sacred Mystery. I can only understand this Mystery when I understand the mystery that I am. Creator cannot be adequately perceived as an object of my awareness—cannot be grasped by conceptual knowing. But God's Mystery, and the mystery that we are, can be experienced in a deeper intuitive level of knowing, which is understood in the Christian contemplative tradition as *unknowing* or as the *apophatic* or *via negativa* path. Standing in this unknowing, I realize that I don't know everything about myself—some aspects of my identity are hidden from me, some will emerge later, and some I will never know. Yet I can trust that I am fully known, understood, and loved by the Creator. Only from the place of unknowing within myself can I glimpse the vast, boundless dimensions of the Creator's love.

Son is Christianity's way of naming the embodiment of the Creator in a visible, mortal person. The Son shows us how the Creator functions in our personal relationships. I experience Second Person awareness when I sincerely say "I love you" to God or to another person.

Holy Spirit is the energizing, creative love that flows ceaselessly between the Creator and the Incarnate One, between the Creator and the created world, between the Creator and us, and between us and others. The Holy Spirit is a sacred "betweening." I experience the Holy Spirit when I sense the dynamic "we space" that connects us to others in a bond of love.

HOW DID I GET HERE?

I've always been drawn to basic questions of existence: Who am I? Why am I here? Is there a way to experience and manifest ultimate truth in a way that transcends the particularities of culture, race, nationality, gender, and politics? When I began this journey decades ago, I knew that my search for ultimate truth would fly into the headwinds of the postmodern assertion that there is no such thing as truth that transcends location, culture, race, religion, and time. But I have persisted. In praying and meditating in Christian and Buddhist traditions, I've come to think of myself as a contemplative Christian who is attracted to the revelatory power of silence. Exploring silence is one of many spiritual practices that draw seekers of all religious traditions to the hidden presence of the Divine. Although each tradition has its own vocabulary and its own ways of framing reality, I believe that, in the end, all traditions point to the same ineffable and compassionate reality.

I didn't begin to understand the power of silence, much less the common experiences at the center of all the world religions, until I was in my twenties. Growing up Lutheran in a working-class family in northern Wisconsin, I never heard that silent meditation could reveal God's intimate Presence. I was taught that divine revelation comes through scripture, belief, verbal prayer, moral behavior, and worship. In fact, it was implied that silence is an unproductive waste of time and an avoidance of work. When I was eighteen, I entered Luther College to become a Lutheran minister. However, within two years my Christian faith had begun to fade. As the war in Vietnam exploded, I transferred to Dartmouth College and majored in government, convinced that religion was irrelevant and powerless to resolve injustice and conflict.

My assumptions about the spiritual life were turned upside down at Dartmouth when I happened to walk into a class on Tae Kwan Do and Ch'an, Chinese Buddhist meditation. I enrolled in the class and gradually learned to sit still in silence, making contact with a reality that transcends intellectual understanding. During my academic classes I was trained in the best methods of Enlightenment knowledge, and after class I would let all of that go as I meditated on a cushion, slow danced the karate moves, broke bricks with the edge of my hand, and walked barefoot in the winter snows of New Hampshire, warming my feet with the sacred energy of *Chi*. I began exploring Buddhism, Taoism, and Hinduism. I still assumed that there must be only one correct way to experience ultimate Reality, one right belief, and I considered becoming Buddhist. But I also wondered whether the experience of sincere Buddhists was so different from that of sincere Christians. Little bridges of thought led me to wonder whether Jesus would have been considered enlightened if he had been born into a Buddhist society. I wondered whether Jesus had experienced *Chi*.

The value of silent meditation gradually rooted itself in me. As an undergraduate I still prayed the Lord's Prayer at bedtime, as my German Lutheran grandmother had taught me, but I was confused about which practice was better—devotional prayer on the Jesus Way, nature-centered Taoist meditation, or Buddhist silence on a cushion. While I pondered these questions, I began reading contemplative Christian texts that suggested I didn't have to choose between silence or vocal prayer. Perhaps they were both avenues into ultimate Truth, into God.

Jesus had always been a source of hope for me. Praying, especially at night, and singing hymns at Lutheran church services nourished my innate longing to feel loved, to love life, and to belong to a caring community. I am sure that attending services and becoming a youth leader at my church during high school gave me a sense of safety that offset the uncertainty, chaos, and danger in my childhood home.

While at Dartmouth I enjoyed being trained in theories of political governance, democratic history and decision-making, public policy-making, and international relations. I avoided worship services. I felt ashamed of my Christian faith, as if it were a premodern relic and fundamentally naive. It took me a while to understand that meditative silence and the artistic forms of Tai Chi could awaken a valid, nonrational kind of knowing. As I look back on these formative years, I think I was beginning to glimpse the Cloud of Unknowing (the term used by an anonymous fourteenth-century English mystic), though I didn't know that yet.[2] My yearning to trust something beyond physical existence led me to the fathomless silence found in Taoism and Zen. I still didn't understand that stillness and wordlessness could also be a Christian experience, and I had no idea how to connect my inner exploration with the demands of a competitive, intellectually demanding classroom. In my twenties, academic knowledge, Christian devotion, and Buddhistic silence were separate categories in my mind, honored in totally discrete arenas.

In the early 1970s I converted to Catholicism and took vows as a lay Carmelite. At The Common, a monastery in Peterborough, New

---

[2] William Johnston, *The Cloud of Unknowing* (New York: Doubleday, 1973, 1996).

Hampshire, I discovered the writings of St. John of the Cross, a sixteenth-century Catholic mystic and poet who practiced both contemplative self-emptying and devotional prayer. Navigating among reason, silence (alone and with others), and prayer gradually became my lifelong spiritual journey.

As I continued to transition from Lutheranism to Catholicism, I discovered the Trappist monk Thomas Merton. Although he had taken a vow of silence, Merton wrote more than fifty books, two thousand poems, and countless essays, reviews, and lectures. This gifted man had found a way to honor both the *kataphatic* (Greek: knowing with our senses, especially images and words) and *apophatic* (Greek: intuitive, wordless, and imageless knowing of the heart) pathways to holiness. I was soon devouring everything he had written. Merton revealed to millions of Christians that the *kenosis* (Greek: self-emptying; Phil 2:7) of Christ shares common experiential ground with the emptiness of Zen, with the proviso that Christian "emptiness" is saturated with divine Love.

THE FIRST KEY PARADOX

The reflections in this book rest on paradoxical assumptions. The first is that God as Holy Trinity is everywhere, beyond and within us, and that God is present in every now moment of clock-time. God's Presence is not limited to a particular time or place.

As a child I was taught that God was "somewhere else" and that if I was faithful and diligent in prayer, God could be called upon to descend into my time and place. I now believe that God is already and always present in our time and place. God as Holy Trinity abides in the depths of our personhood and is at the same time infinitely beyond us. The title of this book reflects this paradox.

Why do I emphasize that God is both inside and outside us? I do so because most believers assume that God is more outside than inside. I imagine that God would be very lonely out there all alone. And we would be lonely too. Instead, I agree with the fifteenth-century German theologian Nicholas of Cusa, who explains, "Everything that actually exists is in God, for God is the actuality of all things. . . . God who is in the universe, is in each thing and each actually existing thing is immediately in God, as is the universe."[3] God is infinite, and infinity has no location and cannot be captured in clock-time. Nicholas experienced the material world and time as a "contracted infinity." Divine infinity is contracted so that we can experience it from our limited perspective. Spiritual practices, such as the trinitarian ones presented here, help us to see through the bounds of reason and language into God's boundary-less Presence. The "everywhereness of God" was expressed by fourteenth-century Dominican friar Meister Eckhart when he exclaimed that we can "expect God . . . in all things evenly."[4] He and other early Christian mystics would say that there is no place that God is not, just as the theologians who created the Nicene Creed would say that there never was a time in which Christ was not.

But if God is everywhere and in everything all the time, what does it mean for a Christian to believe that through the Incarnation of Jesus Christ, God became manifest as a particular person in a specific place at a unique time? Are we, today, completely separate from Jesus of Nazareth, from his Middle Eastern culture, and from his life and death more than two thousand years ago? I've concluded that the incarnation of Christ was both a one-time event and an event that transcends clock-time. Eckhart helped me accept the paradoxical integration of time and timelessness, limited and unlimited reality. Speaking of Christ, Eckhart writes, "The same One, who is begotten and born of God the Father, without ceasing in eternity, is born today, within time, in human nature. . . . St. Augustine says that this birth is always happening. And yet, if it does not occur in me, how could it help me? Everything depends on that."[5] This book offers practices, grounded in scripture and in ancient Christian doctrines, that enable us to release the constrictions of reason, rigid belief, and fear that prevent us from experiencing the birth of the infinite Divine within us.

---

[3] Nicholas of Cusa, *Selected Spiritual Writings*, The Classics of Western Spirituality, trans. and ed. H. Lawrence Bond (Mahwah, NJ: Paulist Press, 1997), 140, 179.

[4] Meister Eckhart, in *Meister Eckhart: A Modern Translation*, trans. and ed. Raymond Bernard Blakney (New York: Harper and Bros., 1941), 250.

[5] Blakney, 95.

God is not a separate being who created the cosmos from some-where outside it. God transcends the limits of time and space. We can acknowledge this while also affirming that the incarnation of Christ two thousand years ago was unique and definitive. The incarnation was unique because it opened a wormhole between eternity and each moment in the clock-time of our lives.[6] God is always right where we are.

When Eckhart said that Christ is born in us, he obviously didn't mean that there can be a literal rebirth of Jesus of Nazareth within a person. He meant that there is a divine formless Presence within the limited forms of our daily lives. This Presence is here, now and now and now. Transcending clock-time and space, this Presence is always present. But we don't always perceive this Presence if we are embedded in clock-time and space, attached to the sensory and material world. Christians name this Presence *Christ,* who *was* born and is *always being born* in the infinity of our hearts. We become aware of this inner birth in an intuitive way as our contemplative practices blossom. When the Divine resides in the deep center of our souls and we choose to be rooted there, we can manifest the fruits of this birth with others. We can become the midwives of the eternal birth in our everyday lives.

THE SECOND KEY PARADOX

A second paradox is that we can only understand God from within God's own consciousness. We cannot prove scientifically that God exists or that God "has" consciousness. But for those of us who experience an eternal Presence called God, we trust that God as Creator has "intentionally" given birth to the cosmos and given creation an essence that is good. We have faith that God creates for good purposes and that the consciousness of creatures emerges from our infinite Source in God. Following the Great Flaring Forth about fourteen billion years ago, consciousness as we humans know it has gradually emerged through the evolutionary process and from the divine seed

---

[6] In physics, a wormhole is a hypothetical connection between widely separated regions of space-time.

of consciousness that is eternal.[7] Consciousness is both within us and beyond us. Our personal consciousness is a unique location of the infinite field of awareness that is Creator's.

Scripture and the recorded wisdom of contemplative Christians through the ages suggest that God's awareness circulates within our own awareness. God is within everything we experience—our sensations, visions, and memories, our feelings of grief and joy, of hope and despair. Our understanding of God changes dramatically when we understand that God's free awareness is the background or infinite stage within which all our personal, everyday experiences occur.

Whether we know it or not, our ego self-awareness is potentially in union with the infinite awareness of God. Our awareness dances across the transparent boundary between our ego-self "I" and the divine Self "I." Our ego self-awareness is grounded in clock-time, in our personality, an identity that is usually bound to our mortal and conditioned experiences. But if we take seriously St. Paul's statements, that our very bodies are members of Christ, that we are temples of the Holy Spirit, and that we have the mind of Christ (1 Cor 6:15, 6:19; 2:16), then we realize that we are each gifted with an unlimited Self that is grounded in the eternal God. Daily spiritual practices help us to know, speak, and act from the Self as much as from the self. When we manifest Self-awareness with others, they will experience not only our personalities but also a certain Light, and a lightness of being in our presence. With God's grace, as we practice meditation and prayer in solitude and with others, we are freed from attachment to our worries, and to the past and future. When we stand in God's awareness, in our larger Self, we witness and bless the everyday concerns of our ego-selves and personalities, but we are also free of them—available to love and be fully alive.[8]

---

[7] The popular name for the initial conflagration of the cosmos is Big Bang, but I favor a name that was coined by Passionist priest Fr. Thomas Berry and cosmologist Brian Swimme, the Great Flaring Forth. See Thomas Berry, *The Great Work: Our Way into the Future* (New York: Bell Tower, 1999); and Brian Swimme and Mary Evelyn Tucker, *Journey of the Universe* (New Haven, CT: Yale University Press, 2011).

[8] St. Irenaeus, Greek bishop (second century CE) is often quoted as saying, "The glory of God is a human being fully alive." Some translations say

Living as temples of the Spirit is a challenge because our ego-selves want to be in control. But actually, when ego is in control, we feel constricted and limited in our love and our creative powers. Our self-consciousness confines us, so we don't feel Nicholas of Cusa's contracted eternity; we only feel contracted. When we surrender to God's awareness within us, we feel seen and known in the eyes of our Creator, known with an ambience of care, mercy, and liberating love. Such an experience of the Divine stands in stark contrast to the belief that has burdened too many Christians over the years: the belief that God is an external, patriarchal being who is eager to find fault and condemn us or who is essentially uninterested in and absent from his creations. Harboring such a belief does damage to one's soul and spirit and limits our understanding of God's true nature. When we realize our own unlimited capacities to love, this is God as Spirit realizing God within us, and it is us realizing ourselves (1 Cor 2:10–11).

TRINITARIAN CONSCIOUSNESS

I believe that consciousness is a product of the biological evolutionary process and is also a direct gift from the divine Mystery. Moment by moment our consciousness springs from our genetic inheritance and also from God's consciousness. There is a holy Presence within us that includes and transcends our personal presence. Science cannot say exactly what or where consciousness is, because we cannot study awareness as though we were on the outside looking in. In the same way we cannot stand outside of God and look at God, because God is both within and outside us. But we are always participating in God's consciousness, if we know how to look.

Christians use the word *Christ* to name a mortal person who lives fully from within God's larger, vastly inclusive awareness. This is why St. Paul, who had experienced a deep spiritual transformation, could say, "Now, not I, but Christ in me" (Gal 2:20). In fact, I assume that when we release our self-centeredness and our

---

simply, "For the glory of God is a living man; and the life of man consists in beholding God." See Irenaeus, *Against the Heresies*, trans. Dominic Unger (New York: Paulist Press, 2012), book IV, chap. 20, para. 7.

self-consciousness, our awareness participates in God's awareness. This can be a frightening realization because our ego-selves assume that our awareness is a personal possession. We can never say that our awareness *is* God's awareness, but neither can we say that our awareness is *separate from* God's awareness. Releasing our grip on the ego-self view, we can participate in the Holy Trinity, allowing the Trinity within us to participate in our personal seeing, hearing, and knowing. Still, detaching from our ego-views will never completely dissolve the ego, so I might amend Paul's declaration. He could have said, more accurately, "Now, my ego 'I' *and* God's 'I' within me." This latter statement resonates most clearly with the Christian idea of incarnation and personhood, wherein we are taught that Jesus Christ was fully human *and* fully divine. Our personal incarnational journey mirrors the incarnation of Christ.

INTERSUBJECTIVITY

St. Augustine described the Holy Trinity as Lover, Beloved, and the Love that flows between. The fifth-century Greek theologians who composed the Nicene Creed suggested that the trinitarian God is a *perichoresis* (a "dance-around").[9] I believe that at the heart of the Trinity, Love is dancing.

According to the mystical theologians who authored this defini-tion of God, three aspects of God's Presence are rotating or dancing as One, and these aspects are called *Persons*—the First, Second, and Third Persons of the Trinity. These three Persons are relationally distinct appearances of Love, but they are not separate. The One God is not three gods. When, in the Book of Genesis, we read that we are created in the image and likeness of God, the Hebrew word for God in this case is *Elohim*, often translated as plural. suggesting to some theologians that the inner life of the Creator is multidimensional and

---

[9] *Perichoresis* derives from the Greek verb *perichorein*, sometimes translated "to make room for one another." The related Greek verb *pericho-reo* is found in Gregory of Nazianzus (d. 389/90). See G. L. Prestige, *God in Patristic Thought* (UK: SPCK, 1964), 291. See also Brian T. Scalise, "Peri-choresis in Gregory Nazianzen and Maximus the Confessor," *Eleutheria* 2, no. 1 (February 2012).

intersubjective. As creatures we are children of the Creator, gifted with divine DNA. All of God's creatures are kin. We are each an ineffable mystery that is multidimensional and intersubjective to the core.

When we practice prayer, meditation, and contemplation, we can visualize and even experience the perichoresis and align ourselves with this divine dance of transcendent Love. Recognizing trinitarian perichoresis as our essence, our spiritual awareness is revealed as a participation in each of the three Persons of the Holy Trinity. We are fully alive, and our awareness moves in a threefold dance of

- being open and present in each moment, letting go of our inordinate attachments to things, events, people, and memories, awakened into Creator's boundless mystery and love (First Person);
- relating with God and other beings in intimate interpersonal ways, in sincere and responsible I-Thou and I-thou relationship (Second Person);
- participating in Spirit-led communities that embrace all persons and the rest of the natural world in an ultimate intersubjective unity (Third Person).

Although what I propose in these pages is a radical reinterpretation of the Holy Trinity, it is one that is entirely in keeping with scripture and with traditional Christian understandings of God. I expect that some theologians will take issue with my approach because I bypass most academic theological perspectives. Still, I will use valuable theological terms that point to spiritual experiences available to any dedicated seeker.[10]

Father Henri Nouwen describes the spiritual journey as a "furnace of transformation."[11] This journey is not easy and can't be undertaken if we settle for understanding the Holy Trinity as nothing more than a religious concept. Living the Holy Trinity is a difficult and rewarding

---

[10] Approaching the Holy Trinity as three dimensions of human consciousness has been explored beautifully in theological terms in S. Mark Heim, *The Depth of the Riches: A Trinitarian Theology of Religious Ends* (Grand Rapids, MI: Eerdmans, 2001), and works by Raimon Panikkar, such as *Christophany: The Fullness of Man* (Maryknoll, NY: Orbis Books, 2008).

[11] Henri J. M. Nouwen, *The Way of the Heart* (New York: Ballantine Books, 1983), 13–17.

discipline that requires seeing through the scaffolding of our personalities. I can't promise that the trinitarian way makes everything easier. In fact, in following this path we might actually feel our inner distress and the suffering of others more keenly. Psychiatrist and Auschwitz survivor Viktor Frankl often said that "what gives light must endure burning."[12] Trinitarian transformation offers us a way to let God burn away all that is not love. This fire does not destroy the ego but renders it *transparent* to divine Presence. This is the dance of love that is always happening and always available to us.

---

[12] See Frankl's excellent book, recounting his experience in the Nazi death camps, *Man's Search for Meaning: An Introduction to Logotherapy* (New York: Simon and Schuster, 1959, 2006).

PART ONE

INTRODUCING THE DOCTRINE OF THE HOLY TRINITY

1

Naming It

EARLY ORIGINS

The Trinity story begins in the Book of Genesis, when Creator "speaks" creation into existence (Gen 1:1–4). According to this mythic story, a divine Voice announces the birth of the cosmos. Christians identify this Voice as the First Person of the Holy Trinity, who speaks to Moses and the prophets, and to Jesus of Nazareth. This Voice conveys a Presence that cannot be seen or heard with the senses. We might say that it comes from an infinitely fecund Nowhere. All creation is birthed from this "formless void" as a sacred wind or breath (Hebrew: *Ruach;* Greek: *Hagios Pneuma*) sweeps over the face of all that is coming into existence. The Voice of the Creator says, "Let there be light," and suddenly there is light. God announces that light is good and separates light from darkness. Our binary complicated world of beauty, good and evil, tragedy and paradox, is born.

First there is nothing—no time, space, or objects. Suddenly there is something, and also *distinctions*. One by one, different aspects of the world appear: light, dark, seas, earth, sky, seasons, green-growing things, and in short order, all the creatures of the world, including whales and humans. Members of the Abrahamic faiths—Jews, Christians, and Muslims—believe that this cosmic unfolding arises from and is sustained by an invisible Presence who "existed" before time and space.

Most contemporary Christians don't interpret this so literally; we value the discoveries of science, which show that over millennia, single-celled, multi-celled, and complex, conscious creatures emerged in the evolutionary process. The creation did not unfold in literally seven days as the Bible states. However, as we integrate faith and science, we do believe that the magnificent seed of all that is, was sown in the cosmos about fourteen billion years ago and has been sprouting and evolving in myriad forms ever since. Genesis tells us that everything that exists, including the ongoing duration of biological evolution, emerges from a conscious Source who is ever present and who pronounces everything "very good." Somehow, our existence is seeded with intentionality, suggesting a purposeful intelligence that is beyond our comprehension. Our faith also suggests that Creator has no beginning or end, and that time and space are born from within this eternity. Yet it is possible to have a direct experience of this formless and eternal Creator—an experience that is discovered and nourished by prayer and contemplative practices.

How is it possible to have an experience of something that is not bound by time and space? Devotees of the Abrahamic religions will likely agree that Creator, who "existed" before the birth of the cosmos, still exists. This ever-present Presence witnesses and sustains everything in the material world. Our everyday moments move along in clock-time, beginning with our births and concluding with our deaths. But all along the way our everyday moments are passing through God's invisible Presence. St. Augustine speaks of this awareness when he writes that he perceives all creation as the immeasurable sea of the infinite Creator.[1] He did not believe that the created world *is* God, but rather that God's Presence shines through every living and nonliving material thing. How did Augustine learn to see the infinity of God in all things? By engaging in what today we would call spiritual practices, such as prayer, liturgical celebration, meditation, and contemplation. Then, as now, spiritual practices are affected by our understanding of the Divine—a topic that the great councils of the church wrestled with in the early centuries after Jesus's death.

---

[1] St. Augustine, *The Confessions of St. Augustine*, trans. Edward B. Pusey (New Kensington, PA: Whitaker House, 1996), Book VII, Chapter V, 1602–6.

THE GREAT COUNCILS

In the Hebrew scriptures, God is One. Who, then, is Jesus, and what is his relationship with God? In the Gospels we learn that Jesus listened and spoke to the Creator, whom he called Father (Greek: *Pater*; Aramaic: Abba). It is important to know that Jesus of Nazareth was a Jew. He often said that he was born from the One he named Father, that he listened only to the Father, and that he perceived only from the inner Ground of the Father. He acted only in accordance with what the Father did (Jn 5:19, 36). He asks his followers to have faith in the Father and to do what the Father wants, but he also tells them, "You have never heard his voice or seen his form" (Jn 5:37, 8:38). Jesus's Abba was, and is, formless and infinite.

Jesus's contemporary followers experienced the Creator (Abba) in Jesus's presence so vividly that they struggled to understand who he was. Was he human just as they were, or was he something more? Why were so many people healed in his presence? What did he mean when he asserted that "the Father and I are one" (Jn 10:30)? How could he fulfill his promise to send them the Holy Spirit after he died—the same holy wind of the Spirit who was there in the Genesis creation story (Jn 15:26)? Wasn't the Holy Spirit already present? Perhaps Jesus was a prophet, a reincarnation of Elijah, or an angel who only appeared to be human. The question of Jesus's identity and his relationship with God (along with extra-religious political dynamics) eventually led to the intense negotiations that culminated in the councils of Nicaea and Chalcedon.

After Jesus died, his followers started many different communities based on their direct experience of Jesus, their memories and stories, and an intuitive, felt sense of his ongoing presence with them in prayer and worship. They developed new individual and communal spiritual practices as they studied Hebrew scripture and the Gospels. Some members of these communities identified themselves as Jews who believed that Jesus had come among them to fulfill the hopes of the Jewish people ("Do not think that I have come to abolish the [Hebrew] law or the prophets; I have come not to abolish but to fulfill," Mt 5:17). Others felt that Jesus's mission required a definitive break with Jewish institutions. Spiritual leaders began to travel from community to community, dialoguing and debating about the emerging spiritual community that would eventually be called Christianity. Would these leaders remain devoted to Jesus the Nazarene while maintaining their Jewish identity, or would they form a new kind of religious community? They were traveling into unknown territory.

One scripture passage that ignited their inquiry into Jesus's identity and the nature of God was Matthew 28:19, in which Jesus says, "Go therefore and make disciples of all nations, baptizing them in the name of the Father and of the Son and of the Holy Spirit." This seemed to inseparably link Creator, Son of the Creator, and the Spirit of the Creator. Early Christians wondered, Are these three gods, three different appearances of the Creator, or a completely integrated Presence? In the first two centuries of the church, this text from Matthew's Gospel was considered a minor biblical passage, but eventually it came to be understood and cherished as the first explicit citation of God as Trinity. By the sixth century Christian theologians were speaking of God as both One and Three; by the eighth century the doctrine of the Holy Trinity was established as a tenet of Christian faith, following several ecumenical councils.[2]

The first two councils—the First Council of Nicaea (convened in 325 CE) and the First Council of Constantinople (in 381 CE)—established the doctrine of the Holy Trinity. In both events emperors gathered church leaders in order to identify common beliefs across the whole of Christendom. Some historians and theologians criticize these councils as politically motivated by leaders who wanted to consolidate their power under the umbrella of Christendom. But I believe that the truth is more complex. I think the motives behind these councils were political, theological, and spiritual; certain leaders did seek political power, but many of the spiritual leaders who attended the gatherings also hoped to decide on a defining and liberating story and creed that would clarify Jesus's identity and his relationship with the Creator and

---

[2] The first seven ecumenical councils are the First Council of Nicaea in 325, the First Council of Constantinople in 381, the Council of Ephesus in 431, the Council of Chalcedon in 451, the Second Council of Constantinople in 553, the Third Council of Constantinople from 680 to 681, and the Second Council of Nicaea in 787.

with Judaism. Ultimately, they worked out the doctrine of the Holy Trinity—perhaps an astonishing accomplishment, given the diversity of the participants and the ongoing struggle to define what was and was not a heresy. Why is this important?

The conciliar theologians could not have foreseen the detailed examinations of words like *consciousness, person, ego, self, Self, spirit, soul,* and *God* that would be conducted centuries later by psychologists, neuroscientists, and philosophers. Nevertheless, I am convinced that the conclusions of the councils have profound implications for twenty-first-century understandings of consciousness and provide an essential foundation for addressing ancient and new spiritual needs, longings, and challenges.

WHO ARE JESUS AND THE HOLY SPIRIT?

In the debates theologians from throughout the Middle East mined the Gospels and the rest of the New Testament for language to describe the God that appears in Hebrew and Christian scriptures.[3] The first two councils established a baseline understanding of Jesus's identity and with it, a trinitarian vision of God.[4] Soon, it was agreed that God is One in Three and Three in One—not (just) one and not (just) three. Formulators of the doctrine contended that although God is One and transcendent, God also fully manifested in a particular mortal human being, Jesus of Nazareth. God could now be experienced both as the infinite Mystery of the Creator and as a mortal human being. And a

---

[3] Many theologians have argued that important spiritual writings such as the Gnostic Gospels were deliberately left out of the canon, but this question is beyond the scope of this book and will not affect our basic trinitarian vision.

[4] The seven Ecumenical Councils (325 CE to 787 CE) did not review all the sacred texts pertaining to Christian belief, because some early documents had not yet been discovered. For example, the Gnostic Gospels, including the recently popular Gospel of Thomas, were not discovered until 1945, when they were unearthed near the Upper Egyptian town of Nag Hammadi. In my opinion, even if they had been included early on, they would not have fundamentally changed the articulation of the Holy Trinity as I explore it in this book.

human being could be experienced both as bound to the timeline of the finite and timeless. It was a bold paradoxical proclamation. Their experience of Jesus as they read the Gospels and as they prayed and celebrated their liturgies led them to believe Jesus when he said, "Whoever has seen me has seen the Father" (Jn 14:9).

By the end of the fourth century the theological conferences concluded that Jesus was *equally and simultaneously human* and *divine*, but this conclusion didn't come easily. Acrimonious debates had addressed a host of paradoxes. For example, Jesus had said that when in his presence one was also in Abba's Presence. But he also declared, "The Father is greater than I" (Jn 14:28). Making their way through the apparent contradictions, the theologians decided that some beliefs could not realize the whole truth of Jesus and his mission. These beliefs were set aside as heresies. Was Jesus more mortal (the heresy of Arianism) or more divine (the heresy of Eutychianism)? Was he actually human, or did he just appear to be human (the heresy of Docetism)? Did Jesus have a human soul or was his soul-place occupied by the eternal Logos (the heresy of Apollinarianism)? Year after year binary conceptual solutions to the paradoxes were pruned away.

In many cases participants struggled because they wanted a logical solution, one that would respect the dictates of reason while looking for a deeper view of mortal and immortal reality. Reason suggested that Jesus must be *either* a mortal human *or* a god, but this view did not survive the debates. In one key move the councils vehemently rejected the works of Pelagius (390–418 CE), who suggested that we can improve our lives by our own free will and by following various ascetic practices without divine help. The theologians felt that this view would tragically separate the Presence of God from our mortal reality. The solution arrived at in the Nicene Creed is one that would be described today as nondual. Not this, not that, but both this and that. Such a conclusion has important implications for all human beings. Like Jesus of Nazareth, we too are human. But we are not only mortal. Like Jesus, our mortal life is vivified by an eternal and immortal dimension. My friend and mentor Fr. Henri Nouwen often declared, "What is said of Jesus, is said of you."

By the fifth century, theologians agreed that God had a third center of subjectivity, the Holy Spirit, envisioned as the One who bridges the gap between the dualities of finite and infinite, mortality and immortality. The idea of a third binding and reconciling energy and presence between apparent opposites was not new. Belief in an ultimate tri-unity is found in ancient Egypt and Babylonia, as well as in Pythagoras's theory of numbers. But the Christian spin on the trinitarian notion emphasized God's personal, interpersonal, and loving character.

Many of the early followers of Jesus were Jews who believed that Jesus was the expected Messiah and that when Jesus breathed the Holy Spirit into the midst of his disciples, he was manifesting and transmitting the very Spirit of God. I wonder if the theologians asked themselves: When followers of Jesus had an experience of what they called the Holy Spirit, were they experiencing God directly or was the Holy Spirit only a poetic metaphor? Was the Holy Spirit something like an angel or was it a divine energy as impersonal as electricity? Was the Holy Spirit simply a channel for God's Presence or was it a direct unmediated experience of God? The doctrine of the Holy Trinity seems to have developed in response to such questions.

Early Christians were certain that Jesus was born and educated in the Hebraic tradition, and they believed that the three Persons of the Holy Trinity were all prefigured in Hebrew scripture. For example, passages like Mark 12:36 and Acts 4:24–25 make it clear that the same Spirit sent by Jesus had also animated the Hebrew prophets.

But how could Jesus send the Holy Spirit if the Spirit had already been present at the creation of the universe and in the lives of the Hebrew people? When Jesus sent the Spirit, was he simply passing along a sacred message or was he conveying a real Presence? They agreed on an answer: the Holy Spirit is a timeless Presence of God that was a principal "actor" in the moment of creation and also lives within everyone in every present now, accessible by faith. Today, a nondual interpretation of scripture and doctrines from the councils of Nicaea and Chalcedon suggests that in sending the Spirit, Jesus was making the Spirit freshly available and with new power because he had given himself to that Spirit, had become transparent to that Holy Spirit, had embodied the Spirit, and was now one with the Spirit. Just as Jesus had said, "the Father and I are one," he might have also said, "the Spirit and I are one," and "when you see me, you see the Spirit."

They accepted St. Paul's claim that we are each a temple of the Spirit, but they must have wondered: If the Spirit *is* God, is it correct to conclude that all humans are temples of God in the same way that Jesus was? They must have also pondered, If Jesus was only a wise teacher, merely sharing his opinions, why should we accept his teachings as ultimate truths? When Jesus spoke, were his followers listening to the human Jesus, to the Father speaking through him, to the Spirit, or to all three? I think these questions are immensely important because for contemplative Christians, and perhaps for others, *our view of God and Jesus affects how we see ourselves.*

THE NICENE CREED

Roughly three hundred bishops attended the Council of Nicaea in 325 CE. They would build a new Christian creed based on the Apostles' Creed, which circulated at the end of the third century and is still recited in some Christian denominations. Tradition claims that each of the twelve phrases in the Apostles' Creed was composed by a disciple of Jesus (thus the name, Apostles' Creed), but today most seminary-trained Christians assume that various spiritual leaders (not the disciples) composed this collection of beliefs and affirmations. The Apostles' Creed does not say directly that Jesus and the Holy Spirit are God. If the conciliar theologians had decided to accept the Apostles' Creed as a complete statement about the nature of God, Christians ever since might have agreed with Jews and Muslims that God is One, not Three in One.

Instead, the Nicaean leaders were strongly motivated to debate and refute the teachings of Arius, a Christian elder from Alexandria in Egypt. Arius contended that Christ was born of God in a moment in time and that he was therefore a creature, a preeminent and holy creature, but not God. Most of those at Nicaea could not accept this duality. Speaking of Christ, they felt strongly that there never was a time when Christ was not. In other words, Christ is eternal.[5] In the

---

[5] In theological terms this belief is called the preexistence of Christ, supported by Jesus's prayer to the Creator in John 17:5, "the glory that I had in your presence before the world existed."

end the council condemned Arius and the movement called Arianism, and Emperor Constantine ordered a penalty of death for those who refused to surrender the Arian writings.

The notion that Christ was (and is) God from eternity to eternity became the key feature of the Nicene Creed. Thus, the creed begins, "We believe in one God, the Father Almighty, maker of all things visible and invisible, and in one Lord Jesus Christ, the Son of God, begotten of the Father, not made." In other words, Christ was born straight out of the holy Ineffable, *not made* from material, biological stuff. Jesus Christ is said to be "consubstantial" with the Father, "God of God, Light of Light, very God of very God." The councils used the name Jesus Christ for the immortal God in the flesh, and they did not explain in psychological, experiential detail the paradox of how a mortal being, Jesus of Nazareth, could also be the eternal Christ.

It is important to notice that the Hebrew Book of Genesis and the Gospel of John each begin with the phrase, "In the beginning." In Genesis 1, the Creator and the Spirit create from nothing and bring life and Light (Hebrew: *'or*), and in John 1, Christ as Logos is represented as the co-creator of life and Light (Greek: *phos*). Thus, early Christian theologians believed that creation came into being through the Word, through the preexistent Christ as Logos. Therefore, the name Christ identifies a formless eternal Presence who "existed" before time and space, who exists in every present moment, and who exists forever.[6]

WHO IS THE HOLY SPIRIT? CONSTANTINOPLE UPDATES NICAEA

Notice again that the Creed of Nicaea describes Christ as *begotten*, not *made*, which means that Christ is said to emerge directly out of the uncaused Godhead, before time, space, and material reality, out of the holy Nowhere. This initial creed defines Jesus as the eternal Christ/God. But while this creed states, "We believe in the Holy Spirit," it

---

[6] The definitive view of Jesus as the Christ was finally established at the Council of Chalcedon in 451 CE.

does not say that the Holy Spirit is God. If the Creed of Nicaea had remained the fundamental belief of Christians, perhaps God would be considered One in Two and Two in One, a "binity"!

The next gathering, the Council of Constantinople, was convened in 381 CE. One hundred and fifty Christian leaders revised and slightly expanded the Creed of Nicaea. The Holy Spirit would be upgraded in status, becoming "the Lord and Giver of life, who proceeds from the Father, who with the Father and the Son together is worshiped and glorified, who spoke by the prophets." The Nicene Creed then presents a vision of God who is simultaneously One and Three—one God in three *Persons*, a creative solution to describe the relational identity of ultimate reality.

The Nicene Creed asserts that God the Father, God the Son (Jesus Christ), and God the Holy Spirit are each, in their own right, God. They are three *hypostases* (Greek: underlying subjective reality of persons) of one *homoousios* (Greek: essence). The three Persons were not to be understood as three gods or as three appearances of one God. Early Greek Christians used the word *hypostasis* (person) to indicate the presence of a someone, a subjective *I* who possesses agency and intentions. The Persons of the Trinity are distinct but not separate from one another. God as *homoousios* is the deep, inner "dance around" (Greek: *perichoresis*) of three *hypostases*, three divine Persons.

IMPLICATIONS FOR US

This is all dizzying for the rational mind: the oneness is ultimately three, and the three is ultimately one. When Christ and the Holy Spirit show up, the Creator shows up; and where God is, all three are present. Yet each is distinct. This idea might seem to make no sense, but maybe there are analogies from our own experience, as when, for instance, we make love, or wander in nature, or listen to music, and feel fully ourselves yet also fully connected. We can feel united with other people and creatures while also being aware that we are distinct.

Because human beings are made in the image and likeness of the Creator, Christians often say that we are children of God. Too often this identity is understood sentimentally, something nice and comforting. But it's much more than that. We know that we were born of mortal parents, but we can also say that we are begotten from the holy Nowhere of the Creator, gifted with divine DNA, and that we participate in the Holy Trinity. Some passages of scripture and some of my fellow Christians assert that we are only "adopted" by God, as if no part of us was in God before and at creation. I cannot accept the view that we humans are completely separate in time and space from the Creator. In my view, Jesus Christ was and is a mortal and spiritual doorway to the revelation that we are all born in and of the eternal God of Love. Through Christ, we too are "begotten," not made entirely of material things.[7] Most important, the contemplative Christian path offers practices to realize our begotten identity.

GOD'S PERSONHOOD AND OURS

I suggest that the English word *person* is a fruitful entry point into the practices of the Holy Trinity. I appreciate this translation of *hypostasis* because it suggests that the positive qualities that we hold dear in persons—such as consciousness, freedom, intention, and love—have their origin in ultimate Reality, in the ultimate subjectivity of God. As a matter of faith, I believe that God is the Root Person, and that each person born from God is gifted with God's infinite freedom and with great power to create or destroy. We are "children" of the Root Person. In this sense all persons, when awake to our mortal-and-divine identity, are to some extent co-creators with God.

Being made in God's image doesn't mean that our bodies look like God's. There is no image for God, and God doesn't have a body. The word *image* refers to personhood, consciousness, and purpose. When awakened in God's Presence, we are dancing the holy perichoresis of intentional, unconditional, and inclusive love. This awakening is not achieved by articulating "correct" words about God or agreeing to any established dogma. Awakening to the mind of Christ is ignited by

---

[7] One must hold this view of our divine DNA lightly because our ego-selves are always prowling for evidence that we are better or worse than others. I believe that humans are begotten in God in the ground of our being, where the ego has no power.

our sincere desire to know ourselves and to know God, because only God knows who we really are. The journey is never-ending; we can never come to a conclusion about God's identity because whatever we say God is, God also is not. God is always greater than we can know, and we, too, are greater than we know.[8] We are standing at the limit of our human understanding, using finite words to point to the infinite. Nevertheless, we must use words. When, with open hearts, we reach out to understand God as three Persons, we are simultaneously reaching inward to make contact with ourselves as whole persons.

Our words about ultimate reality—God—say as much about ourselves as they do about God. As Aristotle and Aquinas discerned in their theories of perception, we can only know what we are. We can only understand what St. Paul called "the mind of Christ" by entering into that mind ourselves. This enlightened mind perceives ultimate Reality as a God of Love, not as a belief, but rather because it has *become* love. Exploring the Holy Trinity as three dimensions of our own awareness opens up a radical new understanding of what it means to be a Christian, and a person.

Maybe the Christian elders who formulated the creeds only wanted to create a theological account of God to consolidate the Christian religious identity, but the architecture of divinity and personhood they fashioned leaves room for, and even invites, a fresh appraisal of what it means to be human. The creeds need to be interpreted in light of our lived experience and in relation to what we know about science. The Christian doctrine of the incarnation tells me that as human beings, we live in everyday clock-time, which is based on the daily rhythms and rotations of our planet and our solar system, but that we also live in nonlinear, unrepeatable time and that our consciousness is a fractal of infinite awareness. Our human personhood is born and dies in clock-time and also mirrors and manifests the infinite Personhood of God.

The word *person* symbolizes an ultimate orientation of spiritual consciousness that reveals and manifests our interdependent identity with others and the natural world. Thus, as we reflect on trinitarian

---

[8] This is a generally agreed-upon spiritual truth and analogous to the insights of psychologists and psychiatrists who recognize that much of our ordinary conscious life is rooted in unconscious dynamics.

consciousness, I'm not suggesting that each of us is fundamentally composed of three persons or of three separate viewpoints. Rather, I suggest that we can't understand God's Threeness unless we explore the trinitarian nature of our own awareness. The dynamic vision of trinitarian personhood presented here points to the deepest qualities that make relationship possible—awareness, intention, empathy, integrity, love, and compassion—all of which are rooted in the Divine. Although we may know nothing about it, we are never out of relationship with the Divine, in whom we live, move, and have our being (Acts 17:28), because we are born from God and the vestiges of God live in us.[9]

In the course of our lives we are always from someone, with someone, and to someone—eternal characteristics that are the essence of an interdependent Origin. Our identities are formed in the context of relationships, and we realize and complete our destiny within relationships. Psychiatrist Donald Winnicott famously stated: "There is no such thing as a baby. There is always a baby and someone."[10] We begin our lives in symbiotic oneness with our mother (or mother figure) and gradually realize the not-me world. In this psychodynamic view, and in the Christian trinitarian view of mature adulthood, as we grow in wisdom and carry out acts of empathy and imagination, we increasingly find others within ourselves, and ourselves in others. As mature adults we can achieve a oneness that includes distinctness and a respectful experience of otherness. We live from within interacting levels of identity. Our ego-self and our divine Self circulate within each other, and both are defined as interpersonal and interdependent. Our awareness never stays still in one position. It is like a crystalline orb that revolves through the threesome of presence and awakened unknowing (First Person of the Trinity), I-thou relationships

---

[9] Of course, we may or may not be conscious of this immanent relationship, and we may or may not be living in alignment with its moral/ethical imperatives. Realizing this relational Self requires intention and practices that we'll explore in Part Three of this book. *Vestigia Trinitatis* (Latin: vestiges of the Trinity) is a phrase often used by Christian mystics to denote the Trinity within us.

[10] Donald Woods Winnicott, *Playing and Reality* (London: Tavistock, 1971).

characterized by interpersonal love and friendship (Second Person), and justice-seeking community participation (Third Person). These three capacities of clear and kind awareness are rooted in the Holy Trinity, continually turning within us to meet the challenges of our everyday reality. This is how we become a true person.

Object relations, the psychodynamic perspective in which I was trained, focuses on the infrastructure of the ego-self, our socially and culturally constituted self—that part of ourselves that remembers and learns from our past relationships, from what we've done, from our accumulated knowledge, and from how we've handled our responsibilities. It is appropriate to honor our ego-self, which gives us a recognizable identity in the timeline of our lives. We continually access the past in order to locate ourselves and our actions in clock-time, and we gradually accumulate important knowledge from the ego-self's rootedness in material reality. We also think and imagine forward in time, planning projects and events that already change our experience of the present. But going backward and going forward in time are always happening in the present, and God is always present in this present now.

For Christians, our maturity as persons is based on our faith in Jesus Christ, who lived in both clock-time and eternity. We assume that when Jesus spoke sentences using the personal pronoun *I*, this *I* was grounded in the linear timeline of his personality as it had developed in this family and community, and also in eternity, because he was at once born of Mary and begotten of Creator. Like Jesus, our spiritual identity (Self) is rooted in eternity and includes and transcends our ego (self) in clock-time.

Viewed in this light, the Christian doctrines that emerged out of the early councils suddenly become much more than theological abstractions or myth. We begin to see that we have a great deal in common with Jesus Christ. Like him, we too live at a crossroads where the timeless meets the time-bound, and it is clear in scripture that Jesus wants us to dance at that crossroad with him. I believe that it is possible to be aware simultaneously from the vantage point of our ego-self and from the vantage point of the Divine within us—from what Thomas Merton called our transcendent True Self. Our True Self infuses and embraces our everyday ego-self but also transcends it, because it is rooted in God, who is the author of time and who has chosen to incarnate (that is, to live within time and space, within our material reality). When we are operating simultaneously from within the ego-self and the True Self, the walls of our ego-self become transparent to our eternal True Self. Living this transparency, our *I* perceives, knows, and learns from the standpoint of everyday practical reality *and* from the standpoint of God's Presence. When I make the sign of the cross over my breast, the horizontal movement symbolizes my mortal life, birth to death, and the vertical movement symbolizes my eternal life. My heart beats at the crossroad of time and eternity.

The contemplative Christian journey is thus a pilgrimage into the Holy Trinity. We can come to know our true personhood and the trinitarian mind by becoming them, and in so doing, discover who we are. We can experience ourselves within the mind of Christ now simply by noticing that we are aware. If you close your eyes now, there is awareness, and if you open your eyes, there is awareness. As long as you live, there is awareness. God's Presence lives within our awareness and can be glimpsed in our daily life and natural capacities—as we touch, feel, smell, imagine, and know. Awareness is free of what we are aware of, and God lives within this free and boundless awareness. For Christians, we might say that awareness itself is God's Presence, which is always here, but we're usually too busy and preoccupied to realize it. Later in our brief time together we'll explore specific practices that release the trinitarian mind from the confines of our ego-self minds.

PERICHORESIS IS OUR INTERBEING

The councils of the fourth and fifth centuries affirmed that God is an everlasting, dynamic, relational Love. They believed that this dance is always taking place in ultimate Reality. I assume that this dance is happening now, within us, and that it animates all relationships in the cosmos. But due to ignorance and sin, it often lies undiscovered, an untapped source of wisdom and creativity.

Another Latin term for this dance-around (in addition to *perichoresis*) is *circumincessio*, suggesting a mutual indwelling. I'm drawn to the perception that all beings are within God, and when we are consciously participating in the holy *circumincessio*, all beings dwell within us. There is, in this sense, no such thing as an individual. The Three of the Godhead circulate within each of us, conveying a Love without conditions in three interactive arenas. We manifest the inclusive trinitarian vision in our communities as different moves in the dance of love. As the author of 1 John declares, "God is Love, and those who abide in Love abide in God, and God abides in them" (4:16). True persons abide and dwell in God and with others, with a keen eye to appropriate boundaries between self and other that avoid separation and honor otherness.

I believe the interdependent dance of awareness (perichoresis) is a Christian near equivalent of *interbeing,* a term coined by Vietnamese Buddhist monk Thich Nhat Hanh.[11] We are individuals, but in our depths we *inter-are* with others and with nature, and we are within the *inter-are-ness* of God. As a child, I was aware that all the farmers in the vicinity of my great-grandparents' land in Berlin, Wisconsin, worked from before sunrise till late at night. On Sunday mornings they gathered for worship at church, and on Saturday nights they met at the grange to dance. My grandfather, Fred Radenz, played fiddle in a polka band. I treasure the memories of these hardworking people dancing, drinking Wisconsin bottled beers, exchanging news, talking about their problems, and then returning to the sawdust-covered floors to smile broadly and whirl each other around. Likewise, when we open our lives to this perichoresis of care, we move among three dance partners and three inward dance floors—perceiving ourselves and others in the humble unknowing of the great Mystery, in the I-thou intimacy of friendship and marriage, and in our communities of care, celebration, and creativity.

Our faith is that the perichoresis of the three Persons was happening even before the Great Flaring Forth, eternally unseen and yet powerfully present. If we are inspired by the Genesis account of creation, we can imagine that the seed of this dynamic dancing consciousness cracked open in the nanosecond after the Great Flaring Forth and continues to be a part of the ever-expanding cosmos of more than two trillion galaxies. I believe that a full flowering of this trinitarian

---

[11] Thich Nhat Hanh, *Interbeing* (Berkeley, CA: Parallax Press, 1987).

consciousness happened in Jesus of Nazareth, and through his life it became available to everyone as the mind and personhood of Christ, within which we are both distinct from, and united with, others. This expansion of trinitarian reality through Christ does not mean that we should become carbon copies of Jesus. I glimpse the perichoresis in the sawdust dancing of my great-grandparents. Each of us is challenged to live the personhood of Christ in our own unique ways.

Thich Nhat Hanh's beautiful vision of interbeing calls to mind Jesus's prayer to the Creator, "As you, Father, are in me and I am in you, may they also be in us" (Jn 17:21). Jesus opens the way to this interdependent, intersubjective reality, and he shares it with us. From within this boundless interdependent identity, we can see ourselves in others while maintaining our distinct identities. This is trinitarian awareness: in each moment, one-and-many.

Spiritual practices of prayer, meditation, and contemplation gradually dissolve the hard boundary between ego-self and Self. When our divine Self opens to the infinite Light of Jesus's Abba, we convey in our relationships a precious power of healing presence that transcends us. Our ability to shine in this way is fundamentally dependent on the grace and Spirit of God, the Third Person of the Trinity. The Spirit's role as our advocate and guide was formulated by council leaders as they reflected on scriptural passages such as Matthew 10:20, where Jesus says, "What you are to say will be given to you in that hour . . . for it is not you who speak, but the Spirit of your Father speaking through you." As our ego-self becomes transparent to the larger reality of Self, our everyday awareness, our speech, and our behavior manifest the sacred Three-ness of unknowing and Mystery (First Person), interpersonal love (Second Person), and community-building Spirit (Third Person). When we perceive reality from this threefold place, the perichoresis is dancing with us, we see the world as a manifestation of this dance, and we convey the dance to others.

I glimpse this perichoretic way of living in Walt Whitman's assertion, "I am large, I contain multitudes."[12] If we mirror Christ's mind and personhood, our bodily senses are awakened, so that gradually,

---

[12] Walt Whitman, "Song of Myself," in *Leaves of Grass and Selected Prose* (New York: Holt, Rinehart, and Winston, 1949), 76.

every sensation, sound, thought, sight, and emotion in our everyday lives becomes transparent to God's Light and is harmonized in the love of Christ. Our bodily senses and our knowing become, as it were, lit from within by grace. Memory, imagination, and pleasant and unpleasant emotions are transformed.[13]

We are complicated creatures, and without a spiritual North Star we can easily become lost in a dark wilderness of reasoning that is based on self-interest and binary either-or thought. John Ruusbroec (1293–1381) was a Flemish priest and mystic. In his great work *The Spiritual Espousals* he describes First Person experience as a "superessential unity" that harmonizes apparent opposites like action and contemplation, self and other, time and eternity, solitude and service, joy and sorrow. I think he would have agreed with the conciliar conclusions that Jesus was a person who perfectly integrated ego-self and Self. But I also suspect he would say that we are all called to embody this superessential unity. For Ruusbroec, our deep interior is a "double mirror," with one face receiving images and insights from the Divine, and the other face receiving corporeal images and information through the senses.[14]

We need a trustworthy and resilient ego-self. One of my colleagues, the clinical psychologist and Buddhist teacher Dr. Jack Engler, often said, "We must have a self in order to empty ourselves of self." I understand the value of the word *empty* in this context, but I would fine tune Engler's notion by suggesting that we will always need a vivid and resilient sense of self and self-agency. Thus, I prefer the word *transparent.* Jesus was fully human, with a culturally defined ego-self, and he was fully transparent to Abba, and he is the

---

[13] Many mystical theologians have opined on the transformation of our physical senses, including Evagrius Diadochus, Origen, Macarius, St. John of the Cross, and Hans Urs Von Balthasar. See Balthasar's chapter "The Spiritual Senses" in *The Glory of the Lord: A Theological Aesthetics,* Vol. 1: *Seeing the Form,* trans. Erasmo Leiva-Merikakis, ed. Joseph Fessio, SJ, and John Riches (San Francisco: Ignatius Press, 1982), 365–407.

[14] John Ruusbroec, "The Spiritual Espousals," in *John Ruusbroec: The Spiritual Espousals and Other Works,* intro. and trans. James A. Wiseman, OSB (Mahwah, NJ: Paulist Press, 1985), 78, 79, 110, 132, 135.

archetype of who we all are. Our everyday self is the location for our transfiguration.

Realizing our True Self can't be "accomplished" as a self-help, ego-self project. It is only realized by God's grace within us, through the Spirit. When transfigured, we *inter-are* in the Spirit. At a given moment we may not be consciously thinking about God, but that doesn't matter. God's presence does not depend on our thoughts. If this were so, when we forget to think about God, God would be gone. But God is never gone. God is always interbeing in our hearts, so we are never alone, even when we're alone.

2

The "Persons" of the Trinity

Living a trinitarian awareness can bring "the peace that surpasses all understanding" (Phil 4:7). In other words, this is a peace that is not based on cognitive reasoning, but rather on something we *are*. Living in this way requires conscious practices, employed both in silence and solitude, and in community. Later I will share practices I've learned and taught in my decades of spiritual guidance. For now, let's look more closely at each of the three Persons of the Trinity as they become manifest in our awareness, recognizing that even though I must consider them one at a time, each of the Three is also circulating within the others.

The First Person of the Trinity is the Creator, who can't be conceptualized or known as an object of awareness. The only way to experience the First Person is to let go of our images, opinions, and judgments—even our cherished theologies—about God. St. Teresa of Avila believed that we can only do this when we descend into the nameless, sacred Self-hood at the center of the soul, what she called the "interior castle." I understand this castle to be a sacred dwelling place in our souls that is free of social conditioning, free of our ego-self narratives. On our way into this castle, we find guidance, inspiration, and comfort by believing in the qualities of God described in scripture, such as love, tenderness, mercy, and forgiveness. But to finally enter, we must be naked, without any belief; our protective clothing of language and ideas has been burned away in a furnace of transformation. Standing in the interior castle we can "know" the Creator only by faith and an intuitive practice of unknowing.

I am attracted to conceptual knowing because that has been my training, but also because it feels safer and somehow more solid than unknowing. Standing on the ground of my intellectual understanding, I feel sheltered by what I know, and in control. Yet I can only experience the total mystery of the Creator when I jump off the edge of my intellect and trust that as I fall into the unknown, I will be "caught" by the ineffable Lord of life. As the Tibetan teacher Choygam Trungpa often said, "The bad news is that we're falling, but the good news is that there is no bottom."

First Person awareness is experiencing everything from within our interior castle, which has no walls. From this spacious perspective, everything flows freely, never impeded by fear, judgment, or attachment. This ancient awareness, gifted to us in our spiritual DNA, is present to all objects of awareness but unattached to them. To be "un-ensnared" is to be free to respond rather than to react. In today's spiritual landscape, being "un-ensnared" is often called detachment.[1] I learned about detachment from Vipassana Buddhist teachers, and I learned from Christian contemplative teachers that the freedom that arises in this practice does not come from self-help efforts, but from the Creator who is the gracious source of freedom and who is within us as the First Person of the Trinity. When we are embedded in our personalities and ego-selves we cannot really practice the First Person dimension of our personhood.

Teresa's interior castle is a placeless and timeless place within us. Christ's self-emptying is this placeless place, kindly and mercifully detached from time and space—always present, witnessing and listening for Love. This interior castle is where we find the eternal life that Jesus promised (Mt 19:29; Jn 3:15, 3:36, 4:14). Buddhist teachers have taught me how to detach from my limited language and give myself to the open and spacious reality beneath my intellect. As a result, I now see a deep resonance between the Buddhist term *emptiness* (Sanskrit: *śūnyatā*) and Christian self-emptying. This awareness witnesses and welcomes everything, whether pleasurable or painful. Thich Nhat Hanh writes:

---

[1] St. Teresa of Avila wrote, "What power is that of a soul brought hither by the Lord, which can look upon everything without being ensnared by it! How ashamed it is of the time when it was attached to everything!" *The Life of Teresa of Jesus*, trans. and ed. E. Allison Peers (New York: Doubleday, 1960), 200.

The word *emptiness* should not scare us. It is a wonderful word. To be empty does not mean to be nonexistent. If the sheet of paper is not empty, how could the sunshine, the logger, and the forest come into it? . . . "Emptiness" means empty of a separate self. It is full of everything, full of life. . . . Emptiness is the ground of everything. "Thanks to emptiness, everything is possible [says Nagarjuna]."[2]

His words echo St. John of the Cross, who counseled that we empty ourselves of all self-seeking mental and emotional operations so that God might infuse the vast inner space of awareness with God's living Presence. St. John's darkness and stillness arise from his longing to love and his desire for the invisible Presence. In this un-ensnared Love, we too are set free for creative, loving, and ethical relationship; we are no longer enslaved by the opinions of other people, by our habitual judgments, or by the unquestioned norms of our culture.

The Second Person of the Trinity lives most vividly in devotional prayer and in the I-thou love that we experience with family and friends. Jesus as the Second Person discloses the First Person. As he says in John 14:9, "When you see me, you see the Father [Creator]." Jesus knew that he was also a mortal person, so I think that he more accurately meant, "When you see me, you see Creator's Divine Love, and you also see Jesus of Nazareth, a faithful Jew and friend."

Second Person awareness invites and blesses friendships, partnerships, and marriages characterized by compassion, love, and commitment. This aspect of our awareness is exemplified by Jesus when he says to his disciples, "I do not call you servants any longer, because the servant does not know what the master is doing; but I have called you friends, because I have made known to you everything that I have heard from my Father" (John 15:15).

Second Person practices invite us into the intimate I-thou relationship that Jesus shared with the Creator. We experience this devotional practice when we pray, sing, or dance as if Creator is right

---

[2] Thich Nhat Hanh, *Awakening of the Heart: Essential Buddhist Sutras and Commentaries* (Berkeley, CA: Parallax Press, 2012), 421.

here and now, as our precious You. The experience might bring to
mind the erotic love poetry in the Hebrew Song of Songs. This is a
delicate awareness that some mystics have described as hanging by
the thread of God's pure love. Catherine of Genoa described this
freedom and love as if she were submerged in an immense ocean
of love, "and nowhere able to touch, see, or feel aught but water."[3]
Whether hanging by a thread or breathing within an ocean of love,
devotional prayer gives us courage to detach from the illusory
ground of our self-centeredness so that we are free to love and be
loved by others.

The Third Person of the Trinity facilitates the infinite love between
the First and Second Persons. In the Third Person we open ourselves
to the Holy Spirit who forms beloved communities of creativity,
mutual care, and compassion. All Three awaken individuals and
societies into this distinctive dance of trinitarian awareness—releasing and unknowing, cultivating friendships, and participating in the
beloved community that Jesus and Martin Luther King Jr. envisioned.
All those who are lit from within by their Personhood in Christ are,
like St. Paul, being transformed—a process that is ongoing and never
fully completed as long as we live. Next, we look at each dimension
of sacred awareness in more detail.

FIRST PERSON IN DETAIL

When we enter the consciousness of the First Person, we witness our
inner and outer experience without attachment, aversion, judgment,
or fear. We are in free fall, because the creation of everything begins
here, where there is no "before" or "after," and no "because." The
Creator, and life itself, has no "because." All we have is a spontaneous
gratitude for this brief duration of life and love.

Why did Creator create the cosmos? Some say that Creator wanted
something and someone to love. I like this interpretation, but I also
think that the Great Flaring Forth was totally spontaneous, for no

---

[3] In Michael Cox, *Handbook of Christian Spirituality: A Guide to Figures
and Teachings from the Biblical Era to the Twentieth Century* (San Francisco:
Harper and Row, 1983), 130.

rational reason. I find it helpful to think that this infinite Love just is. Just as Creator is understood to be outside the causal network of the material world. Some early theologians named God, "the Uncaused." If God had been caused to exist, there would need to be a Creator of the Creator. The Creator, who is not a being in time, just is and is eternal. The name refers to the holy Source of all beings and the entire cosmos. This unknown Source is the wellspring of all spontaneous goodness and love.

In a sense, when we call this Source "Creator," we are pointing nowhere and everywhere, because the Creator has no location. Reflect on this: The Creator has no location. Nicholas of Cusa wrote, "God, the ever blessed, is the center of the earth, of all spheres and of all things that are in the universe, and is, at the same time, the infinite circumference of all."[4] This resonates with how some astronomers and cosmologists struggle with locating the moment of creation. Dr. Stephan Martin, an astronomer in the Consciousness and Transformative Studies program at John F. Kennedy University, says that our cosmos is moving outward from the center of the Great Flaring Forth, but that this center can't be located. He asks, "Where is the center? Everywhere; the expansion is happening everywhere. Every point in the cosmos is the center. The center of the universe's expansion is in me, in you, and in your house. We're all on the edge of novelty. Every place has some subjectivity in relation to the cosmic process."[5] As children of God, we inherit this center of subjectivity and novelty as First Person awareness.

I believe that the moment just before the Great Flaring Forth is woven in our DNA at a subtle level, beneath the apparently firm platform of our intellectual knowing. All the material, causal things in our lives, and our inner narratives about reality, are significant, but deep within us the pure gift of life arises, a gift we did not create

---

[4] Some translators summarize this quotation as "God is an infinite circle whose center is everywhere and whose circumference is nowhere." Nicholas of Cusa, *Selected Spiritual Writings*, Classics of Western Spirituality, trans. and ed. H. Lawrence Bond (New York: Paulist Press, 1997), 159.

[5] This quotation is from my notes at a June 15, 2021, webinar called "The New Story of the Universe and Spirituality," sponsored by the Spiritual Life Center, West Hartford, Connecticut.

and cannot control. The holy uncaused place within our souls is born directly out of the Creator's bosom, a place from which we are free of both past and future from within past and future.

The originating holy Nothing abides within us as the First Person, out of which evolution proceeds, bringing forth diverse forms of life—whales, jaguars, humans, snails. The sacred "Nowhere" of God is eternal, existing before the Great Flaring Forth, before the past and beyond any future. Science can say that the Great Flaring Forth of time and space happened about fourteen billion years ago, but in the instant before it took place, there was only eternity. Science can't say where the expanding cosmos is going or if there will ever be an end. If the cosmos emerges from eternity and expands eternally, it is logical to suggest that this same eternity exists now in every historical moment, and that it will always exist. We were each born, and we will each die in a certain time and place, but the brief duration of our lives also lives forever in God, who is eternal.

The Christian myth of creation is a world of meaning that can peacefully coexist with the scientific view of our origin. Our view was articulated by St. Paul, who preached that the form of the invisible Godhead is named Christ, and that we are all born from the Nowhere of God through Christ, and in Christ, "all things hold together (Col 1:15–17). Born in Christ, all our contradictory feelings, thoughts, memories, and desires are brought into harmony. Of course, this can only happen for us if we consciously choose to follow in the way of Christ Jesus. He is our plumb line, guard rail, and North Star.

Silence is our doorway to eternity. It is difficult, and maybe impossible, to discover this portal to Creator if one's mind is obsessed with worries, fears, aversions, and obsessive desires. Therefore, silence must be a conscious practice. It's best to learn the practice of silence from a good and trustworthy spiritual teacher, and to begin by sitting still and doing nothing. Soon, we become able to access this silence everywhere—even in the midst of discussion and debate, interpersonal conflict, the cacophony of conspiracy theories, and fake news. When we dwell in silence—even in the midst of activities—we bring a deep listening and healing presence to others. When we inwardly access this spacious awareness with others, we move from fruitless argument and debate to truly creative dialogue. Inner silence is essential. It blossoms into action that is more likely to be wise, effective, and infused with love.

Discovering this transforming inner silence is not a self-help project, because it is an ongoing gift from the Creator, who is always present, in every second of our lives. There is a vast difference between experiencing inner silence as something we do—as, for instance, when we try to force ourselves not to think—and receiving inner silence as a free gift from the Creator. We are born into freedom, and it is our challenge to realize this inner freedom even in the midst of outward limits and constraints, and to exercise this freedom by appropriate, compassionate action. This is the way of Christ, "the first born of all creation" (Col 1:15).

These insights into awareness are echoed in other spiritual traditions. Mahayana Buddhism affirms that it is possible to see through the ego-self, which veils reality. It's possible to see things as they really are, not merely through the obscuring lens of personal wants, needs, and fears. This seeing is called *Tathata*, which means "suchness" or "thusness." Seeing things clearly, as they are, is an essential precondition for effective action and is an essential quality of First Person consciousness. This awareness comes first, before our habitual desires, opinions, and judgments emerge. As children of God, our human consciousness is a child of God's super-consciousness. Because every object of our awareness passes through the infinite space of divine consciousness, it is perceived with the fresh and new eyes of love. We are set free to respond rather than react to whatever is happening around us. This view leaves nothing out—it includes our own needs and views as well as the needs and views of others. When we see with the eyes of "suchness," we let go of pretense, wishful thinking, and fantasizing; come to terms with reality; and respond appropriately with clarity and precision when we encounter misunderstanding and injustice.

In the Book of Exodus, Creator says to Moses, "I AM who I am." YHWH adds, "Thus you shall say to the Israelites, 'I AM has sent me to you'" (3:14). God is Being itself (not *a* being), a boundless Presence with no cause, beginning, or end. Naming God as the Uncreated gives us pause. How can we imagine something that is not created, something that's not actually a *thing*? How can the timeless and placeless source of all things exist in time and space, and how can we experience what is beyond time and space? Fortunately, contemplative Christians inherit two millennia of wisdom and practices that help us to find this experience for ourselves.

Catholic theologians often say that we can be in the world, but not of it, that is, not attached to physical reality. If we could run the development of our mortal lives backward, we would see that we are here because our ancestors lived when and where they did, and because of countless material, political, and biological events that preceded us. If we could run the evolution of our cosmos backward still further, we would likewise see that our bodies are composed of elements that once circulated in the stars. And if we could run this movie all the way back to the Great Flaring Forth, we would see that eventually—like everything in the cosmos—we were born from the nowhere and no time before the Great Flaring Forth. This sacred Nowhere is within us, waiting to be set free from our ego's control.

Meister Eckhart searched sacred Nowhere and named it *Wüste*, a desert. When we first fall silent, it can feel like a sterile or boring emptiness, but if we bring a more subtle, vulnerable ear to this ultimate ground, we always discover something new. When we meditate in silence, it's always good to remember that God as ultimate Reality is Love, an infinitely inclusive love, so whatever we notice in silence is happening in love. When we descend into silence, we do so in a stance of faith, trust, and gratitude. We can be aware of and thankful for all the events and beings that have brought us to this moment, yet in the featureless desert of Nowhere, we proceed into the future without attachment to exact causes, reasons, hopes, or results. We summon our God-given courage to face the unknown, and actually to be unknown. Of course, we do value reason and causality in our everyday lives, but in the deepest level of our being—where we share in God's Being—there is no reason and no cause. This view might seem impersonal or even nihilistic, but, as Meister Eckhart contends, that is not the case. In this divine desert of awareness, we love and are loved for no "reason."[6]

---

[6] Reiner Schurmann, trans. and commentary, *Meister Eckhart: Mystic and Philosopher* (Bloomington: Indiana University Press, 1978), 71, 119. See also

Cultivating inner silence is an essential form of prayer. As Mother Teresa observes:

> We need to find God, and he cannot be found in noise and rest-lessness. God is the friend of silence. See how nature—trees, flowers, grass—grows in silence; see the stars, the moon and the sun, how they move in silence. . . . We need silence to be able to touch souls.[7]

We need silence to know our own souls, and in this knowing, we can be available to touch the souls of others.

SECOND PERSON IN DETAIL

As we've seen, I sometimes use the term Second Person to refer to Jesus Christ and sometimes to refer to a dimension of trinitarian consciousness, depending on context. The Second Person manifests the First Person as something personal and interpersonal. We can also say that, in Jesus Christ, the First Person brings the divine to us as a luminous interpersonal relationship. The Second Person as a historical being is called the Incarnation—the First Person in the flesh. Devotion to Jesus Christ awakens our own Second Person awareness, and I believe that something akin to this awareness can be awakened in non-Christians who entrust their lives to a trustworthy Someone who is a source of unconditional love, mercy, and truth.

My focus here is on the incarnation of Jesus Christ, an event that invites a host of important questions. How can Jesus of Nazareth, a man who was born of a mortal mother and who died in the Middle East around two thousand years ago, also manifest the eternal Uncaused, the Creator? If we accept that the Creator is Uncreated, how can the unimaginable, timeless, and invisible Holy Source of

---

Robert A. Jonas, "Loving Someone You Can't See," in *Beside Still Waters: Jews, Christians, and the Way of the Buddha,* ed. Harold Kasimow, Linda Keenan, and John Keenan (Boston: Wisdom Publications, 2003), 143–56.

[7] *Mother Teresa: Essential Writings,* selected with intro. by Jean Malouf (Maryknoll, NY: Orbis Books, 2001), 59.

everything appear as a mortal (created) person in chronological time? What's more, is it really possible that God appeared in only one person at only one time at one specific place on the planet? Was God nowhere else? Was God more present in Jesus's lifetime than God is in our lifetimes now? I won't focus on these important questions or try to answer them. Rather, I hope that as you reflect on the Holy Trinity, you will welcome such important questions as *koans*—questions that may have no logical, fully resolved answer but that can draw us deeper into the mystery of the Trinity.

I favor reserving the name *Jesus* or *Jesus of Nazareth* for the person who lived and died in a specific place and time, and using the name *Christ* for the immortal Presence that shone through Jesus. Jesus is mortal, and Christ is immortal; Jesus Christ is both mortal and immortal. But there is latitude here. Henri Nouwen, for example, preferred to use the name Jesus for the eternal, ever-present Second Person of the Trinity. Nouwen said that anyone's relationship with Jesus can be fully experienced now, two thousand years after Jesus died, because the Presence of Jesus is timeless. Nouwen was more interested in the immortal Jesus than the historical Jesus. Conversely, the Dominican Meister Eckhart didn't refer to Jesus very much, because he was more interested in the eternal Second Person than in the historical Jesus. He preferred to teach about the immortal Christ. But we can say that all great Christian teachers agree that Jesus Christ is simultaneously mortal and eternal. Some favor the name Jesus, some Christ, and some use both names.

Jesus tells his followers, "I am in my Father, and you in me, and I in you" (Jn 14:20). When contemporary contemplative Christians read passages like this, we don't regard them as information about a past encounter. Guided by tradition, we read such astonishing passages as words that transcend time and space, words than are transparent of linear time, words that offer us a direct experience. Jesus is assuring us that the living Christ is within us, too. Such passages can be read as if they were being spoken now and were directed to us personally. The Second Person is Jesus Christ, but through the incarnation, contemplatives affirm that anyone can enjoy the holy I-thou consciousness of, and with, Jesus. This I-thou then becomes the lens through which we experience all mortal I-thou relationships in clock-time.

Awakened in this awareness, our relationships resonate with the love, creativity, honesty, courage, and faithfulness that Jesus exemplified in his relationships.

THIRD PERSON IN DETAIL

When the Holy Spirit is present, God is present. Spirit existed before creation and was there at the moment of creation, facilitating the appearance of what is from nothing: "The earth was a formless void, and darkness covered the face of the deep, while a Spirit wind from God swept over the face of the waters" (Gen 1:2). We can image the Spirit as incredibly powerful—as an invisible living bridge from nothing to something: from nothing to a continuously evolving cosmos imbued with consciousness, governed by impersonal natural laws, and inspiring the dynamism of creative and kind relationships.

In Christian scriptures this Spirit is the connecting, relational love between the First and Second Persons of the Trinity, between Uncaused Father/Mother God and the Incarnate One who appears in ordinary time and space. The Spirit of the Uncaused Source speaks through the Bible, in nature, in each person's interior castle, in liturgies, and most clearly through Jesus Christ. The Spirit is said to live within every person as a guide, counselor, sustainer, and healer.

But this Spirit has no concrete identity—no body, shape, or form. We don't know where She comes from or where She goes. Jesus and all of us are born from within the invisible Holy Spirit, and each of us is home to the Spirit. Scripture often describes the Spirit with images from the natural world, like wind, breath, fire, or, during Jesus's baptism, a dove. This is no ordinary wind, fire, or dove: these figures are vehicles for a holy inner power, for something very real that transcends naming.

St. Teresa of Avila wrote, "The dove of Spirit refers to the flight taken by the spirit when it soars high above all created things. . . . It is a gentle and joyful flight and also a silent one."[8] She uses the image of a dove to describe the Spirit's freedom, a witnessing and a knowing that are independent of all the objects of our awareness.

---

[8] In Peers, *The Life of Teresa of Jesus,* 200.

When in contemplative practice we experience *awareness itself,* the dove of the Spirit soars, taking joyous flight within the infinite "I AM" of the Creator. When Teresa uses the word *above* for the source of the Spirit, she doesn't mean up in the sky. Rather, she refers to the complete surround sound of the Spirit-wind, which flies and sings through the canyons of our thoughts, emotions, memories, and plans. We can't see or hear this Spirit-wind through our senses and our ordinary ways of knowing. However, contemplative silence leads us downward (or upward) into another level of knowing that transforms our senses and our cognitive capacities, awakening them to the mind and heart of Christ.

PARADOX AND THE THREE PERSONS

The One in Three is a glimpse into divine paradox and a portal into ultimate truth. Paradox is not an exclusive mark of theology. In our emotional lives we sometimes experience opposite feelings simultaneously; for example, when a loved one dies, we may experience both grief that they are gone and relief that they are no longer suffering. When our son or daughter grows up and marries, we may feel sorrow as we mark the end of their childhood but also joy that they are stepping into new life. We may remember the pain of a separation or divorce but be thankful for what we learned from the trauma. Similarly, our closest love relationships may include feelings of aggression. Freud famously stated that where there is love, there is also hate. We are each one and many—compassionate and judgmental, fearful in one moment and courageous in the next. Our inner characters, each following their own script, can move within us like a dance-around of perspectives. The Holy Trinity archetype reminds us to recognize and embrace what appears to be our contradictions and opposing feelings, trusting that all can harmonize and "hold together" in the three dimensions of trinitarian awareness.

It is helpful to remember that research reveals paradoxes at the micro and macro levels of the physical world. Newtonian physics describes a linear, either-or reality, but in quantum mechanics and Einstein's space-time relativity, paradox is the norm. Space and time, matter and energy are intertwined and interpenetrating. Light is both a wave and a particle. According to quantum mechanics, subatomic particles can separate, and, even at a distance, can communicate and have exactly the same experience. A single subatomic particle can take different paths at the same time. In addition, simply observing an object can change it. On an everyday level, investigating and witnessing our emotions can change them. Becoming comfortable with contradictions and paradoxes is a fundamental skill in daily life, in science, and in all spiritual traditions. One and three simultaneously? No problem.

Jesus walks a paradoxical path, saying that something can be simultaneously first and last, that there is light within darkness, that powerlessness can be powerful, and that the innocence of a child can be a kind of maturity. In our spiritual lives the portal into the integration of these contradictions is an infinitely inclusive Love that transcends all opposites and the self-centered impulses of our everyday lives. The One in Three of Love and awareness is a dance that we can trust, and one that can bring us into new life in Christ.

MANY WAYS OF NAMING GOD

Images of One in Three have circulated for centuries in Christian churches and writings. My wife and I occasionally attend a small Episcopal country church in Ashfield, Massachusetts. One Sunday there, while singing a hymn, I noticed that the stained-glass window behind the altar has a symbol in deep, resonant primary colors representing the Trinity—Father, Son, and Holy Ghost[9]—each symbolized by a circle in a corner of a rounded equilateral triangle (see Figure 2.1).

Symbols like these are sometimes written in Latin—*Pater, Filius,* and *Spiritus Sanctus.* Each circle is linked to the others by a golden band bearing the words "is not." At the center of the triangle is a larger circle containing the word "God" (Latin: *Deus*). The word "is" links God with each of the outer three circles.

---

[9] "Holy Ghost" is another term for "Holy Spirit." It is no longer in general use in contemporary liturgies or biblical translations. The word *ghost* derives from the Old English word *gast.*

Figure 2.1. Black and white photo of stained glass at St. John's Church, Ashfield, Massachusetts. Photo by author.

This visual representation of the doctrine of the Trinity is said to derive from the Athanasian Creed. Each Person is God, and each of them *is* and *is not* the other. Father (*Pater*) is neither the Son (*Filius*) nor the Spirit (*Spiritus Sanctus*), yet if we move through the center of this symbol, we see that the Father *is* God, just as the Son and the Holy Spirit *are* also each God. This is not only a theological symbol or only a clue to Jesus's identity. It is an image of Jesus's dynamic awareness, and of ours. The First, Second, and Third dimensions of trinitarian awareness are always circulating within us.

Figure 2.2 expands on the one in the stained-glass window, filling in additional names that have been used for each of the Persons of the Trinity, including names that were not articulated by the councils of the church. Each of the three Persons is enfolded in the others as a dance-around called the *perichoresis*.

Naming the First Person as Father stems from Jesus's experience of the Creator. Growing up in a patriarchal culture, he called God his dear Father (Abba). However, given the many ways that God is depicted in Hebrew and Christian scriptures, we may be led, in our prayer and contemplation, to try out other names that refer to the First

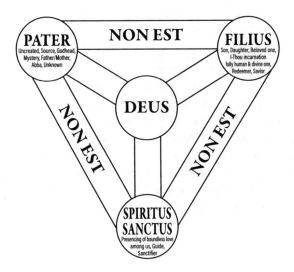

Figure 2.2. Graphic by author.

Person of the Holy Trinity. Biblical texts, mystics, and contemporary theologians have used a variety of names such as Creator, God the Father, Divine Mother, YHWH, Uncreated, Unknown, Uncaused, Jehovah, Source, Mystery, Ground of Being, Abba, Allah, and Font of All Reality. All these names point to the ultimate eternal Source of everything. The Second Person has been named Christ, Son of God, Child of God, Son of Man, Son of David, Lamb of God, Redeemer, Savior, Incarnate One, Emmanuel, the Beloved of God, and Lord.[10] But because Christ (unlike Jesus) has no gender, we can speak of Christ as the Daughter of God as well as the Son of God.

The Third Person has been called Holy Spirit, Holy Ghost, Advocate, Spirit of Truth, Breath of God, Sanctifier, Sustainer, and Counselor.

And in the spontaneity of our own prayer we may find that other terms for God well up within us. Anyone who has fallen in love

---

[10] Jungian psychologist and Episcopal priest John A. Sanford (1929–2005) wrote a fascinating book about the title Son of Man: *Mystical Christianity: A Psychological Commentary on the Gospel of John* (New York: Crossroad, 1993).

knows the pleasure of inventing terms of endearment for one's beloved.

The triune God is not a being, but rather the hidden Source of all
beings, life, and reality. We cannot see this Source with mortal eyes,
because Creator is the sacred source of our eyes and the invisible
source of our seeing. We learn what we can from the maps of the
Holy Trinity and then we let them go, because no image, word, or
framework can contain God. Like Indra's net, an image used by Hin-
dus and Buddhists to describe a cosmic net in which the interstices
of all strands hold a jewel, and each jewel reflects all the other jewels
ad infinitum, each Person of the Holy Trinity is distinctive and yet
also dancing within the other two. This dance is who we are.

3

Trinitarian Awareness

We find clues to Jesus's awareness as we contemplate the Gospels and witness how he lived out his mission of justice-seeking compassion, mercy, and hope. Jesus lived as a healer and died nailed to a cross, and he arose into a life that transcended his mortal life. The promise of trinitarian awareness is that we too can live from within the mind and heart of Christ, which harmonizes everything about us, including our suffering, and invites us to be God's witness to others. Being in the mind of Christ and enjoying eternal life does not save us from death, but it gives meaning and purpose to our lives, consoles us in our suffering, and embraces us as we let go of life into the heart of God.

Trinitarian awareness is intelligent and knows how to navigate time and space from the still point of a life that unfolds within time and space but is not attached to any particular time or place. Thomas Merton called this inner sanctum *le point vierge*, the virgin point that is unsullied by our past experience, by the judgments of others, or by our worries. The eternal life that beckons us is not "out there" in a separate heaven, nor is it "later on" in the future. We discover that eternal freedom is within us as we explore contemplative practices and virtues, and it is up to us to use this freedom for the good. Because we often react to outer events automatically and with fear—fight, flight, or freeze—our first contemplative act is to move our attention from what's happening outside us to what's happening within us, where outer and inner reality meet. That meeting place can most easily be found without distractions in silence. In silence, we carefully witness our experience directly, as it is happening, but are not attached to what we witness. This inner freedom is St. Paul's kenosis, self-emptying. Meister Eckhart reflected on Jesus's awareness: "Jesus was free and void and virginal in himself. Since the masters say that only the likeness of the like establishes union, he who is to receive the virginal Jesus must himself be virginal and free."[1] We can only appreciate Jesus's freedom when we ourselves are free.

When we meditate and contemplate, it may seem as if nothing is happening, but sitting in silence is, in fact, a practice of rigorous honesty. Key questions arise: *What is really going on inside me? What is really true?* When my thoughts, repetitive fears, and memories constrict me so ferociously that I feel claustrophobic, I begin to wonder, *If I'm not my thoughts and memories, then who am I?* If I notice that I am talking to myself, I can wonder, *Who is it within me who is talking, and who is listening?* We may find that we've been holding these questions for a long time but that we've been too busy to notice their importance or too afraid to take a closer look. Part of us wants to know who we really are, and part of us wants to escape, to be somebody else or somewhere else. In contemplative meditation and prayer, all koan-like questions focus our courage and creativity as we face into the unknown. In contemplative moments, practical needs are put aside, but our relationship to those needs can be clarified in silence.

All spiritual practices begin with a search for our true identity. *Who am I?* may be a question I consciously entertain, or it may be a more intuitive and unarticulated search engine that brings me to certain religious traditions. We're hunting for pointers from scripture, fellow seekers, contemporary teachers, and from our own experience. This search brought me home to the bedrock doctrine for Christians, the Nicene Creed. As a child, I received it as the truth, but as I grew into adulthood, I couldn't connect it with my life or direct experience until I realized that it was a map of human consciousness, a glimpse into Jesus's daily awareness.

This trinitarian architecture of awareness suggests that Jesus's awareness flowed effortlessly between a majestic openness to awe, mystery, and fathomless love (revealed through his relationship with Abba) and his encounters with others, always infused by a Spirit of

---

[1] Reiner Schurmann, trans. and commentary, *Meister Eckhart: Mystic and Philosopher* (Bloomington: Indiana University Press, 1978), 4.

Love that inspired beloved community. Jesus's awareness must have participated in each of these three dimensions of awareness, and he longed to share this way of being with everyone.

NAVIGATING ONENESS AND OTHERNESS

Perhaps you've heard from fellow seekers that the ultimate spiritual experience is an experience of absolute oneness. This would be a mistaken understanding of contemplative Christian experience according to most of the teachers who founded and grounded the Christian way. Yes, we affirm that a person can realize a certain oneness with God and others, a unitive experience that we call nondual. But we also assert that this oneness is always dynamic, and that circling within it is a rich, sparkling appreciation of otherness.[2]

For example, I might walk through a field of pollinator plants and slow to a stop in front of a stand of asters that hosts a cloud of Monarch butterflies. I might be keenly curious about the butterflies and intend to see each Monarch butterfly as other than me as I appreciate its radiant colors and its ability to flit so nimbly among the flowers, searching for nourishment before flying thousands of miles to its winter home in Mexico. I might experience admiration and awe at what these Monarchs can do. I might also identify with the Monarch, understanding the challenges of finding food, the joy of fellowship, the dangers of a long journey with no guarantees, and the fragility of existence. I might find myself saying "you" to a Monarch: "You are beautiful, and I wish you a successful journey!" Suddenly, in this experience of otherness, I might feel intimately connected to the butterfly, and realize a kind of kinship that transcends the difference between the butterfly and me. Such a nondual approach draws upon Aristotle's reflection that in sense perception, the relevant sensory faculty must be like the object it perceives. This is how trinitarian,

---

[2] In philosophical reflections on otherness, the positive experience of respecting otherness is known as alterity. See, for example, Emmanuel Levinas, *Alterity and Transcendence*, trans. Michael B. Smith (New York: Columbia University Press, 1999); and Jadranka Skorin-Kapov, *The Aesthetics of Desire and Surprise: Phenomenology and Speculation* (Lanham, MD: Lexington Books, 2015).

nondual awareness moves—navigating back and forth between one-ness and otherness in a stance of empathy, respect, and love. This oneing-and-othering awareness revolves like a flywheel slightly off balance, causing a gentle, long-wave vibration that keeps us awake in each moment. With the assistance and guidance of the Spirit, the frequency and clarity of this revolving awareness are harmonized and fructified.

The mystical theologian Origen (185–254 CE) reflected deeply on Christian oneness. He wrote, "He who is known is mingled in a certain way with him who knows."[3] Whatever we see in others is also within us. St. Thomas Aquinas (1225–74) echoed this theme when he wrote, "The truth is that knowledge is caused by the knower contain-ing a likeness of the thing known; for the latter must be in the knower somehow."[4] Spiritual knowing seems to require a resonant mirroring between us and others, and between us and our Creator.

We come to know the Holy Trinity by surrendering into Holy Trinity consciousness and listening from within it. To do this we must surrender our self-enclosed, dualistic ego's worldview and allow ourselves to become what Martin Heidegger called a "sacred clear-ing" (German: *Lichtung*).[5] In contemplative experience this clearing is where our attachments fall away, as if we were placing them on the altar of our awareness. Awake in a spacious *Lichtung*, we relinquish our grip on habitual thoughts, feelings, sensations, memories, and worries. We become "empty," but it is an emptiness that reveals the fullness of ourselves and others, and it feels unchanging in the midst of change. The great eighteenth-century poet William Blake described it like this: "If the doors of perception were cleansed everything would appear to man as it is, Infinite. For man has closed himself

---

[3] Origen, quoted in Schurmann, *Meister Eckhart*, 25.

[4] For Aquinas's detailed discussion of this perspective, see *Summa Theo-logica* I Q 12.

[5] See George Steiner, *Martin Heidegger* (Chicago: University of Chicago Press, 1978), 115; and Jason W. Alvis, "Making Sense of Heidegger's 'Phe-nomenology of the Inconspicuous' or Inapparent," *Continental Philosophy Review* 51 (2018): 211–38.

up, till he sees all things thro' narrow chinks of his cavern."[6] Living within a "cavern" is to be locked within the hard boundaries of our ego-self, inside the walls of our opinions, complaints, and judgments, and embedded in the linear and limiting boundaries of clock-time.

Cleansing our perception isn't just a lovely poetic idea; it's a deliberate and sacred practice. On the empty altar of awareness, the walls of our ego-cavern are transparent. Through those walls we see a divine light in everyone. We don't "see" it, of course, but with the eyes of faith, we sense that what looks like nothing, or emptiness, is filled with a Presence that touches everything with infinite care. We can't "know" divine consciousness in the same way that we know bits of information or physical things. Sacred scriptures of the Abrahamic traditions describe the entry into this clearing as a "cloud" of Presence or as a dazzling darkness that is permeable to the ineffable voice and Presence of God.[7] From this invisible place within us, all the powers of the ego-self are enlisted in service to God's Love.

Jesus lived from this trinitarian altar, continually emptying himself of all attachments to the passing parades of time and space, and even his attachment to life itself (Phil 2:5–8). I believe that his spiritual practice was to release his awareness into the spacious, caring witnessing of his Abba Creator. Abba was not an object of Jesus's awareness but rather the open field of *all* his experience. Thus, Jesus could say that when you see him, you see the Father. To see Jesus in this way, his friends had to become transparent, stepping into the holy *Lichtung*. Many people who listened to Jesus heard him only from the limited vantage point of their ego-selves, perceiving him as no more than the mortal carpenter from Nazareth (Mk 6:3). According to the Gospels, even many of the disciples who followed Jesus did not recognize the risen Christ after he rose from the dead; perhaps this is

---

[6] William Blake, "The Marriage of Heaven and Hell" [1793], in *The Portable Blake* (New York: Viking Press, 1946, 1969), 258.

[7] See Pseudo-Dionysius, "Divine Names," in *Pseudo-Dionysius: The Complete Works*, trans. Colm Luibheid and Paul Rorem, Classics of Western Spirituality (New York: Paulist Press, 1987); and Clifton Wolters, trans., *The Cloud of Unknowing and Other Works* (New York: Penguin Books, 1987).

because only a "resurrected" or "risen" consciousness can perceive the living, resurrected Christ in our midst.[8]

When St. Paul experienced the altar of Christ's consciousness within himself, he proclaimed, "It is no longer I who live, but it is Christ who lives in me" (Gal 2:20). In his love for Jesus, he had crossed over an empathetic, imaginal bridge between self and other. His knowing and perceiving had become transformed, and his identity was now inseparably linked with Christ's. Christ was the name of his altar. I don't think that Paul's mortal ego-self completely vanished. Rather, I think his ego-boundaries became transparent to divine mystery, to Christ consciousness. In this awareness one sees everything in the horizon of newness. "If anyone is in Christ, there is a new creation: Everything old has passed away; see, everything has become new!" (2 Cor 5:17). Our ego-selves tend to repeat yesterday over and over. But when our ego-selves become transparent, something really new can arise from within our ordinary experience. Standing within the eternal Presence, we see, hear, touch, and feel everything freshly. Eternity doesn't repeat itself; it is always emerging afresh.[9] In Acts 2 the story of Pentecost shows what happens when this eternal clearing shows up in a community: The Holy Spirit alights and graces "the between" of different peoples in a new and awe-inspiring communion of love.

Many sincere practitioners of contemplative silence tell me that as they become comfortable in solitude with the Holy One, they begin to feel that they themselves are a mystery, and that they sense an intimate connection with everyone. Some version of the Sanskrit saying *Namaste* (roughly translated as "I bow to God in you") begins to sing in our hearts as we meet others. In contemplative silence many of us realize that our initial view or opinion of others is often superficial and inaccurate. As we bring our experience onto the sacred clearing—*Lichtung*—we begin to "unknow" our opinions and allow the reality of others to emerge without interference.

---

[8] See, for example, the road to Emmaus story (Lk 24:13–34); and also the resurrection story (Jn 20:1–18).

[9] One caveat: When persons have experienced trauma, abandonment, rejection, or abuse, it is very difficult to achieve transparency. Traumatized contemplatives may find that psychotherapy is an essential adjunct to contemplative practice.

IMAGE AND LIKENESS

Eastern Orthodox mystical theologians name this process of increasing transparency *theosis* (Greek: divinization). It's as though one begins to perceive everything *beyond and within* the permeable membrane of the ego. The new and deeper identity that emerges is a mirror of the *imago Dei*, the imageless image of God. In the process of becoming followers of Christ, Jewish seekers gradually came to understand the *imago Dei* in Genesis as *imago Trinitatis;* that is, from the beginning we are created in the image of a trinitarian God. Becoming transparent to the eternal Trinity of Love within us requires single-minded intention along with meditation and prayer. As our self-emptying and self-othering proceed, we realize that we are intimately involved in the world, and the world is intimately involved in us.

Our vision of a sacred clearing in which the Presence of the Holy Trinity can emerge arises from the teaching in Genesis that something of God is within us—God's image and likeness. Early theologians considered the *image* of God within us to be something we already and always are, but they considered our *likeness* with God to be something that can only develop over time, requiring conscious cooperation with God's will, the intention to live a just and ethical life, and the sheer gift of God's grace. This transformative process was elaborated by many theologians, including St. Irenaeus in the second century, who taught that God incarnated as Jesus, becoming what we humans are, so that "He might bring us to be what He is Himself."[10] St. Athanasius, in the fourth century, suggested that because of the incarnation, we are all called to participate in growing up to our full stature in Christ. This incarnational process requires discipline (practices), yet it depends on grace, along with considerable focus and discipline.

None of us becomes—or needs to become—Jesus, but with our cooperation the Holy Spirit will integrate and harmonize our ego-self with our True Self. We begin by surrendering and joining in,

---

[10] St. Irenaeus, *Against Heresies,* Book V, Preface, trans. Alexander Roberts and William Rambaut, from *Ante-Nicene Fathers*, vol. 1, ed. Alexander Roberts, James Donaldson, and A. Cleveland Coxe (Buffalo, NY: Christian Literature Publishing Co., 1885), revised and edited for New Advent by Kevin Knight.

by believing and trusting that we are participating by grace in a transfiguration that includes us and the rest of creation. When taken seriously and sincerely, this approach gives our ego-selves permission to relinquish control and to trust that when we receive and share God's love, we are being changed in a glorious way.[11] This is difficult to believe in a culture that celebrates competition, greed, self-doubt, and cynicism.

I believe that through the grace of the incarnation of Jesus Christ, there are countless instances and varieties of incarnations and divinizations. The transformative experience of deification has been discussed for centuries in the mystical Christian tradition, but too often it has been ignored in conventional Christianity. Perhaps this stems from fear—fear of the unknown or fear of being carried away by irrationality or grandiosity. But the power of being transformed in the love of the Holy Trinity is freely available. Such a transformation must be intended and practiced in every moment as *awakeness, aliveness, and unknowing* (First Person), *honest, sincere,* and *appropriate interpersonal love* (Second Person), and *sacred community building* (Third Person), each dimension of consciousness circulating in the others.

St. Augustine believed that we already are images of the Holy Trinity, although we don't realize it. This reminds us of a debate that has been carried on in Buddhist communities for centuries: Are we already Buddha nature (enlightened), and don't realize it, or is enlightenment something that we will achieve in the future? Contemplative Christians address this question by answering "both-and." When asked by a divinity school student if we, too, can experience St. Paul's "Now not I but Christ in me," one of my Jesuit professors said, "Already and not yet." We are already the image of God, and we have not yet become the likeness of God. When the *imago Trinitatis* awakens within us, the transcendent qualities of God flow into our work and relationships—nonattachment, generosity, kindness, love, creativity, and a sincere dedication to truth. We are always moving

---

[11] "And all of us, with unveiled faces, seeing the glory of the Lord as though reflected in a mirror, are being transformed [Greek: *metamorphoo*] into the same image from one degree of glory to another; for this comes from the Lord, the Spirit" (2 Cor 3:18).

into the likeness of God, but we only realize this with intention, dedication, discipline, and a desire to help others.

CONTEMPLATION AND DIVINIZATION

The Eastern Orthodox mystics who matured into this tradition of transparency to God were called *Hesychasts*, those who believed that by a practice of prayer, contemplation, virtuous living, and asceticism, they could be transfigured in the same light that enveloped Jesus on Mount Tabor (Mt 17:2; Mk 9:2). In the fifth century St. Cyril of Alexandria wrote that we could become deified (transformed) by *participation* (Greek: *methexis*) in God. This word became popular among later theologians, including St. Maximus the Confessor in the seventh century and St. Symeon the New Theologian in the tenth. We don't single-handedly initiate a spiritual transformation. Rather, we participate in something that begins in the Holy Trinity. Symeon's ecstatic poetry reminds us of Sufi poets Rumi and Hafiz when he writes that in our depths we can "awaken in Christ's body."[12]

The Eastern Church, more than the Western Church, has highlighted the practice of *theoria* (Old Greek: contemplation), whereby one can have a direct experience of the inner Trinity, mediated through the intellect and senses. As this sort of transformation continues, our intellect and senses become clear channels of grace. Our thinking, feeling, listening, and sensing are transformed in a hidden Light. *Theoria* requires watchfulness in silence and solitude, as we sink beneath the monkey-mind of our everyday ego-selves. Although ancient Eastern Orthodox teachers could not elaborate on prayer and meditation in a way that would take into account post-Enlightenment psychological and scientific insights about consciousness, I have nevertheless found their texts insightful. They can point us in the right direction.

One of the Eastern Desert Fathers, Macarius of Egypt (300–391 CE), called his Hesychastic method "a prayer of the heart." He wrote, "When you are praying, do not shape within yourself any

---

[12] Symeon the New Theologian, quoted in *The Enlightened Heart: An Anthology of Sacred Poetry*, ed. Stephen Mitchell (New York: Harper and Row, 1989), 38.

image of the Deity, and do not let your mind be stamped with the impress of any form; but approach the Immaterial in an immaterial manner. . . . Prayer means the shedding of thoughts. . . . Blessed is the intellect that has acquired [this] complete freedom."[13] Those on the Hesychasm path who are gifted with purpose, discipline, and grace become transparent to the eternal love and light of God. It is said that Macarius was so profoundly transformed by the prayer of the heart that his face glowed in the dark. People called him the "glowing lantern."[14]

But the Western church gradually cooled to the idea of divinization, considering it a form of pride. They must have thought, how can mere mortals claim to become God? Isn't this a supreme act of sinful self-inflation? I still find that many of my Protestant friends, and some Roman Catholics, discount the possibility of deification and transformation of the self. They have no conceptual reference point for the True Self or Christ consciousness. Nevertheless, the potential union between Creator and creature continues to be affirmed in the Roman Catholic Eucharist when the priest declares, "By the mystery of this water and wine may we come to share in the divinity of Christ, who humbled himself to share in our humanity." Those mystics who have received the grace of divinization sometimes describe it as a process through stages (purgative, illuminative, and unitive or nondual). This developmental schema, held in great respect by the Roman Catholic, Anglican, and Orthodox churches, was first articulated by Origen (185–254 CE), one of the most gifted mystical theologians of the early centuries.[15] Today, this transformational process is rarely taught in any Christian church.

Even as we live in the real material world of jobs, families, friends, and responsibilities, we can periodically step into the altar of silence,

---

[13] Bernard McGinn, John Meyendorff and Jean Leclercq, eds., *Christian Spirituality: Origins to the Twelfth Century*, vol. 16, World Spirituality: An Encyclopedic History of the Religious Quest (New York: Crossroad, 1989), 399.

[14] "St. Macarius the Great," at www.stmacariusmonastery.org/makar_e.htm.

[15] See, for example, Andrew Louth, *The Origins of the Christian Mystical Tradition: From Plato to Denys* (Oxford, UK: Clarendon Press, 1981), 54.

which we discover by gently detaching from our worries and opening our hearts. This process changes our identity as we find that our deepest center of "I" is hidden in the same eternal "I" that God revealed to Moses, the "I" that Jesus used when he said, "I am the way, the truth and the life." In the *Lichtung*, all our personal pronouns—*I, you, we,* and *they*—circulate and dance freely in joy.

Within this sacred altar of awareness, we are no longer tyrannized by guilt, shame, fear, or what others think about us. Instead, we find ourselves buoyed by a Presence that is not attached to anything that passes in time. James Finley, a contemplative Christian teacher and clinical psychologist, often says that when we awaken to the eternal "I" of Love, we are released from the tyranny of suffering from within the suffering.[16] From this deep identity we can finally relinquish the fantasy of a geographical cure. We may discover that there is no better place to go and no more blessed person to be than where and who we are just now. Now is always the time to be available for divine transformation.

---

[16] James Finley, *Merton's Palace of Nowhere: A Search for God through Awareness of the True Self* (Notre Dame, IN: Ave Maria Press, 1978).

PART TWO

DIVINE THREESOME
IN THE BIBLE

4

First Person as Mystery

From its very first pages the Bible is rich in imagery and stories about divine Mystery—what Christians consider the First Person of the Holy Trinity. The Book of Genesis opens as God (Hebrew: *Elohim*) creates the universe out of eternal silence, before time, energy, materiality, or space. Everything that has evolved over billions of years has an eternal Source that is beyond human conception, measurement, or language. Because we are descended from a holy ineffable Source, we may say that it is our original sacred ancestor, and that this holiness lives in our DNA.

In Judaism, the most important and most often written name of God is the Tetragrammaton, the four-letter name usually written as YHWH (*Yod-Heh-Vav-Heh*), without vowels and so unsayable, yet sometimes pronounced Yahweh. There are several other Hebrew names for the living God. In speaking with Jewish friends about their mystical Kabbalah tradition, I have learned one name in Hebrew that particularly intrigues me: Ein Sof (or Eyn Sof), which is understood as God prior to any self-manifestation in the material or spiritual realms. Ein Sof can mean "unending," "uncaused," "eternal," "infinite," "concealed," or "the Endless One." Ein Sof precedes time and space, and yet exists within time and space.

If I am permitted to borrow this majestic name, I would say that as time and space came into being in the Great Flaring Forth, a seed of life and consciousness emerged out of Ein Sof, and that this invisible and eternal Presence is within us now as pure consciousness, without object, thought, or memory, without past or future. We all inherit this pure awareness and pure presence, but it is unrecognized by the untutored mind and heart. It has circulated within millennia of biological evolution and is hidden within our everyday consciousness. It is usually obscured because of our inherent tendency to focus on immediate survival, tasks, and self-interest—on the objects of our awareness.

Nevertheless, we are all children of the Great Flaring Forth, born from the mystery of God. We can't name specific characteristics of Ein Sof as we can name the qualities of material objects. But we can say that Ein Sof is the sacred source of the entire cosmos, and of our personal qualities of freedom, dignity, creativity, and ability to love. As cosmologist and novelist John Hands writes: We are Cosmosapiens.[1] This sacred Presence transcends us, and abides within us, and is what birthed us into our mortal life. Scripture and our own experience tell us that God transcends time (Job 36:26; Ps 90:4; Ps 102:27; Heb 1:12; 2 Pet 3:8). We come from eternity, and this sacred eternity is within us now.

In Hebrew tradition one cannot know the Creator as one might know a person, an idea, or even a feeling. This is because we are born from within the eternal Creator and can't look at the Creator from the outside (there *is* no "outside"). As Job discovered, we also can't control the Creator—the Creator is free.

In Hebrew scripture God may be experienced in silence, as in "the sound of sheer silence" that Elijah heard (1 Kings 19:11–13) or through a prophet's inner vision, as when Moses encountered God "face to face" (Ex 33:11). Sometimes, Creator communicates through the natural world, as when Moses sees God shining out from within a burning bush (Ex 3:1–6). Humans, nonhuman creatures, and natural elements like stones and water can disclose YHWH's Presence, but they are not *in themselves* God, except insofar as God is the inward reality of everything. No form in nature or religious imagery can fully represent the formless eternity of God's Presence (Ex 20:3–4). Some consider it a sin to create images of the holy Source of existence, lest those images become idols. Names and images can too easily be used to confine the splendor and eternity of God. YHWH's self-revelation in human language is simply, and most powerfully, "I AM who am."

The Hebrew Bible includes twenty-four books called the Tanakh, and the first five books are the Torah. Within the Tanakh, one notices

---

[1] John Hands, *Cosmosapiens: Human Evolution from the Origin of the Universe* (New York: The Overlook Press, 2015).

that drawing close to God is described in many ways. In Exodus 20—21, intimate contact with God is like entering a "thick darkness," the holy context within which all living things are born and die. I believe that this spacious, holy darkness is an aspect of human consciousness, although most of us aren't aware of it.[2] This divine darkness is timeless, never changes or passes, and abides within us. St. Teresa of Avila named this placeless place within us "the interior castle" through which all our mortal experience passes. It is an awareness of knowing that transcends human knowing: "The Lord knows our human thoughts; how like a puff of wind they are" (Ps 94:11, Book of Common Prayer). Human thoughts can point to God, but they are not God, who is holy Mystery. As the prophet Isaiah put it, speaking on behalf of God:

> For my thoughts are not your thoughts,
>   nor are your ways my ways, says the Lord.
> For as the heavens are higher than the earth,
>   so are my ways higher than your ways
>   and my thoughts than your thoughts.
>
> (Isa 55:8–9)

We cannot know or perceive God's thoughts—they are not like our thoughts, yet our thoughts pass through the divine knowing and awareness that are within us. Isaiah notes that God's ways are "higher" than our ways. Contemplatives in both Jewish and Christian traditions do not think that "higher" means "up above" in a physical sense but refers instead to the immeasurable openness of divine consciousness in which humans can humbly participate. It is a consciousness that is unattached to the objects of consciousness.[3]

---

[2] Quoting Augustine and Calvin, Thomas Merton writes that this background consciousness is "the theater of God's glory." Thomas Merton, *Conjectures of a Guilty Bystander* (New York: Doubleday Image, 1968, 2014), 337.

[3] Neuroscientists, cosmologists, biologists, theologians, and philosophers have produced many volumes of work on consciousness. For those who are drawn to this research, see an overview by Rich Heffern, "Consciousness: Science's Biggest Mystery," *National Catholic Reporter* (February 8, 2008).

Everything that is created—including our thoughts, sensations, and emotions—is passing, but YHWH never passes. YHWH is eternally present in each moment but often hidden by the filter of our self-centeredness. Private and communal prayer, contemplation, and the celebration of Holy Days are meant to awaken us to the Presence.

The theme of a Creator who cannot be confined to human categories or chronological time continues in the New Testament. St. Paul declared in a speech in Athens, "The God who made the world and everything in it, he who is Lord of heaven and earth, does not live in shrines made by human hands, nor is he served by human hands, as though he needed anything, since he himself gives to all mortals life and breath and all things" (Acts 17:24–25). God is everywhere, so we cannot limit God to a unique and specific representation that we place in front of us: "We ought not to think that the deity is like gold, or silver, or stone, an image formed by the art and imagination of mortals" (Acts 17:28–29).

In the Gospels, the Creator can't be known by our conceptual minds. We are invited to take up the "mind" (Greek: *Nous*) of Christ, whose human, mortal knowing was transfigured and transparent to the Creator's way of knowing. Jesus counseled his friends to accept the limits of their self-referencing knowing, while trusting that Abba knows all things. One core quality of Abba's awareness is to be awake and alert. "About that day or hour no one knows, neither the angels in heaven, nor the Son, but only the Father. Beware, keep alert; for you do not know when the time will come" (Mk 13:32–33). Jesus likewise affirmed that the kingdom of God—the realm of God—was not something external that could be handled or observed: "The kingdom of God is not coming with things that can be observed; nor will they say, 'Look, here it is!' or 'There it is!' For, in fact, the kingdom of God is among you" [or, as some texts put it, "within you"] (Lk 17:20b–21).

First Person awareness is continually emerging into the present, always detaching from the past and future. This awareness is fully and lovingly present in the passing phenomena of time and space yet is infinitely free. Even as we accept the value and the reality of each precious moment, we are called to realize that this moment is already vanishing. Indeed, everything in our mortal lives is passing, but Creator's Presence never changes and never passes. As St. Paul says, "The present form of this world is passing away" (1 Cor 7:31b). This truth is usually overlooked, perhaps because it can be terrifying—we and the ones we love will die, a lovely spring day is passing, and the household items we recently fixed are already falling apart. The eternal Presence that is found in the altar of each present moment becomes our refuge—the invisible ground of safety. The Gospels present Jesus's Abba, the Creator, as the only trustworthy ground of being in clock-time.

5

Second Person as Divine Interpersonal Love

Interpersonal love happens when an "I" loves a "you." As we've seen, Hebrew prophets respected the total mystery of the Creator (addressed as YHWH, Elohim, Adonai, El Shaddai, Ein Sof, or by other names). But they also often addressed God directly as "You." They did not see a contradiction between God as the totally unknown and God as a You with whom they could be in relationship. Hebrew people expected that the "I-You" dimension of YHWH's Presence might one day appear as a messiah, a mortal who would fully embody the majesty and mystery of God. Yet even now, a Jewish person can be in dialogue with YHWH or Elohim as You.

The opening words of the Bible suggest that there is a kind of personhood in God—therefore making interpersonal relationship possible—because God speaks the cosmos into being as an "other" with whom God can relate. The Holy One, the ultimate source of time, space, and the physical cosmos, creates and speaks, and the earth responds. Of course, God's speech is not ordinary chit-chat. It's an unusual, miraculous, and powerful kind of speech, issuing from a Voice that awakens creation. It is what anthropologists call "performative speech," or speech that creates what it articulates.

The story of creation in Genesis begins the drama of human beings inhabiting the earth: We are created as free from God, with the potential to become "thou" to God's "I." But this beautiful story includes a complicating truth: We struggle between, on the one hand, the impulse to serve and love the Divine as our core relationship, our one and only Thou; and, on the other hand, the impulse to serve only the self. We have a tendency to claim creatorship and godlikeness for ourselves, as if we don't need God.[1] Throughout Hebrew scripture the I-Thou dimension plays out as a drama of blessedness, promise, rebellion, and salvation. This *between* of intersubjective realities—between Creator and persons, between persons and persons, between persons and nature, and within each person—opens into a vast territory of love and hate across which we humans must find our way.

Throughout Genesis, Exodus, Leviticus, Numbers, and Deuteronomy, God initiates lively conversations with Abraham and Moses, and, in later books of the Bible, with other prophets and holy men and women. God is primarily depicted as "He," although in the Song of Songs, God's presence as Sophia (Wisdom) or as Shekhinah (the glory of God, the presence of God in the world) can be feminine. (In some early and medieval Christian communities, Jesus was seen as the incarnation of this same Divine Wisdom.)[2]

> Wisdom is radiant and unfading. She is easily discerned by those who love her, and is found by those who seek her. She hastens to make herself known to those who desire her . . . because she goes about seeking those worthy of her, and she graciously appears to them in their paths, and meets them in every thought. (Wis 6:12–13, 16)

In this passage Wisdom is not abstract, as in the Greek ideal, but is an actual presence of God "in every thought." In scripture Wisdom already lives at the Great Flaring Forth, is always present, and is an interpersonal doorway to eternity within everyone's consciousness. God may be encountered as a person-like Voice coming from no particular place or from within fire, cloud, or an angelic figure. Spiritual seekers must attune themselves to this Voice, or it will not be heard. In the Tanakh, YHWH speaks to individuals and simultaneously to

---

[1] Genesis 3. It is unfortunate that this text seems to blame the woman, Eve, as the source of humankind's original separation from God. Still, Eve is praised later on as being "the mother of all living" (Gen 3:20).

[2] See, for example, Caroline Walker Bynum, *Jesus as Mother: Studies in the Spirituality of the High Middle Ages* (Berkeley and Los Angeles: University of California Press, 1984).

the whole community of the Hebrew people. Individuals and Israel as a community are addressed by God as "you."

One of the most dramatic and memorable encounters between God (as Elohim) and Moses takes place early in the Book of Exodus when Moses notices a bush that is burning but not consumed (3:4ff.). That which should be disappearing in flames seems to burn forever, and the image of this bush becomes a symbol or icon of the Creator's Presence that endures in all things, even as they are born and pass away. Awestruck before this phenomenon, Moses hears a Voice arising out of the bush, "Moses, Moses!" Moses replies, "Here I am." God declares, "I am the God of your fathers, the God of Abraham, the God of Isaac, and the God of Jacob." Of course, Abraham, Isaac, and Jacob had died long ago, but in the eternity of Elohim, they continue to live. In Hebrew scripture one can experience interpersonal, I-Thou contact across time and space. Grounded in this I-Thou relationship, we are passing in time and space, but in a spiritual sense, we live forever.

In the Tanakh we see that God is Being itself, but also a formless Someone who is available for relationship, even conversation. YHWH tells Moses that he sees the suffering of his people and that he is giving Moses a great task: to confront the Egyptian pharaoh and lead the Israelites out of slavery into freedom. God says tenderly, "I will be with you" (Ex 3:12). But Moses resists, insisting that he doesn't have the eloquence to speak for God. However, YHWH does not give up on Moses; YHWH challenges him, saying, "Who gives speech to mortals? Who makes them mute or deaf, seeing or blind? Is it not I, the Lord? Now go, and I will be with your mouth and teach you what you are to speak" (Ex 4:11–12). This is a powerful I-Thou encounter, one that resonates with what Christians might consider a Second Person consciousness, Divine to human, immortal to mortal, Person to person. YHWH's message is that each of us is not alone because God is always with us.

Many conversations in Hebrew scripture between God and humans have the quality of a severe yet loving parent trying to keep the kids on track. Rules are set and then broken. In one of the Bible's most frightening and heartbreaking scenes, YHWH is so disgusted with the evil behavior of his human creatures that he "was sorry that he had made humankind on the earth, and it grieved him to his heart. So

YHWH said, 'I will blot out from the earth the human beings I have created—people together with animals and creeping things and birds of the air, for I am sorry that I have made them.'" Fortunately, one man, Noah, "found favor in the sight of YHWH." After a devastating flood, humans and all creatures are forgiven and given a second chance, and God makes an everlasting covenant with the whole web of life (Gen 6:5–13).

Other Hebrew prophets have direct interactions with God, begging forgiveness on behalf of God's people and urging the people to amend their lives in accordance with God's will. According to the prophets, YHWH cares deeply about social and economic injustice. When the people disobey YHWH's laws for right living, YHWH's reactions, as interpreted by prophets such as Hosea and Jeremiah, can be fierce (Hos 8:1, 4, 14).

We see that YHWH can be jealous, disappointed, and angry. Yet the I-Thou proclamations and conversations between God and the Hebrews often have a more affectionate and intimate tone. Although the people periodically lose their faith and act unjustly, and although YHWH repeatedly threatens them and sometimes brings devastation because of their unfaithfulness, YHWH eventually comes through with a compassionate heart, and the Hebrew people renew their covenant. Through the voices of the prophets God often speaks to the whole community and reminds them of God's blessings: "I led them with cords of human kindness, with bands of love. I was to them like those who lift infants to their cheeks. I bent down to them and fed them" (Hos 11:4).

The personal Presence of God as depicted in the Psalms is a source of guidance, instruction, punishment, protection, wisdom, mercy, love, compassion, judgment, gladness, and joy. In the company of this Thou, the Hebrew people glimpse their essential goodness as it might have been before the Fall, before the stain of guilt, shame, and self-consciousness that spread through the human psyche and community. Over and over the people ask God to forgive, protect, and love them, often speaking like children to a mother or father. The Psalmist prays,

> In You my soul takes refuge;
> in the shadow of your wings I will take refuge.
>   (Ps 57:1)

In my youth I often prayed the King James Version of the Twenty-Third Psalm. I experienced deep comfort and peace as I prayed, "The Lord is my shepherd; I shall not want." And now I often hear the first two verses of Psalm 139 in my silent meditations:

> O Lord, you have searched me and known me.
> You know when I sit down and when I rise up;
>   you discern my thoughts from deep within.

In the Song of Songs the intimate I-Thou relationship with the divine Creator is conveyed through erotic imagery. This book proclaims the goodness, sacredness, and beauty of erotic love, and has been interpreted by the Hebrews as depicting God's love for God's people and the soul's love for God. A maiden hears the voice of her beloved, a presence that is swift and fleeting, yet steadfast and true. The consummation of this love affair between God and the soul is union with the Divine. As in physical lovemaking, the great I AM and the thou of each seeker become one. Later, this imagery becomes the fulcrum for the Christian medieval vision of bridal mysticism and sacred marriage. This divine poetry captures the delight, urgency, and joy of divine-human union:

> The voice of my beloved!
>   Look, he comes,
> leaping upon the mountains,
>   bounding over the hills. . . .
>
> My beloved speaks and says to me:
> "Arise, my love, my fair one." (Song 2:8, 10)

This powerful interpersonal I-Thou experience is central to Hebrew spirituality. The believer puts ultimate trust in the One who transcends the created world, yet who passionately seeks an intimate relationship with his people despite their frequent rebellion. In this interpersonal, interdependent world, the fire of divine love burns at the heart of all relationships. The message that circulates throughout the Hebrew Bible is that we are created to long for the limitless love of God, that

God offers us a vision and framework for right living, and that God is available for intimate relationship.

In Christian scripture the divine interpersonal love in the Tanakh takes mortal human form. Now the I-Thou experience of persons with the Creator can be experienced between persons and a person. As mentioned, Hebrew scripture proclaims that the infinitely transcendent YHWH will manifest as a human-divine being (Messiah) who fully and faithfully embodies the love of God. The Messiah will be a real person, the scriptures say, who will dispel any doubts about God's existence and promises, resolve all conflicts, and ensure Israel's home on earth. Some Jews and others who witnessed the ministry of Jesus of Nazareth concluded that he was the Messiah whose coming and crucifixion were foretold in the Tanakh (Isa 53:1–12; Hos 6:1–3).

Some followers of Jesus of Nazareth experienced the Creator's Presence in him, and, after the proclamation of Jesus's resurrection, their community of fellow believers grew and changed. Entering into an I-Thou relationship with the risen Christ transformed these communities' understandings of the divine-human relationship. When, in the midst of great change and danger Jesus proclaimed, "I will be with you," many Jewish converts heard YHWH's Voice (Jn 7:33; Gen 26:3; Ex 3:12; Josh 3—7).

In the first four centuries after Jesus's death the incarnation story was written by many authors, most of whom are anonymous. It is in four Gospels and twenty-three additional books. In the fourth century, Athanasius, the bishop of Alexandria, distributed a list of chapters with his Easter letter that came to be honored by the Roman Catholic Church and most Protestant churches as the New Testament. In these chapters Jesus of Nazareth, son of Jewish parents, Joseph and Mary, and the Holy Spirit, is presented as the Messiah, the one foretold in scripture.

During Jesus's lifetime, some Jewish religious authorities could not accept that the Messiah would actually show up as a humble carpenter who violated many sacred injunctions, such as carrying out healings on the Sabbath. Jesus said that he could forgive sins, and the religious authorities accused him of blasphemy, since that was a power reserved for God (Mt 26:65; Mk 2:7). They accused Jesus of making himself God (Jn 10:33). Perhaps Jewish authorities felt that Jesus was on what today we might call an ego trip. In addition, the land was occupied by Roman armies, and there might have been some collusion between Jewish and Roman leaders who considered the growing Jesus movement a political threat. So it is that, from the very beginning, seeds of discord were sown between the Hebrew community and Jesus's followers. Many centuries of violence by Christians against Jews ensued, propelled in part by the tragic belief that the Jews killed Jesus, when in fact the truth is much more complex.[3]

Taken as a whole, the New Testament presents Jesus as both fully human and fully divine. He is portrayed as fully human because he is born a mortal in the line of ancestors carefully listed in Matthew 1:1–18 and Luke 3:23–38. Jesus's precise biological lineage has not been confirmed, but historians have no doubt that he lived. Archaeological evidence, independent researchers, and historians have verified the reality of many of the events, places, and characters in the gospel stories. Of course, whether or not Jesus truly manifested divine Presence cannot be confirmed by historical records or scientific inquiry. The divinity of Christ as reported in scripture and in the creeds is a matter of faith and trust. The New Testament makes it clear that the interpersonal relationship between YHWH and human beings becomes powerfully accented in the incarnation of Jesus Christ. God can be met and communicated with on the ground, with a living person in time.

Of the four Gospels, the Gospel of John proclaims Jesus's divinity most clearly. John opens his Gospel as a cosmic story, in which Jesus is named the Word of God (Greek: *Logos*). The eternal Word, who is Christ, was present at the Great Flaring Forth from nothing, just as the Spirit was there at the beginning (Gen 1:1–2; Jn 1:1–18).

---

[3] See the explicit rejection of anti-Semitism in the Vatican II document *Nostra Aetate* (*Declaration on the Relationship of the Church to Non-Christian Religions*), October 28, 1965; and Jon M. Sweeney, ed., *Jesus Wasn't Killed by the Jews* (Maryknoll, NY: Orbis Books, 2020).

In Christian liturgies we hear Christ described as one who was, who is, and who will be (see Heb 13:8), a Presence who transcends linear time, from within time. Jesus is said to be a mortal descendant of David and the son of Joseph and Mary, but he is also conceived by the power of the eternal Holy Spirit. Jesus's followers experienced Jesus's mortal presence as being transparent to YHWH's Presence (Mt 17:2; Mk 9:2; Jn 20:28; Phil 3:8). Through Jesus, the Creator appears as Emmanuel—God with us. Following Jesus's lead (Jn 12:32), the New Testament proclaimed that God's chosen people are now not only the Jews, but "all people" (Acts 15:7; Rom 3:29; 1 Tim 4:10).

Now, YHWH's I-Thou relationship was understood to be universal—all are chosen as God's beloveds. The gospel writers and St. Paul considered Jesus to be the incarnation of the God of Israel, the Messiah for whom the Hebrew people longed, and also the light of God for all, Jews and other people alike:

> Here is my servant, whom I have chosen,
>   my beloved, with whom my soul is well pleased.
> I will put my Spirit upon him,
>   and he will proclaim justice to the Gentiles. . . .
>   And in his name the Gentiles will hope. (Mt
>   12:18, 21)

Jesus brings a universal expansion of the Messiah's mission. Now the Messiah is for everyone. The name Christ (Greek: *Khristós*) refers to the Messiah. The Greeks who considered Jesus of Nazareth to be the Messiah called him Iesous Khristós. When Jewish followers of Jesus experienced him as the predicted Messiah, the sacred I-Thou of the Hebrew people took on a dramatic new meaning. They were relating both to a transcendent invisible other *and* to an embodied, historically grounded person. An I-thou relationship with the person of Jesus was simultaneously a sacred I-Thou relationship with YHWH. The incarnation opens to Christians a new and powerful understanding of ourselves when we, with St. Paul, say that we are "in Christ."

Jesus of Nazareth lived for about thirty years. The Gospels depict him as feeling the full spectrum of human emotions from joy to despair, pleasure to pain. He experienced being loved and being despised. Not everyone he met recognized or appreciated his mission. Not everyone had faith that he was bringing forth the Presence of YHWH in ordinary space and time. But many *did* have faith in Jesus as the Christ, and they had experiences that transformed their hearts, and their very identities. I think that those who glimpsed YHWH in the person of Jesus must have accessed the mind of Christ, because I believe that only the mind of Christ can recognize the presence of Christ. As their awareness attuned to Jesus's awareness, they began to experience their lives as Jesus experienced his, as God's beloved. The incarnation of Jesus Christ perfectly integrates the I-Thou of persons to God with the I-thou of persons to persons. This opens the way for Christians to see others as mortal beings while also seeing them as manifesting the full Presence of God.

What might our lives be like if we begin to experience Second Person awareness? Jesus did not write his own memoir, and no objective reporter recorded Jesus's state of consciousness, behavior, or words. We have no verifiable scan of what Paul called "the mind of Christ." But the New Testament brings us a glimpse of how Jesus lived his Second Person awareness. We can see that he addressed people very personally, often asking what they desired. They responded expressing love, doubt, hope, anger, fear, and gratitude. In reading the gospel stories, we often sense Jesus's compassion. He healed those suffering from illness or demonic possession. He went out among Jews and Gentiles, strangers, sinners, and tax collectors, inspiring the holy and the hopeless, bringing love and healing to the outcast. He challenged those—especially leaders—who were unjust and hypocritical. Jesus wasn't married, and we don't have any accounts of his experiencing sexual intimacy. But we do see that he placed an ultimate valuation on interpersonal love and responsibility, and that he was willing to give his life for the sake of others. In my prayerful imagination I see Jesus looking into people's faces and empathizing with their longing to be seen, known, and loved, for he himself felt seen and loved in this way—not only by his awakened friends, but also and especially by Abba. We might say that the Second Person is the divine archetype of all relationships and reveals the fullest possible expression of God's interpersonal presence on earth.

Jesus's valuation of persons and family was always balanced against his ultimate relationship with Abba and his calling as a spiritual leader. In Matthew 10:37 he counsels his followers, "Whoever loves father or mother more than me is not worthy of me; and whoever loves son or daughter more than me is not worthy of me." And when Jesus is told that his mother and brothers are outside, wanting to speak to him, he points to his disciples and says: "Here are my mother and my brothers! For whoever does the will of my Father in heaven is my brother and sister and mother" (Mt 12:46–50). Jesus believed that his first responsibility was to do God's will, to heal, and to offer his Presence as eternal life, and to carry out this ministry without preferences. His interpersonal relationship with Abba was the ground of all his relationships, even transcending love for his family.

When the Jewish authorities gave him trouble for helping those outside his close-knit Jewish community, Jesus rebuked them, saying, "Those who are well have no need of a physician, but those who are sick; I have come to call not the righteous but sinners" (Mk 2:17). Scripture indicates that Jesus honored most of the Jewish laws and rituals in his community, but he also declared the presence of the Divine to be more important than laws and rituals. He was not a conventional moralist, calculating whether or not people were following the rules. I believe that Jesus's focus was on the present moment—what is happening and what is needed right now. When authorities chastised him for healing people on the Sabbath, he responded, "The Sabbath was made for humankind, and not humankind for the Sabbath; so the Son of Man is lord even of the Sabbath" (Mk 2:27–28). He meant that one who is transfigured and transparent to YHWH perceives reality from God's standpoint, not from the standpoint of any cultural or religious standard or rule. In Jesus's awareness the Sabbath was to be honored, but it was *not* more important than God's healing Presence. For him, the living God was always greater than the rules.

In the Gospels, Jesus sometimes referred to himself as the Son of Man (Greek: *Anthropos*, human being), and he was sometimes called the Son of God. The names Son of Man and Son of God had already appeared in Hebrew scripture, and the early Christians used the terms

to indicate that Jesus Christ was a divinely transformed human being.[4]
His consciousness was fundamentally relational, always aware of
Father, the First Person, even as he related to others:

> Jesus said to them, "Very truly, I tell you, the Son can do noth-
> ing on his own, but only what he sees the Father doing; for
> whatever the Father does, the Son does likewise." (Jn 5:19)

> Jesus said, "When you have lifted up the Son of Man, then
> you will realize that I am he, and that I do nothing on my own,
> but I speak these things as the Father instructed me." (Jn 8:28)

In the fourth century Gregory of Nyssa wrote:

> For as He is called the Son of Man by reason of the kindred of
> His flesh to her of whom He was born, so also He is conceived,
> surely, as the Son of God, by reason of the connection of His es-
> sence with that from which He has His existence. . . . The word
> *Son* claims for Him both alike—the human in the man [that is,
> born mortal, of a woman], but in God, the divine.[5]

As Son of God/Son of Man, Jesus carried out a healing ministry. Encountering two blind men, Jesus touched their eyes and healed them of
their blindness. Crowds of the wounded, longing for his touch, reached
out to him for help, and he responded generously. When he came upon
a funeral, he told the mourners to go away, and then he went to the
deceased, touched her hand, and brought her back to life (Mt 9:23–25).
Simply to be in Jesus's presence was healing and transformative, and
he asked for no credit—indeed, he often asked his disciples to keep
the healings secret (Mt 17:9; Mk 9:9; Lk 5:14; 8:56). Jesus repeatedly
tried to escape notoriety, seeking solitude so he could pray to Abba (Mk
1:35–37). When someone called him Good Teacher, he replied, "Why
do you call me good? No one is good but God alone" (Mk 10:18). Jesus

---

[4] See John A. Sanford, *Mystical Christianity: A Psychological Commentary on the Gospel of John* (New York: Crossroad, 1993).

[5] Gregory of Nyssa, *Against Eunomius* 3.4, cited in Sanford, 98.

wanted his followers to understand that in Abba we experience the ultimate I-Thou relationship, one that transcends our love for family and friends, and even our relationship with the mortal Jesus of Nazareth.

Jesus boldly entered into relationships in concrete ways, but he did not want his ministry to be about himself alone. As the embodiment of Second Person awareness, Jesus shows us that every relationship can be a window into Creator; every relationship can be marked by divinity. When Mary Magdalene realizes that Jesus has died and yet has appeared and is speaking to her, she wants to touch him, but he says, in the well-known Latin translation, *Noli me tangere*, "Don't cling to me" (Jn 20:11). Jesus is about to ascend to Abba, to the Father; he will no longer be limited to one place or time but will be present to everyone, everywhere. Jesus wanted Mary to know that even as she had glimpsed the Mystery of the Creator in his presence, so now, even after his death, Abba would be ever present to her, in Christ.

Jesus assured his followers that, through him, they too would participate in a direct, intimate relationship with God. "On that day you will know that I am in my Father, and you in me, and I in you" (Jn 14:20). Jesus's friends and followers were told that by virtue of their faith and love, they too could participate in the mutual indwelling of Abba and Jesus: "Abide in me as I abide in you" (Jn 15:4). I see his awareness as a continuously evolving dance of love, manifesting in every moment of clock-time. Jesus longed to share his Abba relationship: "My peace I give to you. . . . As the Father has loved me, so I have loved you. . . . The glory that you [God] have given me I have given them" (Jn 14:27; 15:9; 17:22).

A consciousness like Jesus's is nonhierarchical. We speculate about his awareness because we want to align our awareness with his. It's a challenge, because humans generally want to go it alone, without God's help. Over and over Jesus defined the whole and holy person as one who relinquishes the love of power and love of self in order to practice a radically inclusive love. In this surrender one's ego-self bows and gives way to the True Self, to the Christ within.[6] When his

---

[6] See the reflections on Christ as the True Self by Benedictine Brother David Steindl-Rast in his fine book on the Apostles' Creed, *Deeper Than Words: Living the Apostles' Creed* (New York: Random House, 2010), esp. 46–49.

followers grumbled among themselves about which of them deserved the most recognition, Jesus told them, "The greatest among you must become like the youngest, and the leader like one who serves. For who is greater, the one who is at the table or the one who serves? Is it not the one at the table? But I am among you as one who serves" (Lk 22:25–27). Again, when Jesus's friends asked him, "Who is the greatest in the kingdom of heaven?" Jesus answered by inviting a child into their midst, and saying: "Truly I tell you, unless you change and become like children, you will never enter the kingdom of heaven. Whoever becomes humble like this child is the greatest in the kingdom of heaven. Whoever welcomes one such child in my name welcomes me" (Mt 18:1–5; see also Lk 9:48). Second Person consciousness as portrayed by Jesus includes a childlike openness to reality. I believe that such a person is not passive or naive, but sensitive, empathetic, and vulnerable, and available to moments of awe and gratitude. Jesus's way of meeting mortal danger models a striking and powerful kind of vulnerability. This quality is seen in Jesus's ability to fiercely defend those who are being exploited or abused, as when he exposed the hypocrisy of some religious leaders (Mt 23:28; Lk 12:1).

In one of the most tragic scenes in Christian scripture, and perhaps in all of Western literature, Jesus becomes aware that his mission as the embodied incarnation of divine Presence will lead to his death by hanging on a cross. His disciples are shocked. How can the very incarnation of divinity be put to death as a common criminal? When Jesus predicts that friends and disciples will desert him, Peter objects: "I will never desert you." Jesus replies, "Truly I tell you, this very night, before the cock crows, you will deny me three times" (Mt 26:31–34). Indeed, Peter and several other disciples do desert Jesus as he is captured and sent to trial and crucifixion. He makes a lonely journey to the cross, inwardly accompanied by Abba.

I believe Jesus's essential message was that when we realize that we are God's beloved, we will realize that everyone and everything is God's beloved. When we stand within Second Person awareness, we are always in relationship with an infinite, unconditional, and universal Love.

6

Third Person as Divine Spirit

Jesus's early followers included many Hebrew, Aramaic, and Greek-speaking Jews. In their scriptures and liturgies, they had been introduced to the idea of a sacred spirit, called Ruach. As their Jesus-centered community developed over time, Ruach was translated into Greek as *Hagios Pneuma* (Holy Spirit), and by the fourth century this holy spirit would be understood as the Third Person of the Trinity.

All three of the Abrahamic religions include the Genesis story of creation,[1] where God creates the cosmos from nothing and God's Presence is manifest as a wind of Spirit moving across a newly emerging creation. "In the beginning, when God created the heavens and the earth, the earth was a formless void and darkness covered the face of the deep, while a wind [Ruach] from God [Elohim] swept over the face of the waters" (Gen 1:1–2). Saying that Ruach is *from* Elohim suggests that the Spirit is distinct from Elohim. Yet it is implied that Ruach is one with Elohim, that the breath of life is God. This particular interpretation later becomes a critical element in the formulation of the Christian Trinity. The Spirit is holy life and breath that comes *from* God and *is* God.

Christians who read Genesis are invited to embrace this paradox: The Holy Spirit both comes from God and is God. We are invited to understand that Ruach is a sacred "betweening" that connects the boundless powers of the Creator with the enlivening breath of all beings. If one believes that there is a deep and essential connection between the breath of God and the breath of all living things, then

---

[1] Genesis includes two versions of the creation story, but for our purposes, we'll focus on the first story, in Genesis 1, also called the Priestly story.

every breath we take brings us into interbeing, the perichoresis. With every breath, this inexpressible cosmic power is passing through us. Ruach is the inner energy and Presence of cosmic creation and evolution, continually weaving holiness into the impersonal and personal aspects of creation, weaving its creative Presence through our lives.

As the creation story unfolds, both of the names for God in the Tanakh, Elohim and YHWH, are used, and both imply a personal or covenantal relationship with all beings. I'm told that contemplatives in the Jewish tradition sometimes repeat a name of God (there are over one hundred choices) as a spiritual practice, all of which point to, and conceal, the real Presence of YHWH. The four letters of YHWH, read from right to left, are *yodh, he, waw,* and *he*. As a practice, this could be conveyed as *Yh* on the in-breath and *wh* on the out-breath. To live is to breathe and thus to participate directly in YHWH's Presence. To breathe is to participate in Spirit. Contemplative Christians could benefit from this practice too, slowing down to repeat the sacred name of Jesus, or to repeat "Spirit of God" with every breath, as a way to be drawn into the presence of the Creator.

In the books of Genesis, Psalms, Jeremiah, Ezekiel, and Sirach, Ruach is a Presence that bridges immortal God and mortal beings.[2] Ruach conveys a revelatory power to prophets who surrender to God and speak from the God-place in their souls. Ruach gives herself to mortal beings while remaining eternal. Infused with Ruach's Presence, prophets rise to a higher vibration of mortal life (Ex 31:3; Num 11:25; 1 Sam 10:6; Job 20:3; Isa 61:1; Song 1:7). By the power of Spirit the uncreated Creator "speaks" through these mortal beings. Even the Egyptian pharaoh respected and feared those who embodied the Spirit of God (Gen 41:38). Ruach can fill and overflow an individual's mortal existence and speak through the person's own voice. For example, God tells Samuel:

> After that you shall come to Gibeath-elohim, at the place where the Philistine garrison is; there, as you come to the town, you will meet a band of prophets coming down from the shrine

---

[2] Sirach is also called the Book of Ecclesiastes or the All-Virtuous Wisdom of Yeshua ben Sira.

with harp, tambourine, flute, and lyre playing in front of them; they will be in a prophetic frenzy. Then *the spirit of the Lord [YHWH] will possess you,* and you will be in a prophetic frenzy along with them and *be turned into a different person.* Now when these signs meet you, do whatever you see fit to do, for God is with you. (1 Sam 10:5–7)

There is a universal human experience articulated in passages like this. For Christians, becoming a different person might be called a rebirth in the Spirit. Reborn in the Spirit, our breath becomes transparent to Ruach. Whether we are aware of it or not, our moment-to-moment existence depends completely on the power of Ruach.

God declares in Isaiah:

> I will pour my Spirit upon your descendants,
>   and my blessing on your offspring.
> They shall spring up like a green tamarisk,
>   like willows by flowing streams. (Isa 44:3–5)

And in the Book of Joel, in a passage that reminds Christians of Jesus's and St. Paul's inclusionary love and of the powerful appearance of the Spirit at Pentecost, YHWH announces that the Spirit is being offered to all people, not just to the local faithful:

> I will pour out my Spirit on all flesh;
>   your sons and your daughters shall prophesy,
> your old men shall dream dreams,
>   and your young men shall see visions.
> Even on the male and female slaves,
>   in those days, I will pour out my Spirit. (Joel
>   2:28–29)

Humans did not create life. Only the Spirit gives life. In the "Valley of the Dry Bones," told in Ezekiel 37:1–14, YHWH as Ruach brings the prophet into the middle of a valley that is a wasteland of scattered bones. At the Lord's direction Ezekiel speaks to the bones, and miraculously, they come together to form bodies—but are still lifeless.

Ezekiel is then told, "'Prophesy to the breath, prophesy, mortal, and say to the breath: Thus says the Lord God: Come from the four winds, O breath, and breathe upon these slain, that they may live.'" Ezekiel carries out the Spirit's directive and is astounded to look at the bones and to see that "the breath [Ruach] came into them, and they lived, and stood on their feet, a vast multitude."

If God were to withdraw the Spirit's Presence from you in this moment, you would disappear from your chair.[3] This is the message and inspiration I receive when I read the Hebrew scriptures. We are continually appearing out of the holy, ever-present Nowhere of God, and in the course of our lives, it is Ruach who guides us into truth and who inspires us to live virtuous lives (Job 27:3–5). I find it transforming to see out from the center of my life as if Ruach/the Holy Spirit were bringing me to life, moment by moment.

In each moment we breathe in and breathe out the Spirit of God's Presence. When we relax the hard boundaries of our ego-selves and open to the higher power of Spirit, we don't *decide* our way through life's challenges so much as we *discern* our way. We don't own our breath or our existence; our breathing is God's. When we believe this, and realize it, our lives are enlarged, and we breathe each breath with heartfelt gratitude. Ruach is the creative, spiritual engine of life and cosmic evolution—it is so intimate that each breath serves as a doorway from mortal existence to God's infinite Presence.

For Greek followers of Jesus, the holy Pneuma brings life and the full power and presence of God. When Gospel authors such as Mark quote Hebrew scripture, they translate the term *Ruach* as *Hagios Pneuma* (Mk 12:36), which can move through a person's soul, divinizing his or her voice with prophetic messages to the community.

During and immediately after his baptism Jesus is "full" of the Spirit, "led" by the Spirit into the wilderness, and then "filled with

---

[3] The notion of appearing from nowhere in each moment can be found in Reiner Schurmann, trans. and commentary, *Meister Eckhart: Mystic and Philosopher* (Bloomington: Indiana University Press, 1978), 86.

the power" of the Spirit as he returns to Galilee. Jesus's first sermon, delivered in a synagogue in Nazareth, is often considered one of his mission statements. Jesus opens the Torah scroll and reads from the prophet Isaiah:

> The Spirit of the Lord is upon me,
>> because he has anointed me to bring good news
>>> to the poor.
> He has sent me to proclaim release to the captives
>> and recovery of sight to the blind, to let the op-
>>> pressed go free. (Lk 4:18)

All eyes were fixed on him as he declared, "Today this scripture has been fulfilled in your hearing" (Lk 4:21).

In Christian scriptures the Holy Spirit is not explicitly named God. As we've seen, the idea that the Spirit is God was not articulated until more than three hundred years after Jesus's death. But the Spirit makes a dramatic entry in Matthew's articulation of Jesus's genealogy. Jesus is shown to be descended from forty-two generations, stretching from Abraham to Joseph, the father of Jesus—a paternal path spanning twenty-five-hundred years (Mt 1:16–21). But according to the gospel stories, Jesus is conceived in Mary's womb by the Holy Spirit. In Matthew we read that Jesus's mother had been engaged to Joseph, but "before they lived together, she was found to be with child from the Holy Spirit" (Mt 1:18). Matthew does not explicitly say that Mary and Joseph didn't have sexual intercourse. Perhaps they did, before they lived together. Still, the story implies that Jesus's parents did *not* have sexual relations before his conception, and this became the traditional Christian interpretation of the passage.

Yet if Joseph and Mary didn't make love in a physical way before Jesus was conceived, Matthew's genealogy can't justify its claim to be a record of Jesus's biological lineage. If Jesus wasn't conceived and born in a normal human way, he wouldn't belong to the biological lineage of David. What's more, he also wouldn't be a complete human being, despite the claims of standard Christian theology. He would be only an avatar—a ghostlike deity in human form, which is the heresy of Docetism.

My own interpretation is that Joseph and Mary had sexual relations that resulted in Mary's pregnancy, and that, as Jews, their faith in Ruach was so strong that the Holy Breath infused their lovemaking and God chose to become incarnate in their child. In fact, if Jesus is 100 percent divine and 100 percent human, as the Council of Chalcedon declared, Jesus must have been conceived through ordinary sexual relations. For me, accepting this in no way detracts from the wonder of Jesus's conception and birth, nor does it eliminate the power of the Spirit as God's avenue of creation. Jesus is born fully human, and born in the way of all humans, but he is also born of the Holy Spirit. If the breath of the Spirit can bless lovemaking, then sexuality is holy, and so, by extension, is marriage.

We have seen in the Genesis account of creation that Elohim's Ruach brought forth the cosmos and life from nothing. The Christian contemplative view is that as the natural evolutionary process proceeds, the Holy Spirit continues as an indwelling feature of natural laws. This Spirit is eternal, so when we experience the Spirit now, in the twenty-first century, we experience the same Spirit who was present at creation and who illumined Jesus's life. Evolution in all its beautiful, quirky, and violent manifestations is graced by the Holy Spirit. Similarly, all humans are born of the Spirit, even if we don't realize it.

Just as the Spirit makes a dramatic entry when Jesus is conceived, so too does the Spirit play a central role in the story of Jesus's baptism, the pivotal event that launched his public ministry. At the beginning of the Gospels, the prophet John the Baptist is baptizing people with water for repentance, when suddenly he declares, "One who is more powerful than I is coming after me; I am not worthy to carry his sandals. He will baptize you with the Holy Spirit and fire" (Mt 3:11–12; Mk 1:8). The metaphor of perpetual fire would remind Jewish converts to Christianity of the moment when Moses perceived God's Presence in the burning bush. Baptism becomes a sacred Spirit-water-fire that burns and washes away everything that is not God's love, mercy, and justice. The Spirit encompasses many qualities. In the Gospels it can be as gentle and tender as a dove—as when Jesus is baptized by John in the Jordan River and the Spirit descends from heaven like a dove. The Spirit can also be fierce—immediately after his baptism, Jesus is "driven" by the Spirit into the wilderness to face his temptations (Mk 1:12).

The Holy Spirit is often called the Spirit of truth because the Spirit cannot lie and empowers people to tell the truth and to confront those who lie (Jn 16:13). One who lives like Jesus, in the Spirit, speaks words that are "living and active, sharper than any two-edged sword, piercing until it divides soul from spirit, joints from marrow; it is able to judge the thoughts and intentions of the heart" (Heb 4:12). I am reminded of a Tibetan Buddhist *vajra* sword. Wielding the sword is like being in the Holy Spirit: our words and actions cut cleanly, delicately, and swiftly, dividing truth from falsehood without creating harmful unintended consequences.[4]

In all four Gospels the Holy Spirit accompanies Jesus through the temptations and empowers him to cast out demons and forgive sins (see, e.g., Mt 4:1–11). Jesus himself has the power to convey the Spirit through his own presence. Near the end of his life, knowing he will soon be executed, Jesus tells his friends that when he dies, "the Advocate, the Holy Spirit, whom the Father will send in my name, will teach you everything, and remind you of all that I have said to you" (Jn 14:26). A fearless search for truth is a core quality of someone who is led by the Spirit. "When the Spirit of truth comes, he will guide you into all the truth; for he will not speak on his own, but will speak whatever he hears, and he will declare to you the things that are to come" (Jn 16:13). Spirit is a holy inner Advocate, reminding us to live our truth, God's truth, in resonance with our Soul's purpose.

BEING A TEMPLE OF THE HOLY SPIRIT

Becoming transparent to Spirit begins with trust, the willingness to believe that there really is a higher power that we call the Holy Spirit. This conviction is not supported by America's skeptical, secular society, especially by people who are justifiably alarmed by Christians

---

[4] From ancient times the *vajra* sword was a weapon of the Indian Vedic rain and thunder deity, Indra, and was used symbolically by the dharma traditions of Jainism, Buddhism, and Hinduism to represent firmness of spirit and spiritual power.

who use belief in the Spirit to justify policies or practices that are antithetical to Jesus's vision of a God of love. But we need practices to help us stay attuned to the Spirit's presence. Such practices might include regular periods of prayer and meditation, staying inwardly watchful and alert, searching for truth and kindness in every situation, questioning our assumptions and opinions, acknowledging mistakes, being generous, and staying open to surprise—to what is creative, fresh, and new. As we become more transparent to God, the invisible Spirit becomes more visible to others in the qualities of our being and behavior.

The Spirit is not above the clouds somewhere but here in our midst, both among us and within our flesh, bone, and blood. The Spirit is an awakening *energy*, but more than that, there is a subjectivity within the Spirit, which is why our tradition uses the word *Person* for Spirit.

There is also a power within us that defies the Spirit; we inherit a tendency to self-centeredness and selfishness that Christians tradition-ally call sin. St. Paul's word for a life lived from within the limited, self-centered ego is "flesh": "For what the flesh desires is opposed to the Spirit, and what the Spirit desires is opposed to the flesh" (Gal 5:15). It's unfortunate that Paul chose the word *flesh* to refer to the self-centered ego, because it can be interpreted as meaning that our bodies are inherently sinful and are excluded from the Spirit's activi-ties. Paul's word choice was influenced by the surrounding Greek culture and its philosophical traditions that separated body and spirit. Despite theologians who judge Christianity as a body-hating religion, I believe that this is a distortion of the Gospel and of St. Paul's mes-sage. There is evidence that Paul valued the body and the material world; he wrote in one of his letters to the community at Corinth: "Do you not know that your body is a temple of the Holy Spirit within you, which you have from God, and that you are not your own?" (1 Cor 6:19).

Here in this sacred body and in this brief life that we've been given, we have an opportunity to allow the Spirit to become increas-ingly manifest through us. As we become transparent in the Spirit, we cultivate and manifest qualities such as love, joy, peace, patience, kindness, goodness, generosity, steadfastness, faithfulness, and self-control (see 2 Tim 3:10; Col 3:12; Phil 4:4–9), some of which St. Paul explicitly calls "fruit of the Spirit" (Gal 5:22–23).

I have sung the chant *Veni Sancte Spiritus,* "Come, Holy Spirit," in many churches. Although Paul says that we are temples of the Holy Spirit and that the Holy Spirit is within us, the Spirit is also outside us and beyond us; the Spirit transcends us. When we feel a need to pray "Come, Holy Spirit," we may know in theory that the Spirit is already here, but we still need to invoke the Spirit's presence—we need help in perceiving and trusting that the Spirit is here, and here with particular power. Praying "Come, Holy Spirit" awakens us to the Spirit's presence.

The Spirit is often depicted as feminine—an embracing, insightful, and unifying Presence that carries forward the Jewish tradition of Wisdom and Shekhinah. She does not lift us into an imagined, disembodied existence that is separate from the body or from suffering. I think of the Spirit as a spelunker companion, descending into and exploring every corner of our bodily experience, seeking God's Presence in all things—in our fear, anger, and despair as well as in our hope, comfort, and joy. The Spirit investigates every thought, sensation, and feeling as it passes through our awareness, as if curious about every experience, whether pleasant or unpleasant, noble or petty. As St. Paul says to the Corinthians, the Spirit "searches everything, even the depths of God" and is uniquely capable of comprehending the unknowable God (1 Cor 2:11–14). Reason and even human wisdom cannot venture there. When we live in the holy transparent present, the Spirit within us reaches out from, and into, the infinite dazzling darkness of God who is beyond us.

The Presence of the Spirit within us is subtle, and our ability to recognize Spirit is augmented by contemplative practices of listening in solitude and silence. Where does the Spirit come from and where is the Spirit going? We can only "know" this Presence when we realize that we are born of the Spirit (Jn 3:8). This knowing requires a deep listening and longing that are most easily accessed in silence.

In silence, we can release all distractions; we can witness and listen more easily beneath the flow of thoughts, emotions, and sensations. When we feel stuck in a judgmental, remorseful, or angry place, we must first notice that we're stuck. At such moments we can ask for

the Spirit's help and guidance. We might pray: "I'm stuck. Show me
the way through this wall into your freedom." Freedom is available
in each present moment—not yesterday or tomorrow, but always
now. Now is always the doorway to the Eternal. Now is when the
Spirit is available. As Jesus said, "Whenever you pray, go into your
room and shut the door and pray to your Father who is in secret"
(Mt 6:6). In silence we can glimpse the gift of eternal life, which is
mentioned so often in the Bible (2 Cor 3:6; Rom 8:2; 1 Cor 3:17), as
a moment-to-moment reality, not just as a reward after death if we've
been good. We cannot know the Spirit objectively, because the Spirit
moves inside our knowing without separation. And we cannot control
the actions of the Holy Spirit because we don't even know where she
comes from or goes. When we doubt the existence of the Spirit, we
should not get mired in guilt. Instead, we can simply assume that the
Spirit is present in our doubts and that we will see the truth in time.

According to St. Paul, the Holy Spirit is not just "out there" in a
separate heavenly realm. Speaking to the growing Christian community, he says that anyone can be "in" the Spirit, and that the Spirit
"dwells" within us (Rom 8:9). We are "led" by the Spirit, who prays
within us, intercedes for us with God, and helps us understand God
(Rom 8:14; 8:26–27; 1 Cor 2:10–11). Although we differ from one
another and have different personal histories, gifts, and talents, we all
share the same Spirit (1 Cor 12:4–13). When we choose to participate
in this Spirit, we can gradually be transformed into the holiness and
likeness of God (2 Cor 3:18). I believe that the Spirit longs for us to
realize our interbeing with God, with others, and with all of earth's
creatures.

Most Christians recognize the Spirit's role as the awakener of
beloved community, as the "we-bridge" between eternal Mystery
and our interpersonal relationships. In John's Gospel (Jn 7:39) the
risen Jesus breathes the Holy Spirit's Presence on his friends, and
they go forward with renewed energy to spread the good news. The
paradigmatic moment of the Holy Spirit's appearance for the Christian
community, known as Pentecost, comes fifty days after Jesus's resurrection, and is described by St. Luke (Acts 2:1–20).

Before the Spirit arrives, people from different countries gather,
but they can't understand one another's languages. We can imagine

the confusion and the possibility of misunderstanding or conflict. When the Holy Spirit appears, everyone is suddenly lit with the fire of an all-inclusive love that transcends apparent differences. Otherness is honored, as people still speak in their own languages, but now they understand one another. There's an immediate harmony and joy, and some observers even wonder if these people are drunk. But they're only drunk with the wine of the Spirit. This is how the Holy Spirit works, creating harmony in diversity and diversity in unity, and inviting us to experience the field of awareness named by ancient mystics as the perichoresis, the living Holy Trinity. The Spirit initiates and nourishes friendship and love across the boundaries of difference.

As on that day of Pentecost, I have experienced the Spirit bringing a unity of love, creativity, and care to groups composed of seekers from different spiritual traditions. People may give this holy Wisdom and Presence different names, but I believe it is universally recognizable. She brings a sense of warmth, trust, and communion, one that I've experienced in inter-spiritual contemplative Empty Bell[5] groups, even when they're held on Zoom. In the Presence of the Spirit, people's faces light up with a vulnerable and trusting presence. I doubt if many participants *think* that they are manifesting themselves as temples of the Spirit. They may simply feel safe among others, accepting of and acceptable to others without any pretense. When we feel seen, heard, and loved, we quite naturally reach out to others with empathy and kindness. When I sense this ambience in a group, I believe that the Spirit is present.

When we place our ultimate trust in Jesus, we realize that he is manifesting the glory of the First Person (the Creator). The Holy Spirit then guides us into ever deeper relationship with the other Persons. The Spirit is the inner dynamism of Christ-consciousness. This is how we become "new" in Christ (2 Cor 5:17): we are empowered by the same Spirit who was there at the Great Flaring Forth. Those who have become new in this way find themselves doing virtuous things they didn't think they could, radiating beneficent qualities they didn't know they had, creating healing experiences that surprise them,

---

[5] The Empty Bell is a community for the study and practice of Christian meditation and prayer.

and getting to know people they would otherwise have never met. They become less and less tempted to take credit for who they are and what they do, because they are grateful to the Spirit for everything. They realize that they have not created themselves. When they are knocked off balance by suffering, pain, or disappointment, the Spirit helps them to get up and keep walking into the new creation.

SPIRIT CALLS A COUNCIL OF ALL BEINGS

In the light of today's ecological crisis and the growing awareness of White supremacy, I believe God is calling people of White European ancestry to understand that the Pentecostal experience includes not just people who look and act like us but all people and all living things. Buber's vision of I and Thou is fruitfully expanded when we are ready to encounter human beings who are different from us—and also nonhuman creatures—as "thou." Since all living things breathe the same air, and since we are all created as good by the same God, we can envision a Pentecost circle that includes all living beings. Inspired by John's Gospel (14:20; 17:23), we could say: "I am in my neighbor and my neighbor is in me. We are all created in God, and God is in all of us." The Holy Spirit facilitates this deep relational identity of mutual love that Christians call Christ.

When we are immersed in the natural world, we can invite the Spirit into our hiking and paddling experiences—even into our walk in a city park—as we pause to consider the subjective knowing of any creature that we encounter. As I hike through a forest, I might address the Spirit by silently asking, "What do you want me to hear and see?" I have found it helpful to linger in the mutual gaze of king-birds, bullfrogs, monarch butterflies, and even a snapping turtle, and to stand beneath an old oak, listening for their way of being. This is how we realize our true nature as co-beings on this planet. Linji, the founder of a school of Zen Buddhism, called such realized persons "transindividual individuals."[6] Other Zen teachers speak of "a person

---

[6] See Akizuki Ryomin, *New Mahayana: Buddhism for a Post-Modern World,* trans. James W. Heisig and Paul L. Swanson (Berkeley, CA: Asian Humanities Press, 1990), 90.

of no rank," or a "True Person," humbly connected to all other persons and beings. Buddhist activist and teacher Joanna Macy has written extensively about a transpersonal kinship ceremony that she calls the Council of All Beings.[7] Perhaps we glimpse this insight in the social and political realm when we read in America's Declaration of Independence that all persons are created equal.[8] This national aspiration must now be expanded to include all beings.

We come to discover with St. Paul that the Spirit "dwells within us" and that "that very Spirit [bears] witness with our spirit" (Rom 8:9–15). No longer isolated as individual "consumers," we realize with St. Paul that "we, who are many, are one body in Christ, and individually we are members one of another" (Rom 12:5). Paul reflects on this theme in his first letter to the Corinthians: "Do you not know that your bodies are members of Christ?" (1 Cor 6:15). "For just as the body is one and has many members, and all the members of the body, though many, are one body, so it is with Christ" (1 Cor 12:12). "Now you are the body of Christ and individually members of it" (1 Cor 12:27). I believe it is time to understand that this one "body" of kinship includes all creatures, not just humans. The Gospels ask us to live this paradox, to love all others in a unity of Spirit while also valuing their precious "otherness."

In the Spirit revealed at Pentecost we all live alone together; we are distinct, and we also participate in a unity of care. When we're isolated in our separate egos, comparing ourselves to others and complaining about them, we oscillate between clinging and aversion, love and hate, self-acceptance and self-diminishment. But when we understand that the Spirit brings a radically inclusive, transformational awareness and love, good things begin to happen. Under the influence

---

[7] John Seed, Joanna Macy, Pat Fleming, and Arne Naess, *Thinking Like a Mountain: Towards a Council of All Beings* (Gabriola Island, BC: New Society Publishers), 1988.

[8] Meister Eckhart's sermons brim with this inclusive insight, as when he writes: "As long as you love one single person less than yourself, you have never loved yourself. . . . All is well for the person who loves himself and all men as himself." *Meister Eckhart: Teacher and Preacher*, ed. Bernard McGinn, with Frank Tobin and Elvira Borgstad (New York: Paulist Press, 1986), 268.

of Spirit, even what we thought was ugly, marginal, irrelevant, or expendable can be recognized as blessed and essential (1 Cor 12:12–27). I think that those of us who are White are invited to read Paul's letter as a metaphor for how we might look upon all people of color and all creatures. What would it look like if we worked to create communities in which no one was left out, marginalized, or considered inferior?

PART THREE

PRACTICING THE PERSONS

7

First Person

The Mystery Is Us and Not Us

Three pivotal images point us to First Person practices: the first chapter of Genesis, the first lines of the Nicene Creed, and the astrophysical description of the cosmos.

First, the ancient story of creation in Genesis 1:1–5 suggests that all of reality emerges from an intentional, benevolent First Cause, the First Person of the Trinity (who is Uncaused):

> In the beginning when God created the heavens and the earth, the earth was a formless void while a wind from God swept over the face of the waters. Then God said, "Let there be light"; and there was light. And God saw and God separated the light from the darkness. God called the light Day, and the darkness he called Night. And there was evening and there was morning, the first day.

Second, the opening lines of the Nicene Creed state the core confession of Christian faith:

> We believe in one God, the Father, the Almighty, maker of heaven and earth, of all that is, seen and unseen.

Following the guidance of John Scotus Eriugena (810–77), this means that everything I experience—everything seen and unseen— is created from *within* God, not separately from or outside of God.

Scotus asserts that we are perceiving accurately when we see that the invisible and visible coincide:

> For everything that is understood and sensed is nothing else but
> 1) the apparition of what is non-apparent, 2) the manifestation
> of the hidden, 3) the affirmation of the negated, 4) the compre-
> hension of the incomprehensible, 5) the utterance of the unut-
> terable, 6) the access to the inaccessible, 7) the understanding
> of the unintelligible, 8) the body of the bodiless, 9) the essence
> of the superessential, 10) the form of the formless, 11) the mea-
> sure of the measureless, 12) the number of the numberless, 13)
> the weight of the weightless, 14) the materialization [literally:
> "thickening"] of the spiritual, 15) the visibility of the invisible,
> 16) the placing of the not-placed, 17) the temporality of the
> timeless, 18) the definition of the infinite, 19) the circumscrip-
> tion of the uncircumscribed.[1]

Simply *believing* the Nicene Creed is interesting and may provide some hope, but many followers of Jesus want a direct experience of the Creator's Presence in all that is seen and unseen. Contemplative practices make the incomprehensible source of our experience avail-able when we are motivated by a fierce longing to dwell in God's Presence.

Third, contemporary cosmological understanding echoes parts of the Abrahamic creation myth. Both accounts depict a universe of lim-itless origin and dimensions that somehow supports a safe harbor for life to thrive. Our planet is tiny compared to the sun and the trillions of galaxies out there in empty space. Humans are born naked, vulner-able, and mortal on an orb that rotates in a boundless and directionless emptiness with no up or down, no right or left. Nothing is holding us up. In the scientific worldview this surrounding Nothing is a weird fact, but in the contemplative tradition, this Nothing is sacred and a source of both terror and awe. We can be astonished that there is

---

[1] In Bernard McGinn, *The Growth of Mysticism* (New York: Crossroad, 1994), 99.

anything at all! Any experience of the Creator must include qualities of awe, as we touch the sacred mystery of ourselves, and life itself.[2]

We can be amazed that complex biological, intellectual, and spiritual creatures like us emerged in this infinite cosmos. Slight variations in quantum and gravitational dynamics, molecular structure, and temperature at the Great Flaring Forth could have yielded a lifeless cosmos without consciousness. We can appropriately say that it's a miracle we're here. When we, in awe, exclaim, "What a mystery!" we speak the truth. Science cannot give us a final and full explanation of who we are or why we exist, but our raw experience of living on Planet Earth can inspire awe, reverence, and gratitude.

Contemplative practices reveal the awesome and precious Mystery that Christians call the First Person. But they are difficult to follow. For one thing, they bring us straight into the headwinds of our individualistic, capitalistic, entertainment-saturated culture. In addition, throughout the day we must usually focus our awareness on what is immediately in front of us as we address the practical challenges of our immediate situation. We need to survive in ordinary reality—to make a living and to take care of ourselves, our families, and our communities. But even as you read these words, the sun, the moon, the stars, and an endless expanse of Nothing exist far beyond us. This larger view of our situation matters! Recognizing the vast context in which we live our daily lives can be unsettling, even scary, but it can also elicit a deep sense of wonder. If we look directly at the contingency of our lives, and of everything that exists, we can learn to navigate with grace the full range of experience. We may know fear and dread, but we will also know gratitude, curiosity, joy, and an ardent desire to investigate our situation. We enter the gateway to these practices when we look out into the stars at night and ask, "Who am I?" and "Why am I here? Why is anything here?" When these ultimate questions arise, we are dwelling in First Person awareness.

---

[2] As astrophysicist Carl Sagan looked out into space he described our earth as "a mote of dust suspended in a sunbeam" (Carl Sagan, *Pale Blue Dot* [1994; copyright 2006 by Democritus Properties, LLC]). See a dramatic animation of our earth in space based on Sagan's words at Joel Somerfield, "A Pale Blue Dot," YouTube (Dec. 19, 2012).

This cosmological perspective has practical significance in our interpersonal lives and in our relationship with the natural world. In his encyclical on the climate crisis, *Laudato Si'*, Pope Francis suggests a fundamental connection between the experience of awe and a God-given ethical response: "If we approach nature and the environment without an openness to awe and wonder, if we no longer speak the language of fraternity and beauty in our relationship with the world, our attitude will be that of masters, consumers, ruthless exploiters, unable to set limits on their immediate needs." Like St. Francis of Assisi, Pope Francis goes on to describe the cosmos as "a magnificent book in which God speaks to us and grants us a glimpse of his infinite beauty and goodness. 'Through the greatness and the beauty of creatures one comes to know by analogy their maker' (Wis 13:5)" (LS, no. 11).

As I gaze up at the heavens, I feel I'm looking into eternity and at the same time, *the eternity out there is also within me*. The First Person of the Trinity is beyond me and is also within me. Each of us participates in eternity, and the contemplative tradition maintains that one can dwell in eternity while navigating everyday clock-time. As this realization deepens, we can become more and more transparent to God's perspective, transcending time from within time. Many early mystics used the word *deification* for this union of our limited consciousness with that of the unlimited Creator.

Most contemplatives I know find no contradiction between the scientific cosmological perspectives and ancient creation stories. These approaches to truth employ different methods and awaken different aspects of our minds and hearts. But we are gazing into the same unending mystery. We are all living in eternity as time is passing through us. Contemplative practices based on the Abrahamic scriptures, on the Nicene Creed, and on cosmological scientific evidence can give us a direct experience of this eternal mystery. It's a mystery that can be more than thought about; it can be experienced.

MEDITATION AND CONTEMPLATION

I have emphasized that each Person of the Trinity inhabits and awakens an aspect of human consciousness. So, to understand the First

Person, we need to *stand* in First Person consciousness. What is this consciousness? How can we recognize and practice it?

When teachers in the contemplative Christian tradition speak of spiritual practices, they make an important distinction between meditation and contemplation. Meditation is usually practiced in silence, employing certain methods of prayer and reflection that focus and shape our awareness, and may lead to contemplation. The Carmelites, for example, say meditation is an active process. Those meditating are *doing* something—using their purpose and will by employing images, mantras, quiet reflection, and the imagination to place themselves in God's Presence. Methods might include reading scripture, lighting a candle, listening to spiritual music, reciting a mantra, or gazing upon sacred icons. Most contemplative guides will say that these embodied and material settings are necessary meditative preparations for contemplation, which is our portal to the deeper dimension of awareness often called nondual.

Compared to meditation, contemplation is more receptive than active. It gazes *through* words, images, thoughts, and feelings. We aren't doing anything, just opening our minds and hearts and trusting in God's Presence. Crossing the threshold from meditation to contemplation is stepping off the edge of all sensory and cognitive ways and goals. Contemplation lets go of all doing, relinquishing all efforts to achieve. In contemplation, we move from communicating with God to communing with God.

Many Christians aren't familiar with their contemplative tradition, and some are simply uninterested. But changes are afoot. In the last century many seekers in the Christian tradition began to join newly emerging contemplative groups like Contemplative Outreach and engage in practices such as centering prayer. The Trappist monks in Massachusetts who initiated this practice in the 1970s had been meditating at the nearby Vipassana Buddhist Retreat Center and soon discovered that their experiences enriched their prayer life. Buddhist meditation motivated them to uncover their own ancient history of Christian contemplation, beginning with the works of John Cassian (d. 435 CE). This contemplative history and the spiritual practices associated with it were published by Trappist monk and priest Basil

Pennington in 1980. His book, *Centering Prayer,* sold more than a million copies.

Also, during the 1970s the Benedictine monk Fr. John Main, who had learned mantra practices from Swami Satyananda in Malaysia, rediscovered the works of Christian desert fathers and the tradition of *theosis* and deification. Main and his successor, Laurence Freeman, founded a worldwide movement of mantra meditation called the World Community for Christian Meditation (WCCM). Such groups for centering prayer and Christian meditation are inspired by two millennia of Christian mystics; they sponsor many contemplative retreats; and they have produced many books of their own.

Such groups teach students to meditate and trust in silence as the gateway to contemplation. John Main recommended that one repeat a sacred word or mantra with every breath or as one gazes upon on a holy image. Contemplatives in this community often repeat the ancient Aramaic phrase "Maran-Atha," usually translated, "Come, Lord Jesus" (1 Cor 16:22). Repeating this word or phrase with each breath focuses one's mind, allowing the meditator to more easily detach from worries, narratives, and memories in order to be open to God's immediate Presence. Practitioners are advised to maintain the repetition of the mantra no matter what. By contrast, those who practice centering prayer and use a word or image to focus the mind and intention are advised to let the word or image go when it distracts them from the immediate awareness of God's Presence. Quite often, the centering word drops away by itself, quite naturally, leaving us simply and wholeheartedly open in silence to our inner and outer reality. I believe that both of these practices are trustworthy doorways into First Person awareness. Those who glimpse this experience say that it is like a cloudless, star-lit sky.

Both centering prayer and Christian meditation understand that meditation is a steppingstone to contemplation. I have attended retreats in both types of communities. We sit in a quiet place, relax our bodies and minds, sit up straight, and focus our attention by silently repeating a word or mantra with each in-breath and out-breath. As we follow our breathing and silently repeat the word, we notice sensations, thoughts, emotions, memories, and imaginary scenes as they pass through our minds and bodies. As soon as we notice these experiences, we let them go and, if necessary, return to our breathing or to the sacred word or mantra. After years of frequent practice, the power of silently witnessing and detaching from our thoughts and feelings becomes habitual, and a deep sense of freedom and trust arises. We begin to notice our attachments to narratives and judgments, and how these attachments distract us from our direct experience. We begin to realize that we are vastly more than our thoughts about ourselves, others, or God. We begin to trust the silence more than our thinking, and to trust that in this detached present we are very near the Creator, who is the Beyond-Within who witnesses all thoughts and images. Relaxed, awake, and aware, it's as if we are right there at the Great Flaring Forth, when time and space first appeared.

With practice, we begin to pass through the barrier of our self-concerns and become steadily present to the flow of clock-time within and around us. Everything that exists in clock-time is passing, but the First Person's Presence is timeless and never passes. As our practice matures, we often experience the joy and peace of "knowing" without words or images, a knowing that seems transparent to an infinite trust and love. In fact, we might experience what William of Saint Thierry described as *amor ipse notitia est* (loving itself is knowing).[3]

The late Fr. Thomas Keating often said that repeating a sacred word or phrase such as "Lord, have mercy," "Come, Lord Jesus," or "Come, Holy Spirit" is not a self-help method but an expression of intention to let go of everything except God. We understand that our longing for God is also God's longing, which is freely rising within us. In the depths of the eternal cosmos there is a sacred longing (Rom 8:19). Most of us are so attuned to external events, news, and the flow of social media images that we don't even notice that we're longing. Deep longing in deep time is sacred.

Although contemplation can't be experienced by applying methods, methods are a helpful, even necessary, way to begin and sustain the spiritual journey into the First Person; they give us a structure and a holding environment for guidance and inspiration. We trust

---

[3] William of Saint Thierry, quoted in Paul Mommaers and Jan Van Bragt, *Mysticism: Buddhist and Christian: Encounters with Jan Van Ruusbroec* (New York: Crossroad, 1995), 197.

meditative methods like repeating mantras, singing hymns, and reading scripture as bridges to the holy Nowhere of the Creator. This is a holy Nowhere that is everywhere because God has no location. God's center is everywhere, just as the center of the Great Flaring Forth is everywhere. We begin contemplative practices by imagining a path to somewhere better than where we are, a place where we will be better than who we are, but we discover that the path actually leads us to exactly where we are and who we are. We eventually find that the "there" we are seeking is already here, and always has been.

We can trust the guidance of teachers like Meister Eckhart and St. John of the Cross, who wrote that we must eventually transcend all methods of meditation and prayer, continuously cultivating a sense of holy Presence. Then we must actually *be* that Presence to ourselves and others. We are moved to love, serve, and create, and we are given strength to overcome the fears and troubles that might otherwise paralyze us. In that Presence we establish ourselves in the wonder of daily life and the cosmos, where barriers between ourselves and others are transcended in a community of care.[4]

Our portal to this blessed First Person experience is always the present now. That may sound easy, but most of us aren't used to being present. Therefore, I recommend that those who feel drawn to contemplation find a local group to join, in person or on an online platform. It's best to find a group that is hosted by an experienced practitioner and person of faith, and a group that meets regularly to experience anywhere from twenty to sixty minutes of silence. I think it's best to find a group that includes respectful, careful sharing of experiences. Sharing that emerges from silence invites a prayerful and playful sense of communion that is facilitated by the Holy Spirit.[5]

---

[4] Eckhart wrote: "The person who is not conscious of God's presence, but who must always be going out to get Him from this and that, who has to seek Him by special methods, as by means of some activity, person, or place—such people have not attained God. . . . The difficulty lies within the man for whom God has not yet become everything." In Karen J. Campbell, ed., *German Mystical Writings: Hildegard of Bingen, Meister Eckhart, Jacob Boehme, et al.* (New York: Continuum, 1991), 74.

[5] For over twenty-five years I have convened small groups like this at the Empty Bell. I invite you to explore its website. I also recommend the online

CONSCIOUS, KIND, AND CREATIVE PRESENCE

When we access First Person awareness, a fundamental question arises: *If I am not my fears, hopes, memories, and thoughts, who am I?* In silence we become intimate with the changing forms of our perceptions and emotions, directly experiencing the moment-to-moment magic and alchemical transmutation that is always taking place within us. The Flemish mystic Jan Van Ruysbroeck, in *The Sparkling Stone,* described contemplative process as one that combines and stirs salt, sulfur, and mercury into a transformed experience of vision, reason, and love that forms within us and arises like a "sparkling stone," continuously radiant with Uncreated Light. This Light is our consciousness, always rotating and transmitting the refracted Light of the Creator who is sometimes called the Uncreated, because it is a Light that isn't put together with created ingredients and can't be seen with our material senses.

What will we discover as we sit in silence with this intention? On my first ten-day silent retreat at the Insight Meditation Center in Barre, Massachusetts, I folded myself down onto a cushion in the meditation hall, surrounded by one hundred men and women who were also sitting up straight on cushions facing a statue of Buddha and the living Vipassana teacher at the front of the room. I sailed through the first two days, away from work and able to relax. We were asked to remain in silence throughout the retreat, alternating sitting for thirty minutes and then walking slowly back and forth in the meditation hall. We were asked not to communicate with anyone—no letters, phone calls, or conversations with other retreatants. Meals were silent. By the third day I was bored and restless. I imagined quietly gathering up my things, slinking out to the car, and returning to my apartment in Cambridge.

Our spiritual guide recommended that we simply watch our minds and monitor our feelings. I understood the basic Vipassana worldview

---

videos of Contemplative Outreach and the WCCM, two internationally known Roman Catholic contemplative organizations, where you'll find instructions, encouragement, and helpful talks. Fr. Richard Rohr's Living School for Action and Contemplation website also provides useful contemplative instruction.

about suffering and impermanence, but I gradually realized that I enjoyed *reading* about Buddhist spirituality more than actually *practicing* it. In mid-retreat I noticed how judgmental I was, fixating on what fellow retreatants were wearing, or how predictably (and boringly) they would look for a place to sit, and then take so long to settle themselves and become still. Meanwhile, I was continuously wiggling and scratching the various itches that were spontaneously arising on my back and legs. My knees burned, and the muscles in my back ached from sitting still for the thirty-minute meditations.

On day eight something powerful happened. I became aware that many of the thoughts and memories that arose in my mind were repetitious. In one sitting I saw my thoughts constellate and rotate through my mind like wooden horses on a merry-go-round, as if I were sitting in the center of the orbiting carousel, watching a dozen very familiar ideas, opinions, fears, and memories go round and round in my mind and body. I was terrified. I thought, *Is this all I am? Who am I? Am I only this tiresome, humdrum repetition of thoughts and feelings?* I became disgusted, ashamed, and angry at myself for being a totally shallow person. I was nothing—but not the holy Nothing, just the kind that is worthless.

I had thought that I was a good and intelligent person, but no, I was nothing but a roundabout of repetition, a superficial whirl of judgments and opinions. I was just making up stories to impress other people and myself; I was like an actor trapped on a stage, mouthing someone else's lines and unable to make an exit and return to real life. Frightened and appalled, I was relieved to remember what one of the teachers had recommended: that we investigate our mind and feelings. I asked myself, *Why am I so uncomfortable? I'm just another seeker on a retreat. I'm safe, and everyone else seems to be doing fine.* But this narrative didn't help.

I ran out of fresh thoughts, and then I glimpsed sadness. I slid down a long black chute of the heart into deep grief. I tried to sit still as the tears dripped on my clothes. I furtively looked around to see if anyone was looking at me, which only inflamed my self-hatred: *Aren't I always wondering what other people think of me?* As I wept in silence, a memory emerged. I recalled how my maternal grand-parents took in my siblings and me after our parents bought a saloon and disappeared into alcoholism. I remembered how my grandparents tried to shelter and protect us, and I remembered Grandma's wall hangings of Jesus, the shepherd of lost sheep. I was surprised to realize that I was smiling through my tears. Soon, I was being carried on a river of grief, gratitude, and joy, feeling safe and at home on my cushion on the floor.

This is what First Person contemplation can be like. When we sit still in silence, surprising and unsettling things can happen. We soften our hearts and minds and open ourselves to the scary unknown, to the mystery of what comes next. We gradually realize that we are not our conscious thoughts, that in fact we are a vast reservoir of living memories, presences, images, desires, opinions, and fears. We become more aware of experiences that enliven, inspire, hurt, or scare us. With a steady inner gaze, we investigate what sorts of perceptions, memories, and imaginings make our inner world smaller, and which ones convey a sense of spaciousness, awe, joy, love, and hope. We notice that everything we are aware *of* is passing, but that awareness itself is not passing.

We become sincerely curious about who we are. As our practice develops, we find that something new is always taking place. Inwardly, we become an adventure, and we begin to behave with others in ways that invite them to set out on their own journeys. I find that this happens quite naturally, without trying to carefully follow any teacher's advice. Soon, just being oneself is a blessed experience.

In fact, just being oneself is a teaching to oneself. Along the way we can value all the basic teachings we've received as pointers to our own mystery. For example, if, as I sit in silence, something comes up that makes me uncomfortable, I can affirm the contemplative commitment to explore every emotion and memory, looking for its direction and value as sacred. But no teacher can tell me what I will find within myself because no one else is living my life.

First Person awareness invites us to see our minds clearly. In silence we discover that almost all our thoughts have been formulated in the past, and that when we are caught up in thinking, we are probably living in the past. A lot of our thoughts are like Frisbees that we cast forward into the future, thinking that we can imagine or predict what's coming based on what we already know. Some thoughts will yield accurate information about the present or future, some will be creative or helpful, but many will not. When we habitually carry stories and narratives from our past into the present and project them into the future, we overshadow the present moment and what is happening now. Of course, there are times when we need to look closely at the past or to make plans for the future, but we need to do so with clear awareness of our rootedness in the present moment. Nothing truly new can happen unless we are fully present, and God is the most present thing there is.

Thomas Keating often suggested that we let go of thoughts as if they were boats floating downstream as we stand on the shore. Why is this so difficult? Because we tend to believe that we *are* our thoughts and opinions. Relinquishing our hard-won opinions may scare or even offend us, as if we were being asked to give up our very selves. There is a truth to this, because we are indeed being asked to give up the self that we thought we were. Sitting in silence, we may accept the idea that we should detach from our thoughts, and we may try to do this, but then we may find ourselves thinking about letting go of images and thoughts, noticing that we are judging ourselves, wondering if we're doing it "right," or if we're as good at detaching from thoughts as someone else. Thinking about detaching from thinking is still thinking.

Let me hasten to say that thinking and using our imaginations are not wrong or unskillful in themselves. *Attachment* to our thoughts and images is the problem. Letting go of thinking can make us feel vulnerable, because we have inadvertently assumed that our thoughts and sacred images protect us from a dangerous unknown. Our narratives about reality can be helpful, but they can also be bulwarks against reality. If we are protecting ourselves with our thoughts, we are shielding ourselves from the infinite reality of the Creator, who cannot be met in word or thought. Unmindfully attached to our inner narratives about other people, we are also inadvertently protecting ourselves from others who, in their otherness, are not who we think they are.

Sometimes our contemplative practice of detachment is easy: we see that we have been mistaken or judgmental, and we quickly drop those opinions. For some mystics, shedding whatever is not God is a rational process. They notice their unpleasant attachments and entertain a simple thought that releases them, such as, "I'm stuck; let it go," or "God is not this; God is infinitely more." However, for me, detachment is often an emotional process. I take comfort in the writings of the sixth-century monk Gregory the Great, for whom detachment was more than a rational or theological process; it was an exploration into the unknown, often accompanied by grief, fear, or joy. I'm also reminded of Henri Nouwen's image of spiritual growth being a furnace of transformation. Sometimes buried experiences of abuse or abandonment can arise—yet another clue that our habits of conscious thinking aren't necessarily the whole story. We can't think our way out of suffering or think our way to God.

Releasing attachments does not mean forgetting what and whom we love, but experiencing love at a deeper level, along with the grief that accompanies letting go. When we empty ourselves of attachment to opinions, images, people, and material pleasures, we experience loss, and this moves our gaze toward something even more real and eternal. A popular Zen saying is "Die before you die." Dying to our worries, cares, losses, and loves is very difficult. In the presence of transcendent Love, we glimpse our fragile humanity from a much larger perspective. When we love, we open ourselves to grief, and when we grieve, we open ourselves to love.

In the early stages of spiritual development, our grief is awash with self-pity, regret, and guilt—about me and my losses. But as we grow, our tears flow not from ego but from the ground of our infinite souls. Medieval mystics call this *compunctio amoris*, the gift of tears. Echoing the erotic poetry of the Song of Songs, Gregory depicts our awareness of boundless love as a wound in our hearts, and from this sacred wound, God's Love can flow into creation. He quotes the Book of Job: "Because he wounds and heals; he strikes and his hands will cure" (5:18). The phrase "he wounds" is often interpreted as the act of a vengeful God, but I think Gregory means that our increasing openness to God makes us more sensitive and vulnerable to our pain and to all the immense suffering around us. Purity of heart may feel wounding, but God's Love enlightens and transforms our wounds.

Like all mystics, Gregory searches for words to express the inexpressible. He speaks about flashes of light (Latin: *rima contemplationis*) that shine upon the splayed windows of the cathedral of our soul

Figure 7.1. Splayed window, author's composition.

(see Figure 7.1). "The part through which the light enters is narrow, but the interior that receives the light is wide."[6] As we become more naked and open in the infinitude of God's Presence, our minds enlarge in the spaciousness of the Beyond Within.

Sometimes, I must get up from my meditation cushion to sing and dance my overflowing feelings. Arts such as poetry, music, dance, and

---

[6] In Cheslyn Jones, Geoffrey Wainwright, and Edward Yarnold, SJ, eds., *The Study of Spirituality* (New York: Oxford University Press, 1986), 67.

painting are available to help us express ourselves and to release us from who we thought we were. Sometimes I'll play touching worship music that invites my trust in the holy Personhood that Jesus manifested. It may be a hymn, but my grief and love might also be released as I listen to a touching popular song. Soon, the music brings me to a deep, renewing silence. Gazing into beauty also brings me to this Love, and fifty years of photography have trained my eye to appreciate surprising new harmonies and disharmonies of colors and shapes. My daughter Chris is an expert landscape painter. She will stand before her easel and be silent for long periods of time, considering the balance of elements in her work, pondering the colors in her painting and in her collection of oils, watercolors, pastels, and brushes. And she will experience a peace and joy that transcend her clock-time life. Another friend, Vince Redhouse, is a Navajo saxophonist who will play a piece over and over until he lets go of the written notation. It's as if the song begins to sing within him, opening his mind and heart to the Great Spirit. These kinds of deep gazing, listening, and artistic skills are acquired and enhanced in the First Person dimension of awareness.

I have noticed that when I don't know what to do next, I can simply stop, close my eyes, and listen for guidance from the Spirit. In the stillness I may entertain a question: *What are You calling me to do now?* To detach from habitual thinking is liberating; it gives us space to consider alternative actions. But we should never quickly discount an interesting thought or imaginative image. Contemplative teachers, both Buddhist and Christian, speak of the value of relinquishing thoughts, song, memories, and images, but sometimes these experiences convey a blessing. We must be present and awake in the present to receive the blessing.

Sometimes, as I sit in silence, I integrate Christian and Buddhist approaches, inwardly alternating repetition of a sacred phrase such as "Come, Lord Jesus" with the simple Zen phrase "What is this?" Or I might ask, "Who is Jesus? Who within me is seeking Jesus?" Any mantra-like or koan-like question can bring us to a deeper level of mystery. I don't seek answers. The questions are themselves a kind of answer. Questions like these bring me to the edge of the Canyon, and from there I can simply lift my wings and catch the wind of Spirit.

There are as many ways to discover First Person awareness as there are people. For example, I have a friend who grew up in an atheist Jewish household; in her twenties she accepted an invitation to a Hindu kirtan and experienced an illumination that brought her deep peace and a conviction that she is the beloved. One of my clients in psychotherapy grew up in a Lutheran household, felt deeply nourished by liturgies that included music of Martin Luther and Johann Sebastian Bach, but then left the church because these experiences no longer nourished him. His spiritual search led him to a Jewish Shabbat service where he suddenly realized that Lutherans and Jews are devoted to the same ineffable Reality. And I have friends in the environmental-action community who eschew religion but spend many hours in nature and feel drawn to a beauty that is beyond language and thought. All these experiences can be valid portals to Divine Mystery, the First Person, helping us to be available to God in simple awakeness, humility, curiosity, trust, and awe.

GOING DEEPER IS INTERBEING

Imagine you are meditating and find yourself inwardly arguing with someone. Your belly and neck are getting tight. You're angry, convinced that you're right and the other person is wrong. In such moments, we might drop beneath the words and images and bring full awareness to the body. Where is the anger in my body? Is there physical pain? If so, is it sharp, dull, steady, or pulsating? Can I let the emotion be felt exactly as it is, without rejecting or amplifying it? What do I observe in this person that I don't like? How am *I* like that? We can notice our angry thoughts and our constricted body while detaching from the inner argument and exploring the pure energy of anger. Such explorations have often led me from anger to heartache, as I humbly acknowledge my powerlessness to control other people or reality itself. With Gregory, I now assume that my anger often conceals grief, and I've noticed that if I can't find grief, I might not be open to love. As tears of sadness appear, I can usually detach quickly from blame, complaint, and judgment, and perceive how much I need other people, how alike we all are, and how much we have in common. Tears can release the love.

Strong emotions can separate us from others or draw us more closely to others. When I experience vulnerable emotions, I generally feel more connected to others. My sense of self enlarges; my grief (or other strong feeling) connects me with everyone else who experiences it: *my* grief becomes *the* grief. Perhaps, in such moments we "inter-are" in the interdependent field of First Person awareness, which, being infinite, excludes nothing and no one. First Person "unknowing" can open the field of awareness to sudden revelations and memories, informing our understanding of the shame, regret, joy, and love we have experienced. This openness allows us to access our personal unconscious as well as what Jung called the collective unconscious, and what Teilhard de Chardin called the "noosphere" of universal experience.[7] It is possible to experience these contemplative depths while living a householder's everyday ego-self life. Aware of our memories, plans, projects, and responsibilities, we can simultaneously detach from the illusion of our separate individuality and wander in the field of interbeing that some Christian mystics have called perichoresis.

When uncomfortable feelings arise in silence, I sometimes refer to scripture for a phrase or story that holds meaning or brings comfort. For example, when I notice that I'm thinking about a tragedy described in the media, I sometimes imagine myself at the foot of the cross bringing the suffering to Jesus, who suffers with me and embraces everything with love. At the cross, I know that his death opened a doorway to a love that transcends life and death. Perhaps I briefly take on John 1:5 as a mantra: "A light shines in the darkness, and the darkness does not overcome it." When I feel lost or feel exposed and embarrassed, I sometimes accept this discomfort as a sign that God is close. In such moments I might recall Psalm 57:1:

> Be merciful to me, O God, be merciful to me,
>   for in you my soul takes refuge;
> in the shadow of your wings I will take refuge,
>   until the destroying storms pass by.

---

[7] See Carter Phipps, *Evolutionaries: Unlocking the Spiritual and Cultural Potential of Science's Greatest Idea* (New York: HarperCollins, 2012), 162–68.

The unencumbered spaciousness of First Person awareness is the natural territory of our minds and our awareness. It is the cathedral of our true identity in God, the only place from which we can know ourselves and God. I cannot know myself without knowing God, and vice versa. Augustine's autobiography repeats this idea in many different ways: *Noverim te, noverim me* (To know you is to know myself).

BREATH OF LIFE, BREATH OF MUSIC

At top speed we cannot perceive the full scale of reality. Speed kills, obscuring the delicate moments, events, and people who long to be seen and heard. Dashing through our days, we miss the life-giving energies of spirit and *Chi*, and the subtle Presence of the Spirit. We ignore the non-conceptual knowing that is always descending and ascending from our brains and toes down and up through our bodies. Certain kinds of music can liberate us—at least momentarily—from obsessive thinking and from judging ourselves and others and open us to a larger reality. Contemplative disciplines enlarge these glimpses and weave them into our daily lives.

Years ago, I learned to play the shakuhachi, a Japanese bamboo flute. While attending Weston Jesuit School of Theology in the early 1990s, I enrolled in a seminar on Thomas Merton's friendship with the Dalai Lama. One day near the end of the semester the teaching fellow, David Duncavage, played the shakuhachi. I knew immediately that this was my sacred instrument, and I began taking lessons with him. A West Point graduate, David had resigned his commission and entered a Trappist monastery, intending to become a monk. But he soon discovered the shakuhachi and spent many years in Japan, studying this ancient Buddhist tradition with Yoshio Kurahashi.[8]

David considered this flute to be both a Roman Catholic and a Zen liturgical instrument. I was thrilled to begin studying with him.

---

[8] Sensei Kurahashi has recently changed his name from Yoshio to Yodo Kurahashi. His father, Yodo, was also a shakuhachi master. See, for example, the albums by Kurahashi Sensei, *Honkyoku: Musique Zen Pour Shakuhachi*; David Duncavage, *The Empty Bell*; and Robert A. Jonas, *Blowing Bamboo*, all available on iTunes.

At the time, I was forty-four years old and hadn't played a musical instrument for twenty years, but over the next ten years I learned to play the fundamental pieces of Suizen (Blowing Zen) and Honkyoku (Origin music) (see Figure 7.2).

Figure 7.2. A fragment of Kyo Rei (empty bell), a shakuhachi piece. The calligrapher died long ago, and this piece is more than 150 years old.

In ancient times, monks in Japan who played the shakuhachi called their practice *Ichion JoButsu* (to become Buddha in one sound). This didn't mean that the monks would totally forget their everyday life and actually become the historical Gautama Buddha, but that they would discover who they really are—endowed with Buddha nature and witnessing everything from the sacred Nowhere of *Dharmakaya*. Suizen practitioners bring careful awareness to each in-breath, to the smooth outflowing of the breath, and to the silence between the notes, which adds depth and richness to the notes before and after. This rhythm of silence and sound echoes the rhythm of winds that circulate through a bamboo forest, and the swelling and receding cadences of human conversation. In the first few years of shakuhachi practice, I wondered if I, as a Christian, was playing in order "to become Christ in one sound," but this felt too haughty. Instead, I prayed that with each breath I could empty myself of pride and self-reproach and let Christ's kenosis flow through me. Could I let the bamboo take the lead as Christ sings to Creator?

Suizen monks (Japanese: *komuso*, monks of emptiness) trusted that shakuhachi practice would awaken their deep, unseen, true, original Self, which they called non-self (Sanskrit: *anatman*). After playing shakuhachi for thirty years as a solitary contemplative practice, while leading retreats, and in improvising with other musicians, I still find that it grounds me in the moment. If I start thinking while I'm blowing a breath down the bamboo, I don't play well. A scratchy, thin, or breathy note can be a little alarm bell, waking me up to Now. First Person contemplative practices like this require full attention and bring to light our attachments to self-images as they arise, allowing us to discern whether particular images are helpful (Spirit-born) or not.

Rejecting any desire for self-aggrandizement or celebrity, *komuso* wore baskets over their heads when they played to indicate the emptiness from which the music arose. The baskets helped the *komuso* relinquish any attachment to what others thought of them. A Christian *komuso* might think, "No one—not even I—can see me; only God can see me."[9] I think that almost all instruments can be played mindfully, providing spiritual nourishment to us and to others. Those of us on

---

[9] I'm reminded of St. John of the Cross's first lines in the *Dark Night* poem:

> One dark night,
> fired with love's urgent longings
> —ah, the sheer grace!—
> I went out unseen,
> my house being now all stilled.

the contemplative path must find practices that bring us to silence and remind us who we really are, in God.

Kurahashi Sensei, David Duncavage's teacher, eventually became my teacher, too. He taught me to pay attention to the silence of the shakuhachi. I have come to trust the darkness or emptiness between notes, thoughts, moods, and words. During these silences I harbor no self-image, and I'm essentially free of what I think of myself and what others think of me. If I play a note that is too sharp or flat, it matters, but not in any ultimate sense, and perhaps it mirrors more accurately the music of the natural world. I try to play notes in recognizable Western and Japanese scales, but I also make room for the reality that nature is often off-key. As I play shakuhachi, it often seems as if my soul is tracking the silence within me and in the room, adding a richness to the notes and to any words I hear and think.

I believe that Gregory of Nyssa would have appreciated contemplative practices such as Suizen. When we fall silent, we might misinterpret this "nothing" as uninteresting, boring, or a waste of time. But for contemplatives, silence is golden. Gregory experienced silence as a portal to the Godhead. For him, the silence that he experienced was the same darkness in which Moses encountered God (Ex 19:9, 16).

For me, *gnophos* (Greek: holy non-conceptual darkness) is what shines in my heart between shakuhachi notes, and within images and thoughts to which I might otherwise become attached. *Gnophos* is the No Place where God dwells, offering freedom, mystery, awe, and unconditional love. The shakuhachi's rest between notes and Mahayana Buddhism's emptiness point me to the Cloud of Moses, the Cloud of Unknowing, and the kenosis of Christ. Fortunately, we don't have to wear a basket over our heads to remember that we can be empty of our socially conditioned selves.

We'll never catch up with all the news, good or bad, nor with the depth of wisdom that circulates in the cosmos. We can stop trying to figure it all out. When the news of the day threatens to overwhelm us, disciplined silence helps us to respond appropriately. In Suizen practice, the Japanese word *ma* is used for this silence; it is symbolized by a small triangle in the musical notation for shakuhachi. I think of *ma* as the invisible dance of the Trinity. I trust that, when words and notes disappear, I am being held and comforted in not-knowing, as if within a motherly God's generous arms. We are entering into unknown territory, listening for our ultimate identity, for what is ultimately true, and for clues about how to "inter-be" with others.

VALUING AND RELINQUISHING IMAGES

Most Christians begin their spiritual journey in church, singing hymns, hearing sermons, praying with others, and reading scripture. The practice of worshiping in church has been the traditional path that opens into the contemplative journey. For someone who is inclined to contemplation, reading scripture and attending liturgies may at some point lose their revelatory power, and leave the person hungry for an even deeper experience of Divine Presence. Beneath the words and social experiences in church, a longing may arise to follow the suggestion of Jesus: "Whenever you pray, go into your room and shut the door and pray to your Father who is in secret; and your Father who sees in secret will reward you" (Mt 6:6). This "secrecy," an experience most vividly available in silent, solitary prayer, draws us into the infinite spaciousness of the First Person Mystery. However, the theme of personal transformation through the practice of silence is an emphasis that one is unlikely to hear in most churches. Shutting the door to others and to the chaotic and humdrum noise of our senses may be frightening, as if we are entirely too alone. But it is there, in our solitude, that we can be deeply understood and cherished. Paradoxically, when we are alone in God's Presence, we discover that we are intimately connected with others. We realize that the world "out there" is also within us.

It is important to remember that Jesus's Father is the First Person of the Holy Trinity, the One who transcends names and images. Did Jesus have an image of the Father? I agree with Karl Rahner that Jesus did not have a formal image of Abba in his mind.[10] But do *we* have an image for the Father, Abba, the Creator? We need to be aware that our experiences of human fathers will inevitably affect our prayer and

---

[10] Karl Rahner, "Dogmatic Reflections on the Knowledge and Self-Consciousness of Christ," in *Theological Investigations V* (Baltimore: Helicon, 1966), 193–215.

meditations and how we imagine the nature of a God called "Father."
As we review our experiences of real-life fathers, we will likely
imagine some things that may be fearful and some that may be comforting or inspiring. Depending on our personal experience, we might
unconsciously envision "God the Father" as a stern judge; an absent,
dangerous, or unpredictable parent; or as a strong, kind presence.[11]

Images from scripture, prayers, and sacred music can be an open
road to God's Presence, but spiritual teachers such as St. John of the
Cross warn us not to linger too long over images of the First Person,
even those that are consoling, lest we forget that these projections are
never actually God. The name Father borrows from our experience,
but God transcends everything we know about fathers. We might hope
that we'd have some image to work with, but the First Person remains
"unseen," as illustrated by Psalm 77:19:

> Your way was through the sea,
> your path, through the mighty waters;
> yet your footprints were unseen.

Our contemplative practice is most fruitful when we notice our
associations and projections as they arise, and then let them go. This
does not mean that we ignore or repress what we notice. Whether or
not our real fathers were compassionate and loving, abandoning or
abusive, we need to take these memories seriously. Some of us may
benefit from exploring them further, perhaps with the help of a psy-
chotherapist, spiritual director, or AA group. Jesus's Abba transcends
all images, memories, and narratives about fathers, but still, we must
remain alert. It is up to us to know if a particular imaginative image
helps to express our longing for the living God.

Every Sunday morning at the Empty Bell contemplative community, we read passages from the Bible. We recognize that Jesus lived
in a patriarchal culture and religious tradition, and that for him, the

---

[11] See John McDargh, *Psychoanalytic Object Relations Theory and the
Study of Religion* (New York: University Press of America, 1983); and Ana-
Maria Rizzuto, MD, *The Birth of the Living God* (Chicago: University of
Chicago Press, 1979).

experience of fatherhood was a defining portal to God. Our focus is not on the translation of words like *Father*; instead, we look toward the ineffable Mystery to whom Jesus prayed and to whom he dedicated his life. Some of us substitute the word *Mother* for *Father,* and some simply say, "My Holy One." Whether the image of Father or Mother or some other term draws us into the unconditional Presence of God, we support each other to keep dwelling in that Presence.

Sometimes, sacred images are given to us by the Spirit. When we receive these gifts with gratitude, we are following what the early Greek theologians called the *kataphatic* way. By contrast, in contemplative practice we detach from all images of the Creator and enter *apophatic* awareness, what Eckhart calls the "unground" of the First Person.[12] Perceiving everything from this placeless place of consciousness, we value everything we are aware *of*—trees, people, thoughts, and emotions. Witnessing and detaching from our objects of awareness protects us from the idolatry of people, thoughts, judgments, and images, even holy ones. This is a subtle dimension of contemplative practice. For example, we might let go of Father or Mother images, and yet still feel comforted and blessed *as if* God were a holy Mother or Father. An idea or image of ourselves, others, or God may be helpful for a time, but only if we dig beneath the images will we find Pseudo-Dionysius's "dazzling darkness" of pure Presence or Merton's *le point vierge.*

Facing into this unknown isn't easy. Along with trust, we need courage to stand in a transforming fire. It helps to imagine that we are *within* God and that God is feeling the longing, grief, and joy along with us (Heb 4:12–13). Opening to *all* our pleasant and unpleasant experiences in God's Presence ignites a sacred blaze that burns away pretense, self-reproach, and self-consciousness. We recover the sensitivity, awe, and curiosity of a child; as Jesus said in the Gospel of Mark, "Truly I tell you, whoever does not receive the kingdom of God as a little child will never enter it" (10:15).

I grew up surrounded by reproductions of Warner Sallman's Jesus (see Figure 7.3), and biblical stories were passed along to me through

---

[12] I appreciate this neologism *unground* because God is a kind of ground, but not one that can be perceived by our material senses.

Figure 7.3. Warner Sallman, *The Lord Is My Shepherd*. Photo
by author, with permission from Warner Press.

the German Lutheran tradition.[13] They helped me survive my post–
World War II working-class family—a good family, but damaged by
alcoholism and occasional domestic violence. I identified with the
little sheep in Jesus's arms. It wasn't until much later that I learned
that Sallman's Jesus is not the historical Jesus—and that I'm not just
a sheep.

But as I look back, I feel only gratitude. Jesus Christ is still my
sacred plumb line, my ultimate guide. A child still lives within me,
vulnerable to the immense dangers of hatred, selfishness, racism,
climate change, and political polarization—dangers that I, by myself,

---

[13] The paintings and reproductions of Warner Sallman (1892–1968) can
be found at warnersallman.com.

cannot control. But I am simultaneously the mature adult who takes responsibility for protecting others and the natural world. The sacred image of Jesus and the baby sheep that inspired and comforted me as a child still speaks to me, but now I find myself in the sheep, the shepherd, and the hills and rivers. My sense of Self has expanded in every direction, and I see the indistinct image of Jesus everywhere and in everyone.

Even as Jesus guides me, he points me beyond himself to Abba, in whom all live. Jesus often implied, "Look, this is not about me. Follow me into the heart of the Father, where everyone is welcome." He suggested that he was transparent to something far greater—simply passing along what he was hearing and learning from Abba, the Creator. This transparency is available to us as we silently repeat the name of Jesus with each out-breath and receive his Presence with each in-breath. The seventh-century monk John Climacus wrote, "Let your calling to [the] mind of Jesus be continually combined with your breathing, and you will know the meaning of silence."[14] The Gospels suggest that Jesus regularly withdrew from his ministry of service and healing to enter the silence of Abba. We can do the same.

First Person awareness is not an escape from everyday reality with its practical, relational, environmental, political, and economic challenges. Although it emphasizes being rather than doing, it is not an escape from doing. Rather, First Person awareness can serve as a secure platform for living a moral, joyful, and just life. Nobody says it better than Meister Eckhart:

> It depends on the heart and an inner, intellectual return to God, and not on steady contemplation by a given method. . . . We ought not to have or let ourselves be satisfied with the God we have thought of, for when the thought slips the mind, that god slips with it. . . . This requires effort and love, a careful cultivation of the spiritual life, and a watchful, honest, active oversight of all one's mental attitudes toward things and people. It is not to be learned by world-flight, running away

---

[14] John Climacus, *The Ladder of Divine Ascent*, quoted in Olivier Clément, *The Roots of Christian Mysticism* (London: New City, 1993), 204.

from things, turning solitary and going apart from the world. Rather, one must learn an inner solitude, wherever or with whomsoever he may be.[15]

This is an intuitive way of knowing, verifiable by direct experience. Eckhart's "intellectual return" does not mean *to think* about God. We turn inward, in the direction of sacred Mystery, the Godhead, not as a sentimental or comforting image, but as our imageless reality, right here, right now.

Practicing the First Person in everyday life can be simple. One of my Zen teachers, Seung Sahn Sunim, used to say, "Don't add anything." Whenever something happens—an event, a feeling—we tend to look for an explanation. We want to know how to prolong a comfortable experience or how to avoid what is painful. Of course, many things happen for a reason, and it can be helpful to identify causes. But we can get lost in searching for why things happen, and we can get stuck in the perpetually turning wheel of "why?" In First Person consciousness, we set aside our commentary and even our depth inquiry and try to see what's actually happening right now. Contemplative practices clear away our cluttered narratives and bring us into direct contact with our sensory and emotional experiences. We can practice this awareness on a cushion, in a pew, on a subway seat, or in nature.

Contemplative experience trusts God so completely that we want nothing else, want to be nowhere else, and want to be with no one else. We learn to accept *what is*, and to meet reality with resolve to change for the better what is ours to change. We may not *think* that we are having a St. Paul experience—"It is no longer I who live, but it is Christ who lives in me" (Gal 2:20)—but it may be happening. Who is this Christ? Theologically, we can say that Jesus Christ our Savior is present to us, continually manifesting the infinite and loving objectless awareness of Abba, who lives hidden in clock-time. But contemplatives aren't satisfied with a conceptual definition. We want the experience. In each moment of our contemplative journey, we step

---

[15] Meister Eckhart, *Meister Eckhart: A Modern Translation*, trans. and ed. Raymond Bernard Blakney (New York: Harper and Brothers, 1941), 9.

back from what we're aware of, into the gift of awareness itself, the sheer Presence that is Christ.

OUTSIDE OF NOW, IS BEING LOST

Eight years ago I was diagnosed with an aggressive prostate cancer, Gleason 9 on a 10–point scale. Days before the biopsy, I told friends, "Don't worry, I'm not the cancer type." When the oncologist called with the diagnosis, Margaret stood beside me, and we cried. I suddenly discovered that I *am* the cancer type, a human being. I recoiled at the "now" I didn't want. We moved to Cambridge for three months so that I could receive daily radiation and hormone treatments. Five days a week we made the daily roundtrip to Dana Farber Cancer Institute in Boston, a stressful drive in snarly traffic.

Each day I would walk into the radiation waiting room, step into a booth to take off my clothes, and put on a pair of oversized light blue cotton pajamas. If other people were in the waiting room, we would sometimes talk. Men in robes would sit in two rows of chairs, waiting their turn. Sometimes they would be accompanied by their wives or friends. One afternoon a woman a few chairs down from me was crying. A nurse stopped by, stood next to her, and stroked her back. She asked: "Is there anything I can do for you? Do you want to come into the next room and sit with me?" Through her tears the woman said: "I just want to get out of here. I've been here since 8:30 this morning, and things keep breaking and people are late. I just want to go home." On another day I met a Harvard-trained lawyer being treated for prostate cancer. He told me that his wife had advanced-stage breast cancer. He figured that she would die before he did. He looked so sad. Months later we exchanged cards and emails. By the time we lost touch with each other, I still hadn't learned if he or his wife had died.

Every day I was called into the cavernous, windowless anteroom to the "blue table." Young technicians in white uniforms moved about quietly in front of three walls of TV screens and blinking LEDs installed above counters that were covered in digital readouts and keyboards. On the first morning of my treatment a nurse turned to greet me as I entered. She smiled and said hello and asked my name and birthdate. She was very pregnant, and I asked if she was due soon. She said: "Yes, with twins. In two weeks, I'll have a Caesarean." We walked down a twenty-foot-long hallway to the radiation room. The walls on each side featured large photographs of Rocky Mountain alpine meadows, all of them lit from behind by invisible sources of light. As I walked into the blue table room, a young, white-clad operator greeted me, as he would every day, "Hi, Robert. How are you today?" As the weeks went by, I always tried to be honest and creative in my answers. Every day was the same, but completely different, just as my life before and after diagnosis was the same and now, with every treatment, completely different.

The routine was always the same. I'd lie down on the radiation tabletop, which was covered with a white sheet. I'd pull down the waistband of my blue pajamas to my pubic hairs so that the operators, a young man or woman on each side of me, could find the small tattoos that had been marked on my hips and just above my pubic bone. They'd push and pull my hips and the white sheet so that the tattoos would be aligned precisely with the laser lights of their machines. I felt embarrassed as my body was scrutinized so closely by strangers, but hey, my life was at stake, and the promise of a future mattered more than my uncomfortable feelings.

Two machines, big steel boxes of laser power, extended out from the wall and ceiling on swing-arms. A scene from the 1953 movie *War of the Worlds* sometimes popped into my mind—the basement scene where the heroes hide from the long, steel-ribbed Martian cables with electronic eyes that are reaching through the windows, searching for them. I saw it as a seven-year-old, and I was terrified of dark basements for years.

Lying on the blue table I surrendered to the medical team. I let myself imagine that if I was pliant and cooperative, I would receive the best cancer treatment in the world. I had to submit to and trust in the training of the medical team and the skill of the engineers who had created these radiation devices. Precision was absolutely necessary so that other organs wouldn't be damaged and so that I might survive this cancer. I knew that, in order for the treatment to be effective, the laser guns above and around me had to shoot their beams into the exact same spot in my body every day. Following the team's directions, I lay perfectly still when the radiant beams were released. I calmed my mind as past and future dissolved.

After I was arranged properly on the table, someone would say: "All set, Robert. We'll see you in a few minutes." The team would leave, and I would lie in the dimly lit room, looking up at the suspended ceiling. I had asked for yoga music livestreamed from Pandora radio, wanting to hear the long smooth chords of synthesizers, flutes, and harps. I felt that this music might lengthen and relax the cords in my body and soul. I could pray with this music.

In the stillness I would lie motionless, hearing a *clunk-clunk-clunk* to my left, coming somewhere outside the room. Then I would hear a loud, single *clunk* as a large rectangular lightbox on the wall to my right emitted a reddish glow and the words "X-ray In Use." For a few seconds I would hear a buzzing sound. Then the room would fall quiet, and I would lie in silence for a few more seconds until the light and buzz began again. This on-off sequence of light and sound happened several times in fifteen-minute segments, always with the steady background of quiet music. Twice during this sequence someone would slip into the room, reach under the table, pull out an X-ray-sensitive plate, and leave without a word.

I imagined that the radioactive lasers behaved like hungry raptors, swooping down to devour their prey, the cancer cells in my body. Each time the red-light box lit up, I imagined that the beams of carefully calibrated X-rays were diving deep into my body. Their talons would strike the backs of teeming, oblivious cancer cells, and kill them. They would also be killing my prostate gland. I knew that these mysterious, dangerous, and radiant raptors were sent through machines constructed by some of the brightest scientists and technicians on the planet. I suspected that most of these engineers were not interested in the language of spiritual, artistic metaphor and meaning, and yet the machinery and the processes they had invented seemed holy to me. I gave myself unrestrainedly to this process. I imagined a huge drama being played out on the altar of the blue table, as if I were inside the world of J.R.R. Tolkien's *Lord of the Rings*, buffeted by huge forces of good and evil and calmly witnessing and participating in the final battle for life and for goodness. My body and soul were the battlefield.

About halfway through the nearly three months of radiation, I noticed a cross of red light that must have been beaming down toward my prostate the whole time. I figured it was an LED light precisely calibrated to the tattoos on my lower abdomen, but to me, it gradually appeared as the cross, as if Jesus, an innocent and prayerful man, were being crucified right now, a timeless now of grief and love that transcends life and death. I was suddenly accompanying Jesus, and he was accompanying me. From then on I often cried on the blue table. Tears would stream down my cheeks and drip onto my ears. I felt as if I were being held up by a power greater than the awesome technical intelligence that created and operated the machines; I felt sustained. As the days went by, I found myself repeating a mantra through my tears: "Burn away everything that is not love. Burn away everything that is not love. Burn away everything that is not love."

Looking back, I believe that this is what the Creator longs to do in every moment: to burn away everything that is not love. This can only happen when we accept the unavoidable suffering we experience and open ourselves consciously to the mystery, love, and grace that is our heart's deepest desire. When we live in this way, prayer, gratitude, and joy will arise in us in surprising ways.

8

Second Person

Jesus as I-Thou Gateway

For Christians, the Second Person of the Trinity is revealed in history as the incarnation of Jesus Christ. But not all Christians would define *incarnation* in the same way. Believing that the unutterable Divine has fully manifested as a specific human being in a specific time in history might be misunderstood as a singular, never-to-be-repeated event that means that only Jesus is divine, or that Jesus was only divine, and not human. I believe that when we trust that the incarnation transcends time and space, we are changed. A nondual interpretation of the incarnation greatly enlarges our understanding of what it means to be human.

The Second Person highlights interpersonal relationships, including friendship with God, other people, and nature. This dimension of awareness informs us that every one of our relationships is sacred. The great Jewish philosopher Martin Buber, in his book *I and Thou*, contrasts I-It experiences with I-Thou ones. When we relate to someone or something as an It, we treat the other as an object. When we treat the other as a Thou, we encounter them as a subject; we are open to being affected by the other and we relate to them with interest and respect, as one subject to another.

Jesus, the Second Person of the Trinity, highlighted friendship as a critically important location of divine Presence. Practicing Second Person awareness involves valuing and tending our relationships. This is an important antidote to the temptation to become attached to First Person experiences of union or oneness. First Person experiences of oneness in solitude can be so joyous and healing that—

paradoxically—we can become ensnared by them and bliss out on emptiness. We can be tempted to sidestep the responsibilities, joys, and pain of our interpersonal lives.[1] But when we take seriously Jesus's way of living in relationship with God and neighbor, we are invited to stay engaged with everyday life. Second Person awareness is an antidote to spiritual bypass. Contemplative Christians take on the specific challenge of perceiving the divine in every "ordinary" relationship. Every I-Thou is transparent to our I-Thou relationship with God. Seeking and realizing this transparency is a Second Person practice.

Oneness is highlighted in nondual spiritualities such as Advaita Hinduism, in some interpretations of Orthodox *theosis,* and in Eckhart's works. Yet the trinitarian experience of God invites us to realize both oneness and otherness as ultimate dimensions of holiness. We are created in the image and likeness of One who awakens us to the dance of otherness. When relationships are sacred, we commit ourselves to honesty, integrity, reliability, and trustworthiness. We fall in love with others, and we seek to focus that love in appropriate ways. Every friendship honors the love that unites us to another, as well as the love that celebrates the other's particularity. Every encounter with another invites us into this sacramental awareness which frees the other from the fantasy that they are us or are separate from us.

Jesus's relationship with Abba is our template for a love that both unites us and respects our differences. Jesus was both mortal and divine—mortal because, as he himself said, "The Father is greater than I" (Jn 14:28), and divine because "the Father and I are one" (Jn 10:30). He both was and was not Abba. When we develop a relationship with Jesus, a door to Abba opens in our hearts. Second Person awareness invites us to live within a Presence that is both us and other than us, just as Jesus both is and isn't the Creator.

For me, and many other Christians, a devotional relationship with Jesus conveys a sense that we are seen and known for who we really are, understood, loved, and protected across the boundary of life and death. This level of awareness is sometimes called *imaginal,* a liminal

---

[1] This mistake, called spiritual bypass in the psychological community, resonates with Buddhist meditators who become attached to emptiness. Their version is called Zen sickness.

zone of perception between the visible and invisible that can ground and guide all our relationships.[2]

Seekers in other traditions have their own pathways into a personal relationship with the Divine. But I am here to share what happened to me, in case my journey speaks to you. I began my Lutheran Christian life believing that Jesus was the one and only incarnate one, a not-me who was *the* Christ. When I was lost in anxiety and worry, and when I felt abandoned or abused, I trusted that there was One who would never fail me. I could imaginatively stretch out my hand and feel met. This view helped me to survive many lonely and fearful moments as a child and young man. I could count on this Presence, even when I realized that I would one day die. However, gradually, over decades of Christian prayer and contemplation, liturgical experiences, spiritual guidance, and scripture study, my understanding changed in a subtle but profound way. I began to notice that when I assumed that Jesus of Nazareth lived in another time and place—geographically, histori-cally, and in a distant heaven—it was easy to slip into loneliness and fear, for obviously Jesus was somewhere I was not. He was divine, I was not, and I could never match his depth of faith and compassion: end of story. I was prone to self-doubt, self-reproach, and low self-esteem, and this tendency was only amplified by believing that Jesus was above me and separate from me.

Today, the clear dualistic barrier between Jesus and me is not as solid. I still believe Jesus as quoted in John, "I am the way, and the truth, and the life. No one comes to the Father except through me" (14:6). But whereas I once thought that Jesus's "I" signified his his-torically grounded ego-self, which is obviously separate from me, I now understand that his "I" referred both to his historical ego-self *and* to the transcendent "I" of the Divine. The "I" of the Creator is available to everyone. Jesus's pronoun "I" transcends the boundary between clock-time and eternity, between then and now, between

---

[2] The imaginal indicates a reality seen through the eye of the heart. For the French philosopher and professor of Islamic studies Henry Corbin, the word *imaginal* indicates that all creation is a theophany of the divine. See Michel Cazenave, ed., *Jung, Buddhism, and the Incarnation of Sophia* (Roch-ester, VT: Inner Traditions, 2019).

Jesus's specific Middle Eastern Jewish identity and the universal human identity that we share.

For a while, it was necessary for me to believe that only Jesus of Nazareth manifested the "I" of the Creator, because I needed a specific outer focus to ease my anguish; I needed Someone outside of me and my world of troubles to heal and rescue me. I needed Jesus to be separate from me. But as I've matured as a Christian, I feel more and more grounded in a belovedness that Jesus longs to share with me. That is why I appreciate Marguerite Porete's name for God: "My Dear Far-Nearness"—the Christ within. Jesus of Nazareth has died, but his Presence lives forever within me and all others. This change resonates with St. Paul's realization that Christ lived within his "I" (Gal 2:20; 1 Cor 15:10). In his conversion, Paul's personal identity was infinitely enlarged. He was no longer an isolated individual but part of a larger whole: "So we, who are many, are one body in Christ, and individually we are members one of another" (Rom 12:5). As a practice, this understanding inspires me to pay keen attention to moments in which I separate from other persons or creatures and instead to look for kinship.

I think that Jesus might have appreciated this cosmic view of the incarnation. It would have informed the prayer we know as the Lord's Prayer: "Your kingdom come, your will be done." This prayer can be misunderstood as a wish for something better that will appear later, from God as a separate being and in a kingdom that is far away. But when prayed from a nondual Second Person perspective, we are not just asking God to do something while we passively watch and hope from the sidelines; rather, we commit ourselves to *manifest* that holy kingdom as best we can, and *to do* God's will *by aligning our will with God's will*. In Matthew's Gospel the kingdom of God is present tense—it is "at hand" and has "come near" (Mt 3:2; 4:17; 10:7).

Just as Jesus lived out First Person awareness, which is always now, our own access to this experience in relationships is always now. Discovering Christ within us does not mean that we must live in the Middle East, wear tunics and sandals, and "save" the world as Jesus did. We are not being asked to become carbon copies of Jesus of Nazareth. No, discovering Christ within means that we manifest our belovedness in our unique, everyday lives, with our family and friends, and with the community to which we belong.

Like Jesus, we can realize the I-Thou that Jesus experienced in his relationship with Abba and the I-thou of wisdom and innocence that he manifested with others. When we stop and gaze at the world's beauty or well up with tears as we witness childbirth or sit by the bedside of a dying loved one, we might find ourselves saying "you are here," or "thank you" to no one in particular. Contemplative faith tells us that there is a "You" who is listening. Deep, heart-opening gratitude and love that have no particular objective image emerge from the Second Person and address the imageless First Person. Jesus draws us into the I-Thou of the Trinity as an interpersonal love that transcends and connects everyone.[3] Jesus never disappears from our journey into the Oneness of the Creator. Our relationship with Jesus is our gateway to the Creator, and Jesus is always available to receive our longing for a Someone who understands and unconditionally loves us.

We are each alone, but in contemplative silence there is always a You whose eternal, ineffable heart is Love. A young friend used to tell me that believing this was wishful thinking and that imagining a safe Presence in silence was just a mind trick to make us feel better. I responded by agreeing that imagination is indeed a kind of blind faith, but that perhaps it is God who gives us the power to imagine such a great Love. Some meditation teachers tell students to treat all thoughts alike, and to let them go as they arise, and it's true that in contemplative practices we discover that our thoughts don't always match reality. But sometimes a thought, memory, or an imaginative image does bring us into God's Presence. Imagining a boundless, eternal Love that never passes can change our lives and encourage us to live more wholesomely. And yet, this Love does not depend on our

---

[3] When we say "you" to a flower, and dwell in this human-flower communion, we may be having an experience similar to the one that John Muir described after hiking Tenaya Lake in the Sierras in 1869: "When we try to pick out anything by itself, we find it hitched to everything else in the universe. One fancies a heart like our own must be beating in every crystal and cell, and we feel like stopping to speak to the plants and animals as friendly, fellow mountaineers." *John Muir: Spiritual Writings*, ed. Tim Flinders (Maryknoll, NY: Orbis Books, 2013), 41–42, Kindle edition.

thinking or our imagination. We have the creative power to imagine many things—love or hate, trust or mistrust, demons or angels. We can try out different imaginative worlds and faiths, and then, with the careful scrutiny of a scientist, we can observe the effects of such beliefs on our lives. I find joy, meaning, and creativity when I live *as if*—*as if* a transcendent You were here, *as if* a mysterious, loving Someone were present to each of us in every moment. Second Person awareness is the devotional world of You.

PRAYING YOU

When we pray "You" to the Creator, we address an invisible Presence who is listening. For the Hebrew prophets, praying in this way was a practice, one that we too can follow. For the first followers of Jesus, the ineffable You became visible in a mortal person. Of course, this Jesus is not visible to us in the same way he was experienced in his lifetime, but we are invited to trust a passageway that allows incarnation to happen in anyone everywhere. As Jesus said, "Whoever sees me sees him who sent me" (Jn 12:45), and the One who sent Jesus is always here, eternally present. When we "see" Jesus we are praying to him, *through* him, and encountering Abba, because Jesus is transparent to the ever-present Creator. This imaginal seeing of the heart transforms us and all our relationships.

In *Tales of the Hasidim*, Martin Buber highlighted the importance of praying to the holy You. He shares a portion of a song sung by Rabbi Levi Yitzhak of Berditchev. This rabbi's teacher was Rebbe Dov Baer, known as the Great Maggid (Hebrew for "itinerant preacher"), the Baal Shem Tov's central successor. The rabbi would sing this "Song of You":

> Where I wander—You!
> Where I ponder—You!
> Only You, You again, always You!
> You! You! You!
> When I am gladdened—You!
> When I am saddened—You!
> Only You, You again, always You!

You! You! You!
Sky is You! Earth is You!
You above! You below!
In every trend, at every end,
Only You! You again, always You!
You! You! You![4]

I am touched by Rabbi Levi Yitzhak's simple prayer. We are created from within this You, yet we are also distinct from You. We are distinct because God creates us as free of God. Thus, we can choose to seek God's Presence or not. Likewise, we are distinct from Jesus, but because Jesus prayed to the same You to whom we pray, our prayers unite us with Jesus. In the Abrahamic religions any form of devotional prayer to the holy You is a bridge from our mortal lives to the timeless Presence of God. When we cross this bridge, we are changed for the better, but this change requires enhanced alertness because our faith in divine You can be captured by the ego-self—a move that can drive otherwise good people to do terrible things in the name of God. As we pray to You, it's necessary to discern right thoughts and right actions.

THE REAL YOU CIRCULATES FREELY
IN THE EVERYDAY WORLD

The Abrahamic emphasis on the personal and interpersonal dimensions of God does not deny the *impersonal* dimension of the cosmos. Personal, interpersonal, and impersonal dynamics pervade our cosmos. Nor does the interpersonal aspect of reality deny the value of scientific knowing or the random and generative powers at play in the material universe. Countless scientists who adhere to an Abrahamic faith see no contradiction between scientific knowing and spiritual wisdom. In each breath we can pray "You," even as we seek to understand the vast material and biological forces of cause and effect that bring powerful changes all around us. The Abrahamic traditions assert

---

[4] Martin Buber, *Tales of the Hasidim: The Early Masters*, trans. Olga Marx (New York: Schocken Books, 1947, 1975), 212.

that something intersubjective and purposive is going on even in the midst of random interactions of energies and events. We exist because of the underlying purpose of a You who "chooses" to create life and consciousness where there were none. This perspective is a leap of faith that can coincide with an appreciation of rigorous science.

With theologian Elizabeth Johnson, I believe that "the flesh assumed in Jesus Christ connects with all humanity, all biological life, all soil, the whole matrix of the material universe down to its very roots."[5] The incarnation affects all creation, not just human beings, because everything and everyone are transparent to the Creator. Humans are intimately connected with everything and everyone in a sacred bond, a holy community, which means that we can walk down a city street or a forest path and pray "You" to everyone and everything. To live this way is to live within a sacramental universe. When I live as Jesus did—in the awareness that the Creator You is always present—I speak and act responsively, responsibly, and creatively. I am open to I-thou encounters with people and with the rest of the natural world. Second Person awareness lives within every relationship, all transparent to the ultimate You of God.

JESUS AS I-THOU GUIDE

How does Second Person awareness manifest in our behavior? How can we cultivate, or practice, this awareness? We might begin by reflecting on what the Gospels tell us about Jesus. We can imagine our way into his consciousness by listening to his words and witnessing his actions. As we read Jesus's story, we notice his intimate engagement with family and friends. In the Gospels, Jesus is depicted as someone who addresses family, friends, and religious authorities in direct, interpersonal, I-thou conversations. I envision him as smart, compassionate, wise beyond his years, knowledgeable of Hebrew scripture, a healing presence for others, and ready to confront religious and political leaders who are hypocritical and abuse their

---

[5] Elizabeth A. Johnson, *Ask the Beasts: Darwin and the Love of God* (New York: Bloomsbury Continuum, 2015), 196.

authority. Jesus lived on the land and used metaphors from nature to illustrate spiritual teachings. He is baptized in the Jordan River, humbly accepting this sacred ordination at the hands of John the Baptist (Mt 3:1–17). This is a Christian enlightenment story wherein Jesus realizes that he is the beloved child of the Creator. Yes, he is born from Mary, but in his depths, he knows that he is a child from a holy Nowhere of Love, the unnameable and uncaused Creator, Abba.

As we imaginatively participate in Jesus's life, we might feel invited into devotional prayer. Devotion is an equal-exchange dynamic. When we trust and love Jesus, we can imagine that we are simultaneously receiving Jesus's love and trust. In this giving and receiving I am experiencing something like what the Star Trek character Spock introduced to American audiences: the mind-meld. This mind-meld is the mind of Christ, a participation in the Second Person of the Trinity, who blesses every encounter with ultimate significance. Our relationship with Jesus can feel like a sacred vow, so real that we want to be true to this relationship and to be just as open, vulnerable, discerning, wise, and trustworthy as he was.

Entering Second Person consciousness and experiencing Jesus as a companion and friend can transform our lives. In July 1992, my wife, Margaret, went into labor three months early, and delivered our second child, Rebecca. After a few short hours of life in a Boston hospital, Rebecca died in our arms. I held her small body as her breath and color faded away. As Margaret recovered from the operation, a kind nurse brought me a bowl of water, and I baptized Rebecca just before she died. Margaret and I were inconsolable, driving home with a small bundle of items—some photos, a baby blanket, a baby's cap—but no baby. Our son, Sam, was three years old, and leading up to the emergency the three of us had been talking with and singing to Rebecca, as if she were already with us. Each of us wrestled in our own way with sorrow and confusion, and I fell into a period of depression.

One experience helped me through my despair. I called Henri Nouwen, who was in Europe. I poured out my grief, and he said, "I'll come to be with you." Henri soon arrived at Logan Airport in Boston. He sat with Margaret and me, listening and sharing his faith in a life that transcends death. As I sat with him on the couch one day he said, "You know, Jesus lost Rebecca too." In that moment I didn't fully understand the enormity of his remark, but later it dawned on me: I myself couldn't bear the loss of Rebecca, but Jesus could, and Jesus's Presence is within me. And so, for many months, as I wrestled with my grief, I often prayed, "I can't bear this, but you can. You were falsely accused, you were abandoned, and you died a terrible death on a wooden cross. You know how to bear this, and I love you." In the following year I felt a growing assurance that when I let the You of Christ into my experience through prayer and with ultimate trust, that You will help me bear whatever comes.

Of course, after every loss and experience of healing, more tests will come. Immediately after Jesus was baptized in the River Jordan and glimpsed his essential holiness, he experienced temptation. Driven by the Spirit into the desert, fasting for forty days and nights, he was enticed by unholy powers to use his spiritual realization for his own personal gain and to violate natural laws such as gravity and material reality. He was tempted to turn stones into bread, to leap from a great height, and to claim fame and power for himself. But in each case Jesus refused. No one should use the powers that come with spiritual wisdom to violate the reality of the material world or for personal gain (Mt 4:1–11). In the periods of melancholy that emerged from time to time after Rebecca's death, I would turn to Jesus as someone who could look temptation and death in the eye and say: "No. I choose the path of Love. I choose the relationship that transcends death." A prayerful relationship with Jesus gave me the courage and resolute focus to find meaning and hope despite my temptation to despair.

Many traditions bring forward stories in which spiritual experiences are tested. Five hundred years before Jesus was born, Gautama Buddha was tempted by Māra, the Buddhist Lord of the Senses. In the very moment of Buddha's enlightenment (realizing that his essential nature was the Light), Māra appealed to Buddha's selfish desires, anger, and fears. In my imagination the Buddha skillfully investigated these temptations without reacting. He kept breathing mindfully and remained calm and compassionate. Both Jesus and

Buddha remind us that inner barriers to reality and to Love will keep asserting themselves.[6]

Although Jesus and Buddha experienced awakenings to selfless, nondual consciousness, their experiences were not identical. As far as we know, Buddha did not pray to a holy Thou, a Creator. Having been blessed and awakened to an eternal reality, and having passed through the temptations, Buddha continued to live within a vast, spacious consciousness, unattached to any object of his awareness. Buddha probably experienced a materially uncaused and objectless gratitude, but he did not believe or disbelieve in God. It seems that he wasn't very interested in belief, but focused instead on the experience of the believer. From the standpoint of direct experience, I surmise that Buddha's fathomless and clear awareness resonates with a Christian's First Person consciousness. It's not an exact match, but there is a resonance.

Years ago I attended a Buddhist-Christian retreat in Bodh Gaya, India, led by the Dalai Lama and Fr. Lawrence Freeman. The Dalai Lama was asked whom he thanks for the gift of life and compassion. He said that after a person has shed a self-centered worldview, then compassion and a desire to serve others arise spontaneously. Compassion arises naturally, from nowhere. It doesn't come from a Someone. It just is—and is bottomless. I appreciated this wisdom, while I inwardly contrasted the experience with Jesus, who turned everything over to Abba in an interpersonal way. Both Buddha and Jesus go forth from their enlightenment to serve others, but Jesus received everything as the gift of a holy Someone—Abba. Listening to Fr. Freeman and the Dalai Lama, I felt as if I were walking forward on both Buddhist and Christian pathways, accepting the love and compassion that "just is," while also thanking my holy You, Jesus and Abba, for whom I have no objective images.

After his baptism and his sojourn in the wilderness, Jesus's public ministry begins. According to the Gospel of Matthew, early in his

---

[6] Mt. 4:1–11. There is a powerful and beautiful depiction of the Buddha's temptations in the 1993 movie *Little Buddha*. Prince Siddhartha (the Buddha before his enlightenment) is played by Keanu Reeves.

ministry he climbs a mountain where many had gathered to hear him. He offers his first sermon, preaching the Beatitudes (Mt 5:3–10): "Blessed are the poor in spirit, for theirs is the kingdom of heaven. Blessed are those who mourn, for they will be comforted," and so forth. In these words Jesus is passing on what he hears from Abba, who is always blessing those who are downhearted, humble, and abused; those who want to do the right thing; those who are pure in heart; and those who show mercy for their fellows in need. To pray for and to help those who are suffering is a critically important Second Person practice because the Creator You lives within everyone. This isn't individualistic; it's a nondual, relational practice that gradually becomes an inner platform for wise and effective social and political action.

NAVIGATING SECOND PERSON AWARENESS

We can learn something about Jesus's Second Person awareness by reading the Gospels. I believe that the only way to have a direct experience of God is to perceive God from the God-place within us. Jesus says as much when he declares, "No one has seen the Father except the one who is from God; he has seen the Father" (Jn 6:46). Since God can't be seen with our eyes, the word "seen" must mean "perceived" or "experienced." We can experience Jesus's awareness from the Jesus-place within us, and we can experience Abba if we see, hear, and know from the Abba-place within us. We can experience God directly only if we are rooted from a place beyond our self-centered ego; only then we can we discover that we are never separate from God. Realizing that our personal prayer arises from the God-place within us always brings sincerity, authenticity, and humility.

All Second Person, I-Thou practices of prayer, meditation, and contemplation include a kind of First Person emptying. The deeper our prayer, the more we surrender ultimate control over our lives and reality. When I pray to God, who is the "I" who is praying? Is it my ego-self, who wants something from a separate God who, I imagine, is pulling all the strings of reality? Or does my prayer arise from the God-place within me, from my eternal and True Self? Similarly, when I pray to "You," who is the "You" to whom I am praying? If I'm praying from my ego-self, I'm likely to be projecting onto God the resonance of previous human relationships (probably with my parents, teachers, and others). C. S. Lewis wrote that "the prayer preceding all prayers is 'May it be the real I who speaks. May it be the real Thou that I speak to.'"[7] Authentic prayer invites us to keep listening for what is most real and most true within us.

The authenticity and depth of our I-Thou relationship with Jesus is put to the test in our everyday relationships. When I am rooted in the holy I-Thou, I am more likely to listen to others with an open mind and less likely to be listening or looking for criticism, affirmation, or praise. When I'm rooted in the unconditional love of God, I'm less likely to seek it from others and more likely to convey it to others in my speech and listening, in my bearing and my face. Jesus declared, "Whoever sees me sees him who sent me. . . . If you knew me, you would know my Father also. . . . Whatever the Father does, the Son does likewise. . . . The Father and I are one" (Jn 12:45; 8:19; 5:19; 10:30). We don't have much historical knowledge of Jesus's daily life, but the gospel stories show us a Jesus who is transparent to the Divine in all his relationships. Jesus did this by emptying himself of everything that is not Abba's love (Phil 2:7–8), and I trust that his friends felt this open love in his presence. Jesus invites all of us into this way of being.

The Gospels include many stories depicting Jesus doing miraculous things and speaking wisdom in surprising ways, and then telling his followers not to tell anyone what happened. He didn't want the goodness he was manifesting to be about him. He said many times that every good thing he did or said came from Abba. I can imagine that, on a human level, Jesus appreciated being thanked for what he did, but I also imagine that he was free of the impulse to seek credit for himself. This is a Second Person practice, to notice when we seek praise for doing something good. Simply noticing the desire may be enough to drain it of its energy, or we may need to dwell for a while in the loving gaze of God.

---

[7] C. S. Lewis, *Letters to Malcolm: Chiefly on Prayer: Reflections on the Intimate Dialogue between Man and God* (New York: Harcourt, 1992), 81–82.

Did Jesus have a human ego? As a psychologist I read the gospel stories of Jesus's life and see a person with a strong psychological infrastructure—that is, an ego. It seems to me that Jesus's ego-self was bright, humble, compassionate, and powerful. With St. Paul, I believe that Jesus of Nazareth "emptied" himself, allowing an infinite Light to shine out through his ego-self. When we welcome the presence of Jesus Christ into our depths, we have the experience that Jesus describes in Matthew 10:40: "Whoever welcomes you welcomes me, and whoever welcomes me welcomes the one who sent me." By welcoming Jesus we also welcome Abba.

Jesus was a Jew. I don't believe that he intended to start a new religion. He declared, "Do not think that I have come to abolish the law or the prophets; I have come not to abolish but to fulfill. For truly I tell you, until heaven and earth pass away, not one letter, not one stroke of a letter, will pass from the law until all is accomplished" (Mt 5:17–18). For Jesus, the fulfillment of Hebrew laws and commandments was not only a moral challenge. It was an existential one—to surrender to the Spirit who gives the commandments. Jesus sifted them all through the God-place in his heart and discerned the fundamentals. When asked about God's deepest desire for our lives, Jesus quoted Deuteronomy (6:5) and Leviticus (19:18), "'You shall love the Lord your God with all your heart, and with all your soul, and with all your mind.' This is the greatest and first commandment. And a second is like it: 'You shall love your neighbor as yourself.' On these two commandments hang all the law and the prophets" (Mt 22:36–40). All Second Person practices lead us to realize that we are the beloved of God and to recognize that all others are beloved, too. Ethical behavior flows from this free and relational awareness.

SURPRISING APPEARANCES OF I-THOU

A relationship with Jesus is what mystics call "a thin place" where messages and presences from heaven enter our lives. We become "thin" when we love someone, when we suffer, and when we pray and contemplate. Thin places open us to ever-deepening levels of reality, danger, and opportunity—and they can arise at unexpected moments.

One winter night I awoke in desperate anxiety. The day before someone had said something that I experienced as an insult. It might have been an insignificant comment, but it had knocked me off my horse. In the dark I tried to think and pray it through, but I felt thrown into a dumpster of worthlessness. Suddenly, in the imaginal space between sleep and consciousness, I had a vision. Months before, a Tibetan Buddhist friend had shown me an image of a deity called Dorje Drolo, a fierce protector of great spiritual clarity and power (see Figure 8.1). I'd spent a long time reflecting on that image and its meaning. And now, in my despair just before dawn, the doors of my small, worried self suddenly flew open, and for a split second

Figure 8.1. Dorje Drolo reproduction. Photo by author.

Dorje Drolo's presence filled the darkness. My worry, self-attack, and anxiety vanished instantly and completely. It was as if Dorje Drolo had eaten my anxiety. It was gone. Amazed, I got out of bed, and for about an hour I walked slowly around our living room and kitchen in a state of peace and bliss. Somehow, I was able to accept this healing without trying to understand it. Instead of asking why, I murmured "thank you" into the darkness, with no image for this You, and yet I felt surprisingly self-confident, trusting the experience because I knew who I was and I was grounded in Christ.

Reflecting on this event over the next few days, I felt thankful to my Buddhist friend and to the wisdom in his tradition. I did not define the experience as either Tibetan or Christian, but I did think that Jesus's Presence was with me and that he would have honored what transpired. Perhaps I had experienced this Tibetan deity as an angel of the Lord, coming from the holy Nowhere of the Creator, seizing and gobbling up my self-doubt and self-attack. All this is to say that we don't know when or in what form the holy You will appear, or what message it will bring. In this case I learned again, to my surprise, that divine energy can be fierce, cutting through worry and anxiety, just as it can cut through some pious Christians' efforts to be continually "nice."

When praying to, and through, Jesus Christ, we can expect to be surprised by the images that arise in our imagination. Still, it took me a long time to realize that Jesus could take many forms—even forms from other spiritual traditions. I've mentioned that when I grew up in the 1950s in northern Wisconsin, the walls of our Lutheran churches featured reproductions of Warner Sallman's paintings. Sometimes he is gazing into My Dear Far-Nearness, and sometimes he is knocking on the garden gate of our hearts or guiding a young sailor home.

For at least a generation Christian communities have questioned the adequacy of images such as these. Thirty years ago the *National Catholic Reporter* sponsored a contest—Jesus 2000—that invited Christian artists to paint their vision of Jesus. Well-known art critic and TV personality Sister Wendy Beckett served as the judge. A total of 1,678 entries were submitted by 1,004 artists from nineteen countries and six continents. The winning portrait, *Jesus of the People*, was created by Janet McKenzie. You can easily find it online. Her

Jesus is a dark-skinned feminine figure. McKenzie said, "'Jesus of the People' simply came through me. . . . I feel as though I am only a vehicle for its existence." Michael Farrell, then editor of *National Catholic Reporter*, commented, "When the church was overwhelmingly a Western institution, we in the West made Jesus in our likeness. But now at last Christianity has spread to the ends of the earth as the founder once prayed it would."[8] All images of Jesus must reflect his universal and inclusive message.

America is undergoing a cultural, political, and spiritual revolution as we wrestle with truths emerging from the Black Lives Matter movement. People of color and their allies are rightfully protesting the images of an exclusively White Jesus. A White Jesus is a symbol of White supremacy and a Christianity that has too often condoned abusive behavior, racism, and colonialism. New and sometimes surprising images of Jesus can open us afresh to God's Presence, for which no single image can ever suffice.

Our images of God might pass away, but God will never pass away. Some images of Jesus resonate with the deep wisdom of other religious traditions. Janet McKenzie included a small Taoist Yin-Yang symbol in the upper left corner of her Jesus painting to symbolize the dynamic flow of opposites that Christ reveals to her. I think Jesus would have appreciated this inter-spiritual wisdom. On my Empty Bell website I once received an email from a young Christian in South Dakota. He wrote: "How could you talk to Buddhists? They don't believe in God! They will go to hell!" I answered: "Jesus is not afraid of anything or anyone. He wants to know what it is to be human, and maybe what it is to be a Zen Buddhist. He believes that everyone is a child of Abba, and he blesses everyone." When we cultivate our relationship with Jesus, he "in-forms" our heart with universal Love. The material forms and literal stories we have of Jesus Christ are essential, but they point to a Someone who cannot be corralled by images and words, or even by a particular denomination. We can be rooted in Christ while appreciating and learning the rich variety of the sacred images and stories of other traditions.

---

[8] Pamela Schaeffer and John L. Allen Jr., "Jesus 2000," *National Catholic Reporter*, December 24, 1999.

Another way in which Christian imagery is changing is in depictions of the gender of God. Of course, God has no gender, but the traditional Christian naming of God is emphatically masculine: Father and Son, and a Holy Spirit. This male-oriented language for the Trinity was created in a Middle Eastern patriarchal culture and is problematic for many contemporary Christians—men and women alike. I sometimes find deep consolation and peace when I pray to the Creator as Divine Mother.

Henri Nouwen cherished his personal relationship with Jesus, but he was also drawn to the image of the Father in Rembrandt's *The Return of the Prodigal Son*. In his book-length study of the painting, Henri drew attention to the hands of the Father, one of which looks masculine and the other feminine.[9] In his view, the First Person has a balance of what we often consider to be masculine and feminine qualities. Henri followed church teaching in calling the First Person "he," but toward the end of his life he was beginning to feel comfortable with "she." Henri was familiar with the writings of Julian of Norwich, the English mystic (1342–1413) who freely and joyously delighted in both the feminine and masculine aspects of the Divine. She spoke of the Trinity as our Father and also our Mother. This vision of Jesus and the Trinity may confound traditional Christians, but the Second Person Thou touches a universal and relational place in the human heart in which images of time, place, and gender may be fluid.

In Second Person consciousness we love and trust Someone, an eternal Thou we cannot see, but who sees us.[10] Some of us glimpse this You in images, scripture reading, and in nature, and still others in silent prayer on a cushion, or when moved by a piece of music. In a conversation about prayer, a Native American Christian woman once told me that Jesus appeared to her as a black panther. Images like this can awaken the silent and fierce energy of Jesus, who lives so passionately and colorfully in Native American and Black Gospel

---

[9] Henri J. M. Nouwen, *The Return of the Prodigal Son: A Story of Homecoming* (New York: Doubleday, 1994).

[10] I reflect on this experience in my essay "Loving Someone You Can't See," in *Beside Still Waters: Jews, Christians, and the Way of the Buddha*, ed. Harold Kasimow, Linda Keenan, and John Keenan (Boston: Wisdom Publications, 2003), 143–56.

churches. I am also drawn to recognizing the beloved Thou in Sufi poetry.

I-THOU WITHIN EVERY I-THOU

The incarnation is a paradox, the greatest paradox of all: the Divine has chosen to share timeless, placeless Divinity in every time and place. The vertical axis of the cross symbolizes eternity, uncaused, un-conditioned, and timeless; the horizontal axis symbolizes conditioned, causative, chronological reality. The present moment, in the center of our hearts, is where the two axes meet. The Uncreated Source is available in every moment and every sincere heart. This is the sacred Beyond Within of Love. When we address another person, animal, bird, body of water, tree, frog, beetle, or anything else as thou, we are simultaneously addressing the Source who is bringing forth this being. There is Thou in every thou.

When we invite Christ into the center of our lives and stand in Sec-ond Person awareness, we experience ourselves as the meeting place of heaven and earth, immortality and mortality, self and other. This is not merely a philosophical or theological assertion; it becomes a practice that reveals who we really are. How we treat other people is likely to change. For instance, we will no longer seek to serve others because we think we're supposed to, because we want to please a judgmental Father God, or because we want to look moral and virtuous. Our deep I-Thou surrender to Christ gradually begins to manifest as love, empa-thy, compassion, and practical help for others. And, as Jesus explains in Matthew 25:35–40, we meet Christ in everyone we serve.

When we live in Christ, self and other are distinct but also united in God. This is a self-othering love. Franciscan friar Fr. Richard Rohr reflects on the centrality of this sacred I-Thou consciousness as the holy Ground of all relationships:

All of Jesus' rules of ministry here, his tips for the road, are very interpersonal. They are based on putting people in touch with people. Person-to-person is the way the gospel was originally communicated. Person-in-love-with-person, person-respecting-person, person-forgiving-person, person-touching-person, person-crying-with-person, person-hugging-person: that's where the Spirit is so beautifully present.[11]

In *Life of the Beloved* Nouwen maintains that Jesus Christ came to show us that we are each the beloved, just as Jesus is the beloved. This is our true identity: a Self of universal care that includes *and* transcends our everyday ego-selves. Nouwen's spiritual vision is squarely in the center of I-Thou Second Person consciousness when he writes that God is within us, singing a song of love to each of us, enhancing and blessing our relationships:

> I [Jesus] look at you with infinite tenderness and care for you with a care more intimate than that of a mother for her child. I have counted every hair on your head and guided you at every step. Wherever you go, I go with you, and wherever you rest, I keep watch. I will give you food that will satisfy all your hunger and drink that will quench all your thirst. I will not hide my face from you. You know me as your own as I know you as my own. You belong to me. I am your father, your mother, your brother, your sister, your lover and your spouse . . . yes, even your child. . . . Wherever you are I will be. Nothing will ever separate us. We are one.[12]

Our transformed identity as the beloved is already complete, but we tend to run away from this reality, thinking we must reject certain feelings, memories, or thoughts, or thinking that we must become someone different in order to be worthy of love. We need to learn that even our wounded, jealous, resentful, guilty, and self-hating inner voices can be drawn into an all-inclusive love. Nouwen always emphasized that we are already loved, just as we are—despite the many inner voices that may tell us otherwise. Instead of lashing out at others because we've been hurt or because we are afraid, Henri

---

[11] Richard Rohr, *The Good News according to Luke: Spiritual Reflections* (New York: Crossroad, 2002), 153.

[12] Henri J. M. Nouwen, *Life of the Beloved: Spiritual Living in a Secular World* (New York: Crossroad, 2002), 36.

would encourage us to notice our feelings of existential aloneness and abandonment. He often affirmed that Jesus is with us in our aloneness, with all its trauma, melancholy, and abandonment. Henri trusted that our honest and prayerful self-reflection and healing would lead us to amend our lives. When we hear negative self-talk, we can notice the critical voices, befriend them, detach from them, and place ourselves consciously in the presence of God's unconditional Love. We can imagine that God hears our negative self-talk, and rather than reacting with judgment or condemnation, receives us with mercy and forgiveness. When we realize that the Divine loves us, all our inner voices eventually become integrated and aligned. We learn to relinquish our anxious efforts to earn God's love and approval—efforts that actually separate us from God and others. Instead, we receive our ultimate unique identity simply by accepting Jesus's commitment to us—his friends—that we are one in Christ with him.

Our prayerful, private experience of belovedness gradually becomes the template for our everyday relationships. Our capacity to be open, vulnerable, and honest with the holy Thou strengthens and enlivens our capacity to be real and undefended with other people. We cannot keep secrets from this Source, who sees all with compassion. Therefore, when we interact with others we can be grounded in a place in our soul where everything about us is already known, forgiven, and loved. We have nothing to hide and there is nowhere to hide, because the holy You is everywhere. We are less susceptible to shame and self-consciousness. When we know that we are unconditionally loved in every situation and relationship, we are empowered to speak the truth, even when it may be risky or dangerous to be that open and vulnerable.

Loving others and being available to be loved by others in friendship is a fundamental Second Person practice, one that is inspired by our relationship with Jesus Christ. Many of us are better at loving another person than consciously receiving and valuing someone's love for us. But authentic Second Person love is always mutual. I am in this dimension of the perichoresis when I cultivate trust, care, and compassion for others, when I take the risk of saying "I love you" to others in appropriate ways, and when I am humble enough to receive and value the love I do receive. When walking in nature, I might stop beneath a tree, look up, say "you," and sense that the tree, as a you, is saying something to me. What message is being shared?

Imagine all the people around the world who, right now, are saying "I love you" to someone and hearing the response "I love you, too." How precious it is to know that we are participating in such a universal experience! The desire to exchange love is universal because this impulse comes from an infinite place that is everywhere and in everyone. Second Person awareness offers this goal—to leave every conversation with the assurance that those with whom we have interacted feel respected, cared for, and happy to be themselves, just the way they are.

9

Third Person

Spirit as Transformation

The Holy Spirit may be the most difficult Person of the Trinity to practice. Like the First Person, She never appears in a particular material form. She is *in* the wind and the breath, but not visible as Herself. We can't control the Spirit's whereabouts, Her coming and going. Nevertheless, there are ways we can make ourselves available to the Spirit. Indeed, the Bible speaks of the possibility of being "born" of the Spirit (Jn 3:8).

Jews and Christians believe that it is possible to align our human spirit with God's Spirit. As we've seen, such an alignment might be called deification, salvation, the mind of Christ, enlightenment, holiness, or True Self, a graced integration of self and Self. Samuel, the first prophet after Moses, declared,

> The spirit of the Lord [YHWH] speaks through me,
> his word is upon my tongue. (2 Sam 23:2)

So too, Jesus often proclaimed, "The word that you hear is not mine, but is from the Father who sent me" (Jn 14:10–11). Jesus promised his followers that he would send them the Holy Spirit (Jn 14:16). In several Bible passages we hear that if we trust the Spirit when we face evil, the Spirit will speak through us and defend us (Mk 13:11).

Still, Jesus makes it clear that aligning the human spirit and Holy Spirit will not be easy. The ego-world (Buber's world of "It" and Paul's world of "flesh") can tempt us to ignore the Spirit. We engage in empty chatter with others, and we mistakenly believe that our stories about reality match reality perfectly. We begin to realize how easily we are deluded. With a steadfast practice of silent meditation and calling for the guidance of the Spirit, we begin to witness the source of our delusions—our moment to moment attempts to escape our aloneness. At this point we can turn to Jesus and remember his assurance that he has sent us the Spirit as our comforter and guide. We are cared for, safe, and inwardly accompanied: "This is the Spirit of truth, whom the world cannot receive, because it neither sees him nor knows him. You know him, because he abides with you, and he will be in you" (Jn 14:16–17). This intuitive sense of a deep abiding presence releases us from fear, and gives us confidence that living Jesus's core message, to love others as we love ourselves, is actually possible.

How do we practice this Spirit of truth? First, we understand that contemplation requires rigorous honesty—the ongoing willingness to see ourselves as accurately as possible, without pretense. As I sit in silence, I admit to myself that I am afraid, alone, and longing for something I can't articulate, something that will bring me peace. I summon sacred imagination, asking the Spirit to accompany me, to sit beside me, and to witness the doubts, fears, worries, and self-reproach that are jumping around in the wild tree of my mind.

We also might ask koan-like questions that don't provide immediate answers but that do give us direction, questions such as "Spirit, what are You seeing here? What are You hearing?" Such questions allow us to step back and witness our situation from a "higher," more inclusive place. I can summon courage and patience as I listen for what the Spirit is hearing within me. I trust that the Spirit is hearing everything within me and is also guiding me toward qualities such as being mindful of the poor and outcast (Lk 4:18); being ready to forgive (Acts 2:38); seeking wisdom (Acts 6:3, 10); maintaining a stance of respect, humility, and gentleness, and bearing with one another in love (Eph 4:2).

Jesus sends his followers the Spirit as an inner guide in their effort to live the commandments. Our spiritual happiness and the fulfillment of our longing depend on our intention to love God and to realize that each of us is no better or worse than others. But we can't meet this challenge or practice this life-enhancing adventure if it is nothing more than a self-help project. We need the power of the Spirit.

A second element of practicing the Holy Spirit is to take the risk of believing. Honestly, this may be difficult. As I discovered in my secular education both in public schools and Ivy League universities, trusting in the Spirit runs counter to all the ways of knowing that we have been taught in our post-Enlightenment, reason-driven, and secular educations. It is a belief that questions the legitimacy of our capitalist culture, which focuses on quarterly returns and often reduces our identities to what we do, how much we earn and own, and what social status we have achieved—rather than focusing on who we are. Believing in the Spirit is likely to be scoffed at as a magical, pre-rational, and premodern fantasy. Therefore, in order for the belief to bear fruit in us, it must be consciously chosen. When we choose to believe in the Spirit, we step into an unknown future, one that is not pre-digested by the dominant culture. As we go forward, we cooperate with the Spirit in this uncertain path by practicing skills we've learned in the First and Second Persons—how to navigate the unknown with discernment and grace, and how to co-create relationships that help to build up a culture of kindness.

In addition to believing in the Spirit, we must seek Her and make ourselves available to receiving Her. Christians have discovered over the centuries that certain contexts are especially helpful in attuning us to the presence of the Holy Spirit: (1) gathering for worship and prayer, especially the practice of Eucharist (Greek *eucharistia:* thanksgiving); (2) practicing meditation and contemplation in silence, alone and with others; (3) being mindful of the Spirit—alone, in one-on-one relationships, and in community; (4) following the Spirit's lead toward a more just society; and (5) seeking the Spirit's guidance in nature and, inspired by the Spirit, doing what we can to protect the natural world. I will briefly address each of these practices. None of these practices guarantees that we will experience the Third Person of the Trinity, but these, and others you may discover, can make us available to the Spirit's Presence.

EUCHARISTIC TRANSFORMATION

For over two thousand years Christians have gathered in churches all over the world to pray and sing "Come, Holy Spirit." Many branches of Christianity teach that liturgies, especially the Eucharist (also called the Lord's supper, the mass, and holy communion) are essential practices that invite this Presence. In the Catholic mass congregants are asked to listen in reverent silence and to relive a scene from the night before Jesus died, when he sits at a Passover meal with his friends:

> While they were eating, Jesus took a loaf of bread, and after blessing it he broke it, gave it to the disciples, and said, "Take, eat; this is my body." Then he took a cup, and after giving thanks he gave it to them, saying, "Drink from it, all of you; for this is my blood of the covenant, which is poured out for many for the forgiveness of sins." (Mt 26:26–28)

Here, Jesus is identifying his body and blood with elements of the earth: bread and wine. He is telling his followers that spiritual friendship with him is just as nourishing and essential as eating and drinking. He tells his friends, "Do not work for the food that perishes, but for the food that endures for eternal life, which the Son of Man will give you," and, "The words that I have spoken to you are Spirit and life" (Jn 6:27; 6:63).

Growing up Lutheran, I treasured communion as a special memory. Something miraculous had happened long ago, and I could be blessed by imagining the event. My understanding deepened when, in my twenties, I became a Roman Catholic and was introduced to the mass. Having never experienced it before, I was struck by the elaborate, colorful ritual which seemed to transport me directly to the very moment of that dramatic Passover meal. I fell through ordinary time; suddenly the past was vividly present. The last supper wasn't just a memory anymore, and not even in the past. The solemn demeanor of the priest as he slowly moved around the altar in a cloud of incense brought tears to my eyes, for I felt that I was in the presence of a magnificent, awesome, and transcendent beauty and love. I imagined myself in Jesus's terrifying situation—knowing that he would soon die. In an act of profound gratitude and generosity, he released his life, giving everything away to Abba and to his friends. As the priest lifted up the bread and wine, we members of the congregation were invited to surrender our lives—body, blood, and spirit—to the Holy One, as if to say to God, "You have given me this life, and in thanksgiving I give my whole life back to you." What freedom, to sail through life and death without regrets, grudges, unmet needs and plans, and fears! What a gift for those who witness this openhearted acceptance of death. Don't be afraid, just give it all away! Deeply moved, I resolved that my life must align with this Presence.

In the Christian denominations I know best—Roman Catholic, Episcopal, and Orthodox—the faithful believe that through the Spirit, Christ is truly present in the Eucharist. When the gathered worshipers pay close attention and become fully present, we experience holiness within us and among us. Drinking in this experience begins with a belief in the power of the Eucharist, but soon transcends belief, as one offers existential trust to the invisible, invincible power of the Spirit who makes such time-transcending and transpersonal experiences possible. As we stand joyously in this transforming Presence, we mirror Christ's suffering, death, and resurrection, as if they are taking place within our own lives.

The celebration of the Eucharist shouldn't be laid aside as a routine ceremony. We can attend a Eucharist and just go through the motions without paying full attention or realizing the power of what's happening, but eucharistic transformation is a fire we shouldn't step into unless we are prepared to face the Almighty. Are we ready to give up the life we knew, the one that was so attached to being comfortable and being right? As we sip the consecrated wine and eat the morsel of consecrated bread, we take in Christ's Body and Blood and join our lives to his. St. Paul declared that on the Jesus way, our mortal bodies are becoming more and more transparent to Christ's eternal Body, and that the two bodies are becoming one Body in the timeless Spirit. "For in the one Spirit we were all baptized into one body—Jews or Greeks, slaves or free—and we were all made to drink of one Spirit" (1 Cor 12:13). "Now you are the body of Christ and individually members of it" (1 Cor 12:27).

Experiences of mind-body radiance in the Spirit don't just happen at the Eucharist; they can happen anywhere at any time, depending on our heart's availability. However it happens, undergoing sacramental transformation leads us to experience Christ's transfigured or radiant body, "the body of his glory" (Phil 3:21). This luminous body is not an object of our awareness, but instead involves a transformation of awareness itself. Once, when I described this vision to a Tibetan geshe, he smiled and said, "Oh, yes! We too glimpse a Body of eternal Light! Our spiritual identity doesn't stop at our skin. We live within a larger Body. From this place we see a Light that we have become."[1] My geshe friend used the term "subtle body" for this larger identity, when our spiritually infused inner life becomes so radiant that it shines out across the boundary between our individual self and all others, out beyond our material body. We Christians might call this body the Body of Christ, the True Self, or our transfigured Self. Those who are attuned to the marriage of spirit and body, of eternity and time, will notice this luminosity and feel safe and safely known. Again, this Eucharist transfiguration isn't something we see outside of ourselves. It is not something that we see with our material eyes but is something that we become.

Transformed in the Spirit of the Eucharist, we go forth to live our everyday lives, maintaining relationships and holding jobs, but we experience subtle changes of perception and emotion. We are less likely to get stuck in the confusion of our monkey-minds. Our larger Self infuses our body and breath with a knowing that discerns reality clearly even when our reasoning mind doesn't understand what's happening. Through practice, it is possible to live more fully from within the subtle body, the transcendent Self that is holy and infinite, and lit by the radiance of the Spirit. Ego-level knowing is transformed as the knowing of the Spirit is awakened (1 Cor 2:11).

One of the most cherished stories in scripture is the story of Jesus's transfiguration, an account of his bodily transformation in the Spirit. Jesus ascends a holy mountain with Peter, James, and John, and suddenly Jesus's face shines like the sun and his clothes become dazzling white. Within this aura of holy Light, Moses and Elijah appear and are talking to Jesus. Of course, Moses and Elijah have been dead for hundreds of years! How can this be? To me, the story indicates that every moment of transfiguration is a window through clock-time facilitated by the Spirit. This event is a Christian analogue to what Tibetans name the "subtle body"—when a divine, eternal Light infuses

---

[1] *Geshe* in Tibetan Buddhism literally means "spiritual friend."

someone's whole being, enkindles their presence, and opens them to eternal life (Mt 17:1–8). Such experiences have also been recognized as a reality in many ancient and Indigenous spiritual communities.[2]

We all must be willing to risk everything when we step through this fire, and we emerge in joy. The founder of Methodism, John Wesley, is supposed to have said, "Catch on fire, and people will come for miles to see you burn." We need examples of people who are on fire with spiritual passion. This fire of love is stoked by how we see ourselves and God. Jesus commented: "The eye is the lamp of the body. So, if your eye is healthy, your whole body will be full of light" (Mt 6:22). When our consciousness is healthy we see holiness in all things, and we convey the living Light of the Spirit to others.

SPIRIT IN SOLITUDE AND STILLNESS

As we sit in silence, the detritus and graces of our everyday lives— thoughts, memories, opinions, sensations, and voices—flow in and out of the temple. Our rational minds, rooted in the ego-self, may get confused with what seem like conflicting and opposing messages and emotions. From moment to moment we might shift from despair to hope, suffering to joy, trust to distrust, peace to annoyance, love to hate, and back again. This should not disturb us, because we inherit an ancient gift of the Holy Spirit as the steady, eternal One who harmonizes all opposites. Being "in the Spirit" is subtle—it's not driven by or dependent on thoughts or feelings.

We might say that the Holy Spirit loves pure silence. Benedictine priest Henri Le Saux suggested, "Quiet and silence alone make it possible for the Holy Spirit to work freely in the soul."[3] Sitting still in silence and listening to the Spirit who is listening within our listening is a powerful practice. When we sit still in contemplation, we do not leave outer reality. We are simply entering a deeper dimension of

---

[2] See a discussion of subtle body in the Hindu Yogic tradition in Swami Kripananda, *The Sacred Power: A Seeker's Guide to Kundalini* (South Falls-burg, NY: SYDA Foundation, 1984), 58: "The subtle body is a body of energy or light interpenetrating the physical body."

[3] Abhishiktananda, *Prayer* (Delhi, India: I.S.P.C.K, 1967; Philadelphia: Westminster Press, 1967), 40.

divine time as we descend beneath the cacophony of images, sensations, emotions, associations, and memories that streams through our
minds. As we make this descent, we take nothing for granted, and we
prepare to discover something new about ourselves, others, and God.

Zen teachers speak about the ancient contemplative practice of the
tea ceremony (Japanese: *chanoyu*), where participants relax into a
delicate and mindful awareness that brings a harmonious blending of
heaven and earth. In this ritual a quiet place is prepared as tea is brewed
and carefully poured into one's cup. The surrounding shapes, colors,
and sounds of nature blend into the taste of the tea, which awakens
one's interbeing with all the elements of the natural world. The beauty
and heart-awakening experience of *chanoyu* can only be appreciated
in the ambience of slow-moving silence. Those who give themselves
to the spirit of *chanoyu* enter "Heavenly Reason." They relax all doing
and trying, dwelling in a timeless space of consciousness that D. T. Suzuki called a "psychosphere," a sacred inner field of intuitive knowing.

Relaxing one's ego-control "in the Spirit" is a kind of *chanoyu*, a
respectful state of no-self that allows infinite room for the Spirit's Self
to illuminate every corner of our mortal lives. When the ceremony
is over, the inner luminance continues to shine, guiding our behavior
according to the gifts of the Spirit. Ceremonies like the Eucharist and
chanoyu can awaken our spiritual senses if we are willing to know
that there is nowhere else to be and no one else to be.[4] Partaking of
heavenly reason or being in the Spirit aren't experiences that one can
achieve by efforts of the ego. In fact, trying to achieve these blessed
states shows a lack of respect for the independent power of the Spirit,
who comes from and goes to nowhere. We also don't respect this
sacred power if we try to attain it because we're supposed to. It's not
a goal that makes one a good Buddhist or Christian. In these quiet,
Spirit-full practices our spiritual capacities are harmonized with our
reason and our practical considerations. Our left-brain activities of
categorization, analysis, and reason don't disappear. Rather, they are

---

[4] Daisetz T. Suzuki, *Zen and Japanese Culture* (Princeton, NJ: Princeton
University Press, 1959), 276–83, 295. Of course, Eucharist and *chanoyu* are
not exactly the same, because the Eucharist is meant to convey a transcendent
interpersonal Presence. The purpose of *chanoyu* is to awaken one to the present moment.

transformed within the spacious sky-like consciousness of the Spirit, who lives within and from the First and Second Persons of the Holy Trinity.

In some contemplative practices imagination is to be avoided, with teachers suggesting that we note in silence any images that arise, and then let them go. But I disagree. Some images, and even some narratives and stories that travel silently through our minds, bring blessings and revelations that deserve awe, gratitude, and love. What images of Spirit work for you? What is most important is that we guard against the tendency of the ego-self to calcify and possess our insights and imaginations. The world is at a crucial turning point as we struggle to reweave the web of life and to forge a more just and resilient way of inhabiting the earth. The only way forward is to realize that everyone and all creatures are the beloved, that a transcendent Goodness is moving within and among us, and that we can trust what the Spirit will bring.

ONE-ON-ONE RELATIONSHIPS

Each of us is unique, but when we attune ourselves to the field of the Spirit, we hear resonances of our inner voices in others and in nature. On the ocean, I hear my gray-whale voice; in the mountains, I hear my kestrel voice; and in the forest, I hear my yellow-warbler voice. We are always going out of ourselves and coming back. As we do so, we are blessed and our identity is enlarged, for we find ourselves in everyone we meet. I value the statement attributed to the second-century Roman playwright Terence: "I am human, and I consider nothing that is human alien to me." This reveals a challenging practice: as soon as I notice myself recoiling and judging another, I ask myself, How am I like that person? I can forget to do this, and sometimes I want to forget this, but when I remember, I bow to the Spirit, who is remembering from a higher level within me.

The Spirit helps us notice when we are "othering" someone in a negative sense. Awakened, we can rotate the lens of negative otherness to "alterity," wherein the ways in which we are different from others become the doorway to a deeper level of empathy and compassion. For example, my irritation with someone's behavior can shift into sincere curiosity and a desire to understand the other and myself. In such moment I might realize that my annoyance is unpleasant and constraining *for me*. Negative judgments of others wound and captivate me. The next step in understanding, inspired by the Spirit, is to imagine asking the other person, "What's it like to be you?" "What are you afraid of?" "What are you longing for?" Learning something new about others also teaches us something new about ourselves.

If we are drawn to the idea of spiritual oneness, we also must be alert to what we might call spiritual narcissism: a consciousness that obscures the richness of otherness. From within ego-driven narcissism, we see others only in ways that help us avoid pain or find pleasure. Seeing another as an opportunity for newness and surprise is a more joyful way to live. The Holy Spirit is always nudging us to seek what is new within ourselves and in others. This is a commitment, a moment-to-moment discipline, to become lifelong learners of the mystery that we are. This special experience of newness is known in Zen Buddhism by the name *Ichi-go ichi-e*, which means to treasure the unrepeatable nature of a moment. The Holy Spirit facilitates *Ichi-go ichi-e*, inviting those of us in interpersonal conversations and those in contemplative groups to see each momentary interaction as unique and even revelatory.

The Spirit is there dancing between self and other, honoring oneness and appreciating otherness. In the oneness of true love a deep and inclusive kind of individuality flourishes. When the wife of Christian mystic and author C. S. Lewis died of cancer, what Lewis missed most was "the rough, sharp, cleansing tang of her otherness."[5] This is the paradox of trinitarian awareness, as well—God is both "out there" and within us, both other and not other, both three in one and one in three. We need a power with more oomph and freedom than our egos—the power of the Holy Spirit—if we are going to dance this paradox wisely in our relationships.

As I deepen my appreciation of how my wife and I are different, I actually feel closer to her. In our everyday dialogues and decision-making, we experiment with new ways to relate to each other. I can imagine us, in the early years of our marriage, carrying out various

---

[5] C. S. Lewis, *A Grief Observed* (New York: Bantam Books, 1961), 2.

tasks in the kitchen, she making an observation about world news or a family member, me listening with only half attention, silently weaving her narrative into my already established opinions about the topic and about her. But lately, when she shares a thought, I follow a new model of behavior: whenever possible, I drop what I was thinking about, turn, and look her directly in the eyes. I've made it a practice to gaze with warm curiosity as if to ask: Who are you being now? This movement in awareness awakens me from the slumber of thinking that I already know her and why she is saying or doing a particular thing. I feel closer than ever to her now, and I've been honored to see that she also turns to me with a quality of curiosity and love. We are fortunate to be on similar spiritual paths, both of us believing that God creates the cosmos as an "other" to love, and that God has seeded a distinctive, lovely kind of otherness into our marriage. When we are irritated or annoyed with each other, we are alerted to the danger of separation and to the possibility of a deeper love.

To accept the idea that the Holy Spirit lives in our awareness is to believe that interpersonal relations are a window to the divine. Because we are created as creatures distinct from God and because we have been gifted with freedom, we are free to love or reject God. When we allow others to be different from us, we grant them the same freedom that God grants us.

The practice of trinitarian awareness affirms that appreciating otherness is a holy practice, since otherness circulates within the Being of God. Otherness is seen as a path to the limitless New of God, whereby God is making all things new (Isa 43:19; 48:6; Rev 21:5). Our name for the story of Jesus is called the New Testament for good reason. All along this path we are invited to become new. This invitation reminds me that I do not know everything already, and that what is now in the shadows, whether comforting or frightening, will further my knowledge of self and God. The Spirit is inviting me into the sacred unknowing of the First Person of the Trinity.

If we are honest, we know that we can bring self-centered irritation, self-pity, annoyance, and anger to our relationships. But we shouldn't use this self-knowledge to reject ourselves or to separate ourselves from others. I assume that the Spirit knows us better than we know ourselves and sees through our selfishness to the core of our belovedness. God says to us what God said to St. Paul: "My grace is sufficient for you, for power is made perfect in weakness" (2 Cor 12:9). Again, Paul knew that human wisdom is insufficient by itself to transform lives. That's why he said, "My message and my preaching were not with wise and persuasive words, but with a demonstration of the Spirit's power, so that your faith might not rest on human wisdom, but on God's power" (1 Cor 2:4–5). Freed from the tyranny of our small ego-selves, a beloved community of ever-renewing relationships is born.

SPIRIT IN COMMUNITY

We have considered images and experiences of the Holy Spirit in scripture and as articulated by several Christian mystics throughout the ages. These accounts offer clues about how to practice Spirit awareness, but many are culture bound, historically dated, and lacking in precise psychological, perceptual, and emotional detail. I am grateful for the work of contemporary spiritual teachers like the Dalai Lama who have inspired and supported neurological, psychological, and medical research into the effects of meditation, but I am not aware of studies into the practice and experience of the Holy Spirit. Identifying specific practices of the Holy Spirit is also difficult because I believe that people who are not Christian receive glimpses of the Spirit and either don't have a word for their experience or use different, often psychological words for Her appearance. When in my graduate studies at Harvard we read Abraham Maslow's description of "peak experiences," I heard the Holy Spirit's voice.

I see evidence of contemporary sightings of the Holy Spirit in stories about people's experience in music and sports. In my teens and twenties I played many different sports, and I sometimes felt "in the zone" with teammates.[6] In moments like this, one's self-consciousness drops away in an atmosphere of interpersonal trust. One feels as if the

---

[6] Michael Murphy and Rhea A. White, *In the Zone: Transcendent Experience in Sports* (New York: Open Road Integrated Media, 2011); Andrew Cooper, *Playing in the Zone: Exploring the Spiritual Dimensions of Sports* (Boston: Shambhala, 1998).

participants are one body of awareness, and that, somehow, what will happen is already known. There is a sense of ease and a seamless flow of collective awareness and energetic readiness to respond. There may be exuberance, an unfailing self-confidence that is perfectly timed and choreographed with the skill and confidence of others, and joy. When this kind of experience happens for Christians, we say that we are "in the Spirit." The ambience is safety and kindness, along with the other "gifts of the Spirit."

But there is a shadow side to experiencing the Spirit in community. Feeling safe and at one with others can lead to an over-identification with the group—a kind of negative tribal consciousness that condemns or simply excludes others. We've seen this phenomenon in the incendiary climate of Nazi Germany and in the insurrection at the US Capitol on January 6, 2021. The Nazi "Spirit" was a form of group narcissism that rejected respectful relatedness to people outside the Party. Tribal participation can help individuals and families survive in hostile environments and can support a sense of healthy social cohesion. But tribal consciousness can also be toxic and dangerous, and we must keep asking ourselves whether or not a particular movement or group activity is cultivating compassion, empathy, love, and alterity (as the appreciation of otherness).

After decades of self-monitoring, I have become used to listening within myself for the unseen presence of the Spirit when I'm in a group or community setting. When I host spiritual groups, I usually begin with twenty minutes of silence and offer basic instructions for newcomers. I suggest very few rules or methods, asking members only to remember their ultimate purpose—encountering our Higher Power—and to listen inwardly as we speak and listen to others. I ask everyone to notice when they form an opinion or judgment about themselves or other people, to inquire into it, and then to let it go, always ready to notice what is new. I ask them to listen deeply to themselves as they formulate something to share with others and to entertain questions such as:

- What do I really need to share?
- Why do I want to speak now?
- Will my contribution add to the flow of listening that is happening in this room?

- Am I being careful to facilitate the flow of mutual understanding that is happening, or is my glib, cynical, or judgmental comment taking us down a rabbit hole of confusion?
- Am I merely sharing information about my recent activities, simply wanting people to know what I did or what I think?
- Am I telling my story in a way in which listeners can find common ground? Is there something universal in what I am sharing?
- Am I trying to be right or trying to be smarter than someone else?
- Am I mindful of the overt or subtle judgments I'm projecting onto participants?

This self-questioning can facilitate our availability to the Holy Spirit in interpersonal and group interactions. When we care, and intend to communicate our caring, there is always a transcendent and holy Listening within our personal hearing.

At the Empty Bell contemplative sanctuary I've made the transition from considering the Holy Spirit to be an It of theological symbolism and impersonal energy to recognizing Her as a Thou of relationship. My relationship with the invisible Spirit is like a marriage. I've made a vow to go nowhere without the Spirit, knowing that I will often fail and seek forgiveness. Saying "You" to the invisible Spirit seems to sanctify my relationship to others in the room. I hold myself accountable to this Presence. Also, assuming the Presence of the Spirit enlarges my sense of Self beyond ego concerns, inviting me to see and hear inner voices or the concerns of participants that I might otherwise override in fear or haste. Having faith in the Holy Spirit means choosing to be awake, present, and vulnerable to what is, while simultaneously listening for signs of what help we can bring to every situation. I feel beholden to the Spirit, and also pledged to the Spirit's Presence and vision for human flourishing.

Being fully awakened to the Spirit in community requires First Person openness and unknowing. I'm reminded of what Japanese Zen Buddhist teachers describe as *mushin* (literally, no thinking mind), a state of focused presence that flows beneath our thinking with an innocence of heart that overrides the brain's dualistic habits of categorization and judgment. Living in the Spirit does not negate the ego or our power of logical thought and discernment. Rather, we live from a larger frame of reference imbued with care and love. D. T. Suzuki describes *mushin* as

> going beyond the dualism of all forms of life and death, good and evil, being and non-being. . . . This state of mind gives itself up unreservedly to an unknown power that comes to one from nowhere and yet seems strong enough to possess the whole field of consciousness and make it work for the unknown. . . . [One is] "unconsciously conscious" or "consciously unconscious."[7]

I would say that in the Christian experience of *mushin*, everything that is in us—conscious and unconscious—is in God, known by the Spirit who accompanies us. Therefore, we are not alone and need not fear the unknown.

Experiencing Spirit-accompaniment in solitude and silence and in one-on-one relationships will enhance our self-confidence and insight as we participate in groups and as we serve our community.

SPIRIT INSPIRES AND GUIDES ACTION FOR JUSTICE

The Spirit yearns for the reconciliation of human beings with one another and with the rest of the natural world. So it's no surprise that the Spirit is often active in nonviolent movements for social and ecological justice. Religious faith can be distorted and exploited for private and political gain and used as a force that resists social change and efforts to promote justice, and Christianity has often been used to justify injustices such as slavery, White supremacy, and ecological destruction. However, the Christian God of love is always luring us to form relationships based on kindness, justice, and mercy, and to take part in co-creating the beloved community.

When the Holy Spirit is present in groups, appropriate outrage against injustice can be shaped and channeled into effective action for the common good. Countless churches have been nesting places for the Holy Spirit in this effort. In the struggle for justice it is helpful to be skilled in mediation, conflict resolution, and listening, but what

---

[7] Suzuki, *Zen and Japanese Culture*, 94.

matters most is a basic trust that a Higher Power is present and has a stake in the outcome. We are accountable to this Power.

When we give our lives to God's mission of love, we put our-selves on the line in an ultimate way. Mortal fear can prevent us from confronting evil, but the Spirit can empower us to take risks despite our fear and self-centeredness. For example, trusting in the Spirit's presence and vision has helped me to accept revelations about myself that I would otherwise be unwilling to face. The Black Lives Matter movement has opened my eyes to the ways in which I as a White Christian man have unknowingly accepted and tacitly approved rac-ist practices in my life. I've inadvertently harbored and expressed thoughts and ideas that justify and maintain White privilege, and I have failed to intervene to stop injustice when I had an opportunity to do so. Dropping my excuses for White privilege opens me to the Spirit-work of learning to participate in justice building.

Social transformation takes time. We may recognize the urgent need for radical changes in society, yet we cannot force others to agree with us. As a psychologist I have worked with many social change agents who threw themselves so deeply into the struggle that they became ideologically rigid and stopped listening to their better angels. The Spirit within invites us to be vulnerable, strong, resilient, and humble, speaking and acting with clarity and commitment. Our work for social and ecological justice will bring us into contact—and often conflict—with other people. When we meet with allies to figure out how to address the damage caused by greedy individuals, rapacious corporations, or corrupt governments, such meetings usually focus on legal and political actions, which is necessary. But the Spirit who calls us to participate in movements for justice also invites us to grow in self-awareness and compassion as we interact with allies and opponents.

Meetings to plan social action can be sidetracked by interpersonal squabbles and unpleasant power dynamics. Even when our intentions are virtuous and worthy, we can hurt one another and undermine our effectiveness. Deliberately or inadvertently, every one of us can hate and hurt people whose race, gender, class, opinions, sexual orienta-tion, or religion is different from ours. We can also hate and hurt people with whom we simply disagree. This is true because we are all complicated human beings. We often bring past wounds, resentments, and rigid opinions to our interactions; we generally want other people to resemble us; and we don't want to change. Ego-self wants to be who it wants to be, thank you very much, and we can become fearful, annoyed, or angry when others aren't like us or don't agree with us. When participants in social and environmental action meet to act, I believe it is beneficial to begin meetings in silence, and especially helpful if the leaders have spiritual resources such as the Holy Spirit that can be inwardly tapped to release them from attachment to their strong opinions.

We often resist the truth that the seeds of everything we view (and perhaps condemn) in other people also exist within us. When we reject particular aspects of other people, we often don't notice that we are disavowing some aspect of ourselves. For example, perhaps I notice someone who does something unkind, and I secretly harbor unkind thoughts about that person. The other person's unkindness may be real, but it is also real right here, in me. What we see outside ourselves is entwined with who we are. Many advocates for justice say that the Holy Spirit is like a miner's light that guides us out of the dark cave of our self-righteousness. We need this transcendent light because when we are trapped in our ego-selves, we will always justify our own, limited perspective. Ego-self sees dualistically: others are (or are not) members of our tribe; their ideas are (or are not) like ours; and their habits and behavior are (or are not) acceptable to us. But the Spirit is a bridge builder, always searching for connections, mutual understanding, and compassion, as we've seen in the Pentecost story (Acts 2). The Spirit expands our vision and understanding from a private and constricted "I know" to the intersubjective knowing of the True Self.

In recent rallies, I have stood among crowds that include all age groups, races, genders, and religions, and I've been brought to tears by some of the music, speeches, and chants that open our hearts to deep levels of outrage, grief, joy, and solidarity with others. It's as if we are in the zone, being carried along in a stream of good will. I've also been present when speakers and marchers bring a level of rage that taunts those who are different and even incites violence. In such groups the Spirit of interbeing has been captured by the clannish spirit of fear, loneliness, and self-satisfaction.

Living the challenge of authentic otherness is especially important now, in the midst of the Black Lives Matter crisis-opportunity. In the late 1960s I spent a year as a VISTA volunteer in the Wayne Minor projects in Kansas City, Missouri—one of only a few White people in a Black community. As I began this period of immersion in the poverty and violence of cheaply constructed public housing projects, I was shocked by my first glimpse of what too many Blacks in this country have had to endure. I was also touched by the love and courage that I witnessed. Mama Bohannon was the president of the Housing Association, and her son Wayne was a leader of the Black Panthers in Kansas City. I'd often walk down from my eleventh-floor apartment on the dark and garbage-filled stairs to sit in Mama's apartment with her children and grandchildren as she hosted residents who were discussing community problems, singing, and, often, hungry and looking for work. I keep a photo of Mama Bohannon on my desk. She was my tutor and protector, and she introduced me to the dynamic heart-opening liturgies at her Black gospel church. It soon became clear to me that the singing and dancing presence of the Holy Spirit in her church was a fundamental source of the community's emotional and spiritual resilience.

The civil rights movement hit the public stage in the 1960s because people like Dr. Martin Luther King Jr. and others opened their hearts to the Spirit of a justice-seeking, mercy-loving God. King had grown up in the segregated South. His father and maternal grandfather were Baptist ministers, and King received his theological training at Morehouse College, Crozer Theological Seminary, and Boston University. Inspired by his love for God and by his admiration for Mahatma Gandhi's nonviolent opposition to colonialism in India, King returned to Alabama, to his Baptist ministry, and to leadership in the Southern Christian Leadership Conference, which promoted nonviolent tactics to combat racism.

Some said King was moving too fast and that reaching equality would take a very long time. But King and his friends continued to pray, worship, strategize, and organize, reporting that they felt the presence of the Spirit as they undertook their impossible task. Of

course, King was painfully aware that White Christians in the South
had created and enforced the culture of slavery in his community.
But he also knew that if Jesus could bear the humiliation of the cross,
the Black community could bear the scourge of racism and co-create
the beloved community. King assumed that Mahatma Gandhi's heart
was open to the Spirit when he fought for independence and justice
in India. Gandhi's nonviolent political activism inspired King, offering him a method for revolutionary change, and the gospel gave him
the spirit of hope when it seemed that real change might be beyond
reach.[8] The civil rights movement of the 1960s scored legal victories,
and, according to Dr. King, it was the Spirit who gave his people the
trust, energy, and vision they needed to live with dignity.[9]

This movement for racial justice is just one example of the ways
that people of faith can feel empowered to realize God's love, justice,
mercy, and harmony in our communities. Gandhi's *Satyagraha* (Sanskrit: soul force for truth) campaign, with its Hindu-Christian flavor,
was animated by Gandhi's steadfast faith in a God of truth and love.
Similarly, the Truth and Reconciliation commissions in Argentina,
Chile, and South Africa, the last led by Archbishop Desmond Tutu,
Nelson Mandela, and other religious leaders, remind us of the power
of acting in the Spirit.[10] Migrant farmworkers in America's Southwest
have experienced over a century of racial and economic discrimina-
tion, and the hopelessness and despair that White supremacy bring.
Their fight for honor and justice was once led by Cesar Chavez
(1927–93). Chavez was raised Roman Catholic and motivated by the
vision and moral principles of Catholic social thought. Inspired by his
faith and by *Rerum Novarum* (1891), the papal encyclical concerning

---

[8] See Martin Luther King Jr., *The Autobiography of Martin Luther King Jr.,* ed. Clayborne Carson (New York: Warner Books, 1998).

[9] Martin Luther King Jr., *The Essential Martin Luther, Jr.,* ed. Clayborne Carson (Boston: Beacon Press, 2013), 76, 80, 256.

[10] Nelson Mandela did not speak or write much about his Methodist faith and his belief in the Holy Trinity, but those who were close to him knew that his faith gave him the courage to fight for justice. See Dennis Cruywagen, *The Spiritual Mandela: Faith and Religion in the Life of Nelson Mandela* (New York: Penguin Random House, Kindle edition, 2018), esp. 144.

the rights and duties of capital and labor, Chavez placed the Spirit in the center of his "Prayer of the Farm Workers' Struggle":

> Show me the suffering of the most miserable;
> So I will know my people's plight.
> Free me to pray for others;
> For you are present in every person.
> Help me take responsibility for my own life;
> So that I can be free at last.
> Grant me courage to serve others;
> For in service there is true life.
> Give me honesty and patience;
> So that I can work with other workers.
> Bring forth song and celebration;
> So that the Spirit will be alive among us.
> Let the Spirit flourish and grow;
> So that we will never tire of the struggle.
> Let us remember those who have died for justice;
> For they have given us life.
> Help us love even those who hate us;
> So we can change the world.[11]

This kind of Holy Spirit awareness seems comparable to the experience of one of my Native American colleagues and friends who speaks of the Great Spirit, the One of many names who blessed his people's living on the land for millennia. I resonate with this Great Spirit prayer of the Iroquois:

Oh Great Spirit, whose voice I hear in the winds, and whose breath gives life to all the world, hear me. I am a (human) before you, and one of your many children. I am small and weak. I need your strength and wisdom. Let me walk in beauty and make my eyes ever behold the red and purple sunsets. Make

---

[11] Cesar Chavez, "Prayer of the Farm Workers' Struggle / *Oración del Campesino en la Lucha*," available online.

me wise so that I may know the things you have taught my people.[12]

SPIRIT IN NATURE

The idea that we can "practice" the Holy Spirit in nature may startle some Christians, for we have inherited a long-standing suspicion of ancient pagan beliefs. We have been told that we should worship God, not nature. But as the ninth-century Celtic master John Scotus Eriugena pointed out, the natural world is born of God, who proclaimed at the birth of creation, "This is good." Nature manifests the goodness of God. Nature itself is not God, but nature is a theophany of Presence.[13] The beauty we find in nature reflects the infinite Beauty in God, and in us. Scotus and other Christian mystics such as Nicholas of Cusa felt that the Holy Spirit empowers us to see the eternity of the First Person in all natural things.[14] St. Francis of Assisi likewise reminds us that because the holy You of God abides in nature, we can say "you" to all creatures and elements and feel addressed by them.

Nature is transparent to the Spirit, and the spirit within us leads us to discover the Spirit in the natural world. We awaken to this truth when we allow ourselves to be fully present in nature, especially when we have no practical agenda. The Holy Spirit, the Voice of sacred interbeing, guides us into creation in two ways. First, She awakens gratitude for the planet's wild, quirky, complex, and beautiful living systems and creatures. Second, She reminds us of God's charge in Genesis that we steward the goodness and integrity of the natural world. Given the ongoing destruction of nature, we humans are finally awakening to the Spirit's core message: we "inter-are" with

---

[12] "Iroquois Prayer," www.ya-native.com.

[13] See, for example, John Scotus Eriugena, *The Voice of the Eagle: The Heart of Celtic Christianity*, trans. Christopher Bamford (Great Barrington, MA: Lindisfarne Books, 2000), Kindle edition, loc. 1541.

[14] *Nicholas of Cusa: Selected Spiritual Writings*, trans. and ed. H. Lawrence Bond (New York: Paulist Press, 1997): "In the First Book it was shown that God is in all things in such a way that all things are in God . . . as if, by mediation of the universe it follows, then, that all are in all and each is in each" (140).

winds, waters, and lands. Treating the natural world from within "the It-world" is destroying the web of life and threatening human civilization—a terrifying, ongoing tragedy of ecocide and suicide. As our appreciation and awe deepen, the Spirit leads us out into the public square to advocate for public policies and protections that safeguard the natural world. Stewarding nature is stewarding ourselves and God.

The Spirit challenges city dwellers to come out of our houses and off our screens to make direct contact with nature, and She invites all of us to take practical actions that contribute to a sustainable and habitable earth. This is not a sentimental or romantic charge; our lives and the lives of our descendants hang in the balance. We—and the whole living world—are temples of the Holy Spirit, and rejecting the voice of the Spirit is self-destructive.

Many of us need to learn how to bring a contemplative gaze to the natural world. For example, I might embark on a slow walk on a New England field near wetlands. I might ask myself, *What am I being called to see, hear, and touch? Whom am I being led to encounter?* On a summer afternoon my eyes are drawn to plants that are woody, flowering, grass-like, ferny, saturated in glowing colors, or, at first glance, ugly. But as I gaze, welcoming everything as part of the whole, I perceive beauty in the unusual shapes and colors that at first repelled me. Underlying my walk and gaze is a trust that I will, indeed, be able to see beyond the boundaries of what I already know. My gratitude for this moment is enhanced because I know that the whole natural world is beautiful, evolving, suffering, and being reborn.

Gazing at the new green birch leaves, I recall them as buds just a few weeks ago, and I remember how, last fall, the leaves yellowed and then dropped and drifted across the field when the first frost came. Gazing into nature I witness the passage of time. The leaves and their radiant greens will be gone in a few months, and the bare oak limbs will be outlined with snow. I walk slowly toward a stand of white pines, noticing the nearby hemlocks, beeches, and ashes, all of them endangered by climate change. Memories and reflections pass through my mind, and I bring my attention back to what is here right now, drinking in the fresh presence of the stones, the cattails, the tree frogs beginning their late afternoon symphony. Each footstep in the grass is like a step into the cathedral of eternity that is hosting and blessing all that passes in time.

As I walk, my mind may wander. I may feel flashes of anger, fear, and grief about what we humans are doing to the planet. My practice is to try to stay here on my feet, inside this communion, in the I-thou presence of natural things that I am experiencing now. The lovely kinship Presence of the Spirit reminds me to bow toward everything, to the "you" in everything I see. I appreciate the beauty and feel grateful, even in the midst of fear and outrage. Is the Spirit leading me to turn toward the shade at the edge of the field or out into the goldenrod to watch the bees? What are the swallows, mallards, and beetles saying? I listen as I step, and the Listening is happening within me. When I return home, I feel free, enriched, and more connected to the natural world, as if I have just walked out of a landscape liturgy. If my mind gradually becomes a tree full of monkeys, I am more inclined to listen for what the monkeys are saying to one another.

In his groundbreaking book *Living Buddha, Living Christ*, Thich Nhat Hanh reflects on common spiritual ground between the revelations of Buddha and of Jesus. He believes that Shakyamuni Buddha was a definite historical person, like any other person, but that his presence is eternal because he manifested the timeless light of the eternal Dharma, that nameless place from which everything appears. For Thich Nhat Hanh, the transforming power of Buddha's presence appears everywhere and in everything. Nature is transparent to this presence:

> The trees, the birds, the violet bamboo, and the yellow chrysanthemums, are all preaching the Dharma that Shakyamuni taught 2,500 years ago. We can be in touch with him through any of these. He is a living Buddha, always available.[15]

In this spirit, contemplatives of all religious backgrounds, or none, wander in nature, listening to the preaching of Canada geese, blue jays, cicadas, and turkey vultures. Contemplative nature lovers may

---

[15] Thich Nhat Hanh, *Living Buddha, Living Christ* (New York: Riverhead, 1995), 146–47.

be scientists, experiencing awe and wonder even as they record the names, behaviors, interactions, and histories of trees and birds, frogs and wetlands; as they study forest degradation and how to increase carbon sequestration; or as they study coral reefs and how to save them. There's a noble place for science—studying and discerning precisely what's happening, what's causing what, and how to understand and safeguard the natural world. But when we embark on a contemplative journey into nature, we are not seeking causes, not trying to analyze what we see or trying to figure out how nature can be useful to us. We might even let familiar names, like crow, kingfisher, salamander, and owl, fall away. We are simply present to what is, noticing and appreciating without a why. We are available for an encounter with other creatures and with the rest of the natural world—animate and inanimate—and ready to receive whatever they wish to communicate to us. In this practice of sacred "betweening" of a living human to the living nonhuman world, we let go of trying to put words on everything. The only fact that interests us is the fact of inter-presence: we look into the eyes of a turtle as the turtle looks at us.

And the Spirit invites us to protect the web of life. Converging political, economic, and psychological forces are conspiring to destroy the natural world as we have known it. The challenge can seem overwhelming, but each of us has a particular role to play and all of us together can make a difference. If we keep listening for the Spirit and seek the Spirit's guidance, we may be surprised to discover how we can contribute to the restoration and regeneration of the earth. As we commit ourselves to the goal of a sustainable future for life on this planet, we need to double down on eco-friendly scientific research, technological innovation, and political, legal, and financial policies. However, we also need a transformation of consciousness, the invisible inner platform of our knowing and our ethics. We are learning a new way of being, which values reciprocity and mutuality instead of domination.

This revolution of awareness is now profoundly affecting the environmental and conservation communities as science itself begins to confirm what Indigenous people have always known: the trees, birds, whales, fish, wind, and waves are speaking and listening to one another.[16] Many Americans are learning how to participate in that conversation, attuning ourselves to the "betweening" of the Spirit in nature and discovering how connected we are with—and dependent on—the rest of the natural world. Trusting in the presence of the Spirit is not a sentimental hope. It is an actual practice—the discipline of slowing down, gazing, and listening to the Listening within and among us. When we perceive the earth with prayerful attention, we come to understand that the earth is sacred. As the Psalmist says, "The earth is the Lord's and all that is in it" (Ps 24:1). We are not only *on* the earth—we are *in* the earth, and the earth is in us. A trinitarian revolution of consciousness reveals this truth and can lead to different kinds of effective action.

---

[16] See, for example, Peter Wohlleben and Jane Billinghurst, *The Hidden Life of Trees: What They Feel, How They Communicate* (Vancouver/Berkeley: Greystone Books, 2015); Robert MacFarlane, *Underland: A Deep Time Journey* (New York: W. W. Norton, 2019); Diane Fossey, *Gorillas in the Mist* (Boston: First Mariner Books, 1983).

10

Practicing the Trinity in Personal Relationships

The Trinity as a mandala of spiritual consciousness revolves luminously within all our relationships. When we are fully present with others in First Person awareness, we continually step off the edge of our opinions and narratives, maintaining an attitude of curiosity about ourselves and other people. Everything I know about me and everything I know about others and God is already changing. While dwelling in this Person, we notice feelings and thoughts as they arise and quickly ascertain if they lead toward or away from compassion and truth. Our inner compass is Christ. We realize that we cannot walk forward into new life on the shifting ground of self-centered thoughts, memories, and opinions. The only reliable and ultimate ground is the invisible foundation of transcendent and inclusive Love.

When we are fully present with others in Second Person awareness, we likewise cut quickly through conditioned judgments and opinions and respect other people's unique ways of living with a discerning eye focused on relationships. We dwell in the "you" world, where our inner detachment frees us to be available for friendship. As we abide in the freedom of our I-Thou relationship with God, we can imagine the invisible thread of You within other persons and creatures. Since our need for unconditional love is already met in Jesus, we can more fully appreciate the limited love that others can give us. Abiding in this awareness, we offer someone a safe presence that is neither invasive nor abandoning.

When we are fully present with others in Third Person awareness, we are drawn to participate in the co-creation of a compassionate

181

and respectful family, community, and world. We consider every interpersonal relationship as situated within the unity-in-diversity of perichoresis. Third Person awareness naturally evolves from total Mystery, and from the you-world to the we-world, where we are invited to participate in creating a beloved community.

How do we know if we have been listening on God's Personal channels of contemplative awareness in our relationships? We know because, as we practice this awareness, we gradually become less reactive, less fearful, more kind, more curious and generous, better able to love ourselves and others, and more willing to take risks to help others. Rooted in the Persons of trinitarian awareness, we feel safe enough to risk being vulnerable with others. As practices, none of the three divine dimensions comes first, because each is a microcosm of the infinite Divine which shines within every relationship. Where there is one, there are three, and where there are three, there is one.

Here are some tips for practicing the Trinity in interpersonal relationships, Person by Person.

FIRST PERSON PRACTICE IN RELATIONSHIPS

First Person awareness is always happening *now*: as we converse with someone, we may notice that we are thinking, remembering, daydreaming, or worrying, but our practice is to keep bringing ourselves back to the present moment, to the person who stands before us. Now is the only time in which something new can happen within us or within our relationships. When present with another person, eye contact is important—not merely looking into someone's face but bringing our eyes in direct contact with the eyes of the other.[1] We're careful not to be invasive; we are simply present and open to what is happening within us and between us. From this place of open awareness, we listen to the other person with care and curiosity, noticing if memories, feelings, and sensations are triggered by what the person is saying or doing. What is happening now? This question is always alive within us as we move through a conversation or a relationship

---

[1] Of course, I am speaking of cultures in which such eye contact is welcome. That is not the case in all cultures.

in the First Person. Dwelling in now, we take on what some Zen masters call the "Don't Know Mind." We are certainly aware of what we already know about someone, but we assume that we are not fully aware of the other person, or of ourselves.

In addition to the raw data of our senses and thoughts, we usually perceive others through the veil of our opinions and memories. Isolated behind this veil, we don't see and hear our conversation partners as they really are. Rather, we see and hear what we think about them and who we prefer them to be for us. This is an easy mistake to make, for we all tend to play a character with predictable things we say and do. Still, our responsibility is to notice our tendency to label people and events in private narratives that we've developed over the years, narratives that may be invisible, even to us. As we become more present, curious, and observant, we become aware of the habitual inner narratives and filters that we place between ourselves and others. As we become more present, we begin to see new dimensions of the other person and of ourselves. In the present moment, God is always new, and everything is being born anew (see Rev 21:5).

Our personal and cultural filters relate to our momentary practical and long-term goals, only some of which are consciously known to us. Past experiences have imprinted themselves in our psyches and become templates for current and future relationships. Images and narratives from others and from the media circulate through our minds. We prefer certain images of faces, body types, genders, and skin color—inner images that affect how we relate to others. As Sigmund Freud and Carl Jung understood, we all harbor resonances of painful past relationships and unconscious fears and impulses, which Jung called the shadow, that is, those parts of ourselves we don't want to see, parts that we sometimes project onto others. The free-gazing of First Person awareness makes us more available to notice the parts of ourselves that have been hidden from us. When we are truly present to someone, our narratives about self and other and the places where we get "triggered" become easy to spot against the vast story-less sky of Creator-consciousness.

When I was a young man who learned and then taught Tae Kwan Do, I was trained to employ 360-degree awareness, always prepared to encounter an enemy who could approach from any direction. I was trained to bend my knees slightly, so that I could quickly pivot in the opposite direction. This bodily motion became rooted in my everyday awareness, alerting me not only to dangers but also to blessings that might come from within or from outside me. All our experiences, narratives, and opinions are passing through the infinite and free awareness of the First Person. We are free because we are not attached to being a particular somebody with required opinions. When we stand in this holy No Place, we can see clearly that when things are going well, we might suddenly become afraid and then try to stabilize and retrieve that good feeling. We may try to hold on tight to a pleasing identity and the feeling that goes with it. If instead we simply notice our unease, we may feel as if we're falling—falling through the walls of our prefab identity into emptiness. In fact, in an ultimate sense, we *are* empty of any firm identity. Nevertheless, we are not alone. We are inwardly accompanied by Someone who knows that we are free of any fixed material or psychological identity. In this emptiness we are participating in the kenosis of Christ, who emptied himself of everything and lives forever.

As we relinquish our habitual story about any relationship, we step into a mode of careful and yet detached witnessing. This allows us to experience something new in ourselves and others. It's like being present in the nanosecond before creation—first there is nothing, and then there is something new! In First Person awareness we respect and honor the silent pause between knowing and unknowing self and other, trusting that a new knowing will emerge from the unknowing.

I've mentioned my wife, Margaret, who leads climate-change retreats from a spiritual perspective. One day she received a call from a Roman Catholic retreat center in the South. A woman on the phone invited Margaret to lead a retreat for a contemplative social action group that would focus on Pope Francis's encyclical on climate change, *Laudato Si'*. I happened to be nearby in the kitchen, and I overheard some of the conversation, because Margaret's speaker phone was on. I suddenly remembered that I had once led a Henri Nouwen retreat with that same group and had really enjoyed the experience. But after listening for a few moments, I realized that I was getting upset. I grabbed a piece of paper, wrote the words *Henri Nouwen,* placed it on the counter in front of Margaret, and left the room. Why was I upset, why had I written Henri's name on that paper, and why had I left the room?

As I walked away from the kitchen, I realized what had triggered me. I had done a lot of research and planning for my retreat at that spiritual center; I had even produced a short video in which I narrated Henri's thoughts about the sacredness of nature, integrating his words and my voice with images of America's natural beauty. I realized that I wanted the leadership of the retreat center to remember Henri and me. I wanted them to remember my teaching that Henri's message of universal belovedness was not only about people, but also about all creation and about issues like climate change. I realized that I was upset because Margaret hadn't even mentioned Henri, my friendship and work with him, or my video! How could she have forgotten that? How could she have forgotten me?

After several minutes of reflection in my study, I understood that I'd placed that paper in front of Margaret because I'd wanted my work—and me—to be recognized. I'd also wanted her to do what I would have done in her situation. In short, I'd wanted her to be me! My hurt and anger were replaced by shame, and I felt as if I'd been hurled into a dank, dark cell with no room to move. My neck and belly were tight. Noticing this constriction, I breathed deeply, relaxed my body, and recalled the spaciousness of the Creator, who is the temple of my consciousness and unattached to any momentary feelings and narratives. Breathing in that sky Presence, I resolved to talk with Margaret after I had settled down. I'm certain that my ability *to notice and accept* my anger and shame, and the pain of my body's contraction, was a result of contemplative practice. When feelings arise in relationships, I notice them more quickly than I once did. Fortunately, when Margaret came into my office later, we could discuss what happened and complete our dialogue with a hug.

This experience illustrates First Person awareness in a long-term relationship: we notice inner reactions and return our awareness to an Unknowing whose powers transcend our own. Anything is possible: Who are you now? Who am I now? Perhaps we've been holding a grudge against someone and suddenly realize that we're not angry anymore. In First Person awareness we *let this new now be so.* Hoping to reconnect, we might want to share our change of attitude with the other person, as appropriate in the context of mutual trust. However, we must be mindful, since the other person may be uncomfortable with the goal or process of resolving misunderstandings and conflicts. When we dance the perichoresis in relationship, we are always noticing what arises, letting go, and discerning our intention and our next behavior. When we lose our footing and stumble on this holy invisible dance floor, we try not to react but just to pick ourselves up and start again. Creator awareness is always new. Within this dance we are always seeking a larger harmony of personal and interpersonal reality, even when we must move through conflict to get there.

First Person awareness may inspire us to say to our partner of many years: "I know you so well, but I also don't know you, and I want to know more. I expect this will always be true until I die." Our ability to empathize accurately depends on our capacity to "unknow" ourselves and others. What we think we know of ourselves and others can be valuable, but it can also be a defense against the raw experience of living openly, without the ersatz protection of our opinions. Yes, I have decades of marital memories that can haphazardly come to mind as I encounter Margaret around the house, but my practice is to see her as a surprise. This practice supports our marriage vow, and it is one way to escape the relational trap that the poet Rainer Maria Rilke observed when he wrote:

> how little at home we are
> in the interpreted world. . . .
> Is it easier for lovers?
> Ah, but they only use each other
>   to hide what awaits them.[2]

I don't want to live in a secondhand, interpreted world, and I don't want my marriage to be an unconsciously conceived den where I hide from myself, from my spouse, or from life itself. In the incident above I eventually understood that behind my initial reactive response to Margaret was my longing to be recognized, remembered, and appreciated. After this incident I reflected on the shame I'd felt.

---

[2] Rainer Maria Rilke, *Duino Elegies*, bilingual ed., trans. Edward Snow (New York: North Point Press, 2000), 5.

According to my self-image I was a long-time, enthusiastic supporter of the feminist movement, yet here I was interfering with a woman who was exercising her power and skill to lead spiritual retreats. Perhaps I wasn't as liberated as I thought. First Person awareness is being awake to what is happening inwardly as we relate to another person. Almost always our thoughts and opinions are accompanied by emotions. My thoughts about Henri, Margaret, and her retreat were intertwined with my need to be seen and valued, and these needs were bundled with anger, loneliness, desire, guilt, and shame. All such packages of thoughts and emotions are unfolding within Creator's boundless consciousness. These packages are not solid and not eternal. Only God is eternal.

The sky-like consciousness of the First Person invites a continual investigation and unfolding of ourselves in relationship. As we grow in awareness, we often discover that we have been misinterpreting who we are and misjudging our parents, children, neighbors, and friends. Then, as Rilke points out, we can suddenly realize that we've used our secure love relationships to hide from truths we don't want to face. We carry narratives from past relationships, and sometimes they are helpful, steering us away from dangers and leading us toward friends who will support our belovedness. But in any moment of contact with others, it's best to notice filters of thought, memory, desire, or emotion that may screen out the truth and obscure direct contact with another person or living being. When we are in truth, we are in love. We are born with First Person consciousness; this birthright is within us, ready to be awakened by our prayer and practices.

Humanistic psychologist Arthur Deikman recognized this kind of knowing in *The Observing Self: Mysticism and Psychotherapy*.[3] The observer self is sometimes called the witnessing self, an awareness first described in Sigmund Freud's psychoanalytic work as "evenly suspended awareness."[4] For Christians, this practice of witnessing

---

[3] Arthur Deikman, *The Observing Self: Mysticism and Psychotherapy* (Boston: Beacon Press, 1982).

[4] Ken Wilbur uses the term "witnessing self" in *One Taste* (Boulder, CO: Shambhala Publications, 2000). For a discussion of evenly suspended awareness, see Michael J. Tansey and Walter F. Burke, *Understanding Counter-Transference: From Projective Identification to Empathy* (Hillsdale, NJ: The Analytic Press, 1989), 41ff.

and discerning was popularized by St. Ignatius of Loyola in the sixteenth century. He named this spiritual practice *indiferencia*, "a state of inner freedom, openness, and balance that allows us beforehand not to incline more toward one option than to another."[5] Although, as far as I know, Ignatius did not explore how this awareness functions in interpersonal intimacy, this capacity is always available to us. Christians who practice witnessing, evenly suspended awareness, and *indiferencia* in their relationships do so with faith that this aspect of consciousness is infused with love—not a romantic or lightweight love, but one that touches everything with a transforming Presence and care. To give full attention is to love. It can't be forced, and it blossoms from sincere faith rather than from being a self-help project. Deikman's insight is a contemporary, secular reinterpretation of the ancient *apophatic*, or *via negativa*, the way of the First Person—*non-attachment* to objects of consciousness. In my experience those who practice this detachment *as they interact with others* discover a rich vein of new energy, insight, and care.

My interaction with Margaret shows how detachment can work in relationship. We notice our thoughts and feelings as they arise—especially reactive and judgmental ones—and inwardly we ask ourselves, *What is this?* This is a characteristic First Person mantra, a manifestation of the detachment at work in all our relationships. As we breathe, we might silently query: *I'm uncomfortable and want to push this person away. What's going on?* This is a practice of humility. We jump off the loud train of what we already know, stand still in the grass, and listen for something new to arise. Perhaps we have to abandon our desire to be right as we make the other person wrong. This practice of detachment requires patience as we wait for something beneficial to say, something that, perhaps, we've never had the courage to share before. Contents of awareness are always passing through, and if we don't notice and quickly discern the importance of the opinions, memories, desires, and emotions that flow by, we will be swept downstream and never really know what's happening or who we are. Our relationships will become stale and unsatisfying.

---

[5] See "Introduction to Inspired Decision-Making: Personal and Communal Discernment," Xavier University, Resources of Ignatian Spirituality.

First Person consciousness is not a dispassionate, analytical stance, but rather a warm, compassionate, and merciful witnessing that brings kindness to the content, no matter what it is. Our intention is always to benefit the relationship, even when giving and receiving uncomfortable feedback. When angry with someone, we might need to separate ourselves, but somehow we know that the other and I will always live in the same world, and that someday, in this life or the next, the relationship will resolve. Trinitarian awareness is always moving, rotating like a transparent crystalline orb, always opening to the emerging present moment, alone or with others. If I realize that I'm upset about what someone just said or did, I might give myself trouble for being upset, but then I go spelunking into the feeling, seeking the source. I ask myself: *Is there a problem? Is this something I need to address right now or can I let this go?* I discern a response and keep navigating into First Person spaciousness.

THE MYSTERY OF THE CREATOR
IN RELATIONSHIPS

One might think that the Creator of the cosmos is infinitely distant from our everyday lives and relationships, but this would be a great mistake, because we and time itself are created *from within* the Creator, who is present in every second of time as it passes. Because we dwell within the eternity of the First Person, we share in God's free, un-ensnared attention, even as we interact with others. This is why the Creator chose to incarnate in a person, so we can trust that God knows what it is like to be human and so that God's freedom can manifest in all persons and relationships.

The Creator is free of attachment to anything, and free of time. Creator has no past or future and is always now, always a new now as we communicate with others. This word *now* can sound like something that exists only in time and space, but "now" is actually a river that is continually "now-ing" within and among us—ever new, yet never changing. Now is not something that happened in the past or will happen in the future. When relationships are difficult, we might draw on lessons learned in the past, and we might glimpse some hope for the future, but the only possible pathway to forgiveness, reconciliation, and love is now. Now is when we must discern what to say or do in a conflict. I have experienced spiritual teachers who say that only the present moment is real, but I believe that past and future are also real, and that they are continually up-welling into every present moment. First Person "nowing" is a kind of past-present-futuring. When is it happening? Now, as you read these words. Follow these suggestions, closing your eyes occasionally:

> Take a deep breath and, for just a moment, open all your senses—smell, sight, touch, emotion, thought, hearing—to what is happening right now. See if you can do this without narrating your experience. Relax, stay awake, listen, and remain alert. Let a train of thoughts pass through without getting on board. What do you see? What do you hear? Try to see and hear something you've not noticed. Simply be in the surrounding experience of Now, and trust that even as you sit and do nothing, our planet is revolving, people, robins, and whales are being born, and others are dying. For a few moments, there is nothing you can do about it. Life goes on in this Now, and God is communing with you right now. Now is where you can listen to the grandeur, trauma, and ecstasy of life as it passes over this planet and through your heart.

> You may feel drawn to add a Second Person aspect as this meditation unfolds: In silence, imagine a person who you care about, and notice your honest response. Imagine saying your truth to that person, perhaps "I love you," "I'm afraid of you," "I could use your help right now," or "I need some distance from you right now." What do you say to the oceans, now so damaged by over-fishing and plastic pollution? What do you say to the forests, being chopped down to clear land for cattle and crops or burning in the grip of climate change? Now is always the time to be honest.

When we stand in the freedom of the First Person, we are standing in a nonreactive presence with others. Reactivity happens when our awareness is captured by something, and we're sidelined from the flow of now-experience. Being reactive to someone in anger, fear, jealousy, or judgment is not necessarily bad, but reactions must be explored. When we're stuck inside of reactive emotions, we've stepped away from now. When clarity returns, we can always step out of the tight enclosure of reactivity into the spaciousness of the First Person; from here, we are free to respond honestly, as appropriate.

This way of detachment or unknowing in relationships is an exemplar of what St. John of the Cross refers to as the "dark night" and the *nada* (Spanish: nothing), which he considers the pinnacle of the spiritual journey. John's *nada* is not nihilism or meaninglessness, and it is not experienced only in monasteries. It is a free openness (darkness to the reasoning mind that tends to focus on problems, memories, and future thinking). For St. John, the darkness of Now is the only source of something new. John didn't discuss how the dark night relates to interpersonal situations, but I think he might agree that the *nada* he experienced goes on continuously in every situation, alone or with others. This unknowing can't be a pretense or a manipulation. It must be real, as if our lives were at stake—for they are. Life is short, and each precious moment in every relationship is an opportunity to experience and to manifest the Creator's free awareness and care.

I believe that Jesus's awareness was rooted in *nada* when he came upon a village in which an adulterous woman was about to be stoned (Jn 8:1–11). According to then-current religious laws, a woman accused of adultery should be stoned to death. We might surmise from scripture that the local religious authorities resented Jesus's increasing popularity as a rabbi, and they tried to trap him, asking him if indeed the woman should be killed. They knew that Jesus was representing himself as an authentic Jewish spiritual teacher, but also that he portrayed himself as manifesting YHWH's inclusive mercy and forgiveness—not just his own opinions. If Jesus affirmed the execution, he would, in effect, bow to the local religious laws and authorities, but this would undercut his unique focus on God's extra-legal love and mercy. On the other hand, if Jesus said that the authorities were wrong to allow the killing, he would be exposed as a radical who disrespected Jewish laws. It seemed that there was no way out. In my opinion Jesus realized the mortal danger he faced, and inwardly stepped back into Abba's free awareness where impossible choices are transcended. He had no programmed reaction, no prefigured response when he dropped to the ground and "wrote" with his finger in the dirt. I imagine that he was silent as the authorities railed at him and at the woman. Then he slowly and deliberately rose up and declared, "Let the one who is without sin cast the first stone" (Jn 8:7). Jesus's response was not a quotation from Hebrew scripture. I believe it was something unpredictable and new, a response that not only set him free from the trap that had been set for him, but also one that set the woman free. His response also reframed the situation: everyone is accountable for what they do, and everyone needs God's mercy.

I believe that as Jesus moved his finger through the dirt, his mind was open to infinite possibilities—his categorical thinking and problem solving were stilled. When a comet of truth sped across the sky of his heart and mind, it illumined what he should do next. Jesus's quick response was brilliant, but something more than human intelligence was at work. I believe that when Jesus put his finger into the dirt, it was as if he had touched a dark, transforming fire. Something new for himself and the world suddenly burned away his self-concern. The Spirit's firestorm of clarity silenced the angry crowd and blessed the woman.

Most mystical theologians prior to the twenty-first century did not leave explicit tutorials and practices for practicing *nada* or kenosis in relationships. As with all our traditions and teachings, it's up to us to update our spiritual software. The mystics may not have mentioned this, but we can affirm from our own experience that practicing honesty and not-knowing during every conversation often introduces something new and opens a pathway to greater self-understanding and greater intimacy. When we are free of opinions about others, they often feel heard in an unusual and refreshing way. People feel safe with us because they sense that we are not distracted and not critical, invasive, or abandoning. We can do this when our own deep needs for unconditional, loving presence are being met in prayer and from trusted friends and counselors. When we can be unconditionally present to others, they will often feel nourished, whether or not they are conscious of what happened. The worst thing we can do is to leave a conversation imagining that we have completely figured out ourselves or the other person, for we can never get to the bottom of the mystery of being human. The capacity to honor, even to protect, the unknown dimension of our self and others is rooted in the First Person of the Trinity, who is unfathomable Mystery.

SECOND PERSON PRACTICE IN RELATIONSHIPS

Let's turn now to Second Person consciousness, the interpersonal inscape of what Martin Buber called the "You world." In contrast to First Person awareness, this is more focused, paying close attention to the other with a sense of commitment to their well-being. Hebrew prophets tapped this relational awareness with God when they shared YHWH's comforting vow to his people, "I will be with you" (Gen 26:3; Ex 3:12; Deut 32:23; Josh 1:4; Isa 43:2). Likewise, Jesus, speaking from the place of Abba within him, tells his followers, "Abide in me as I abide in you" (Jn 15:4). We might call this interpersonal abiding a holy friendship. Speaking to his followers, Jesus said, "I do not call you servants any longer, because the servant does not know what the master is doing; but I have called you friends, because I have made known to you everything that I have heard from my Father" (Jn 15:15). I believe Jesus named friendship as a kind of interpersonal intimacy that reveals the mystery of Creator. Rightly conceived, friendship is a relationship that closely connects the "I Am" Mystery of the Creator with the incarnate I-thou of mortal personhood. Friendship is rooted in ultimate mystery and in the most intimate of all I-thou questions and declarations, "Do you love me?" and "I love you" (Ps 18:1; Isa 43:4; Jn 21:15–17; 2 Cor 12:15). To say "I love you" with sincerity releases us into the depths of the Second Person (Christ) consciousness that Jesus lived.

Jesus stood in the You-world, addressing the infinite as You, and giving his life to his You-Father and his you-friends. In all his relationships Jesus's self-awareness was infused with this unarticulated mantra: I am seen, known, and loved by Abba, and I see, know, and love you in the same way. He didn't desperately need love, for he was already living Abba's unconditional Love. He expressed love for his friends and wanted them to thrive. It is within this You-world that human beings become fully alive because we have dropped all pretense and removed the veils that we wear to hide our True Selves. This transformation is something glorious, as St. Paul announces when he tells us that with unveiled faces we will see "the glory of the Lord as though reflected in a mirror and know that we are being transformed into the same image from one degree of glory to another" (2 Cor 2:18).

Jesus's love arose from the Nowhere of the Uncaused Creator who loves for no reason. He was passing along the Uncaused Love of the Creator who has no cause. In Jesus's love-relationship with God and other people, he did not stand on the ground of causality, judgment, or opinion. He was not saying, "I see you *because* you believe me; I know you *because* I'm a good judge of character; I love you *because* you will therefore love me in return and do what I want." When we, like Jesus, stand in the uncaused and unconditional First Person, we love God and others from within the You-world where there is no "because"—only care, commitment, and love streaming through the permeable boundary of the self.[6] Our practices bring us to a place where we spontaneously love for no reason.

Look how Jesus manifested his Second Person reality: the Jesus we meet in the Gospels is exquisitely sensitive to people—respecting them, listening to them, noticing where they might be getting lost, and extending compassion. When he confronts someone, he does so because he discerns that something ultimate is at stake. He acts to stop harmful behavior and to heal what has been hurt. We have no historical, archival records of Jesus's daily life, but I believe that everything Jesus did sprang from the font of an Uncaused Love. His faith and love inspire mine. When, like Jesus, we love others without conditions, we pass along what we ourselves are receiving. When God's love flows through us, we embody the Jesus archetype and participate in the life of the Trinity.

It is likely that we feel grateful when we're in the company of persons who are established in God's love; it's as if they are transparent to the ultimately important qualities of goodness, truth, and beauty.

---

[6] St. Bernard of Clairvaux (1090–1153) taught that the highest stage of love is to love for no extrinsic reason. See "On Loving God," *Bernard of Clairvaux: Selected Works*, trans. and foreword G. R. Evans (New York: Paulist Press, 1987), 173–205. Since all things are born from the Uncaused Source, we can agree with Emily Dickinson who wrote the poem "Beauty Be Not Caused It Is."

We feel safe with such people, for they don't invite us to pretend or hide. We sense that they see us as we really are, and we feel freer to be ourselves. Relationships enhanced in this Second Person way convey healing, delight, and creativity. We feel loved for no reason, so we don't have to try to be loved. It's a done deal, and we know that we have a friend.

Many non-Christians have an inner Thou who ignites this kind of love and empowerment. I have friends whose holy Thou is Muhammad, Buddha, Kwan Yin, Tara, Sophia, the Dalai Lama, Moses, or Rumi—Someone who inspires them and brings them a peace and joy that radiates into their everyday relationships. If you have a holy Someone within you, you will want to be true to that Presence in your relationships, because that Someone already knows everything about you and loves you. That inner I-Thou relationship allows and supports you to live with honesty and integrity because you already know that you are fully known and loved. I do not claim that every holy Thou is the same Thou, or that the various experiences of Thou in disparate religions and cultures always yield a Christian You. I can only say that I experience a unique and clear quality of interpersonal Presence in Jesus Christ, the Second Person of the Trinity. Our everyday relationships are the practice field for Second Person awareness.

YOU WILL BE PROTECTED

This kind of friendship, which is transparent to a deathless love, doesn't come easily. We might fear I-Thou friendships because we've been hurt in the past and have set up inner defenses, or because we've grown up in a culture that rewards self-centered thinking and behavior that divides us from other people and from nature. Perhaps we've been traumatized, abandoned, or abused by others. Perhaps it's a challenge to make friends with others, and to love them, because we fear what might be asked of us or fear that we will be rejected. We might not trust ourselves enough to love others while maintaining good interpersonal boundaries. Loving others and receiving the love of others may also be scary because as we enter Second Person awareness from the invisible ground of the Creator's spacious openness, we become more sensitive to what is happening within and around us, and therefore we may feel more vulnerable. The pain that others experience may affect us more keenly. Then again, we may be apprehensive because if we commit ourselves to care for someone, we fear that we won't be able to follow through with our care when times are tough, or we fear the loss of the other person through death.

Surrendering to God's Love in prayer readies us to receive the love of others because we enter a zone of trust that strengthens our ability to navigate worldly friendships. We can risk vulnerability with others because we realize that if we stop protecting ourselves, we will be protected. Even if we make mistakes and fall short—even if we have been hurt by others—we know that the abiding Love that we have found in prayer will always be with us. We can trust that this Love will be a resource of strength and courage when we notice that someone is disappointing or mistreating us. We can trust that the Spirit will help us to discern how much we can give and receive in any particular relationship. Growing in such trust gradually enables us to relinquish pretense, deceit, and posturing, because we are loved just as we are.

When we address the Father or Jesus in I-Thou prayer, we trust that God loves what and who God created. We can feel released from trying to be someone else and we gradually learn to experience the freedom of being exactly who we are, without self-consciousness or self-rejection. We will discover that this inner freedom and security are with us throughout the day and can help us act with wisdom and clarity in our daily relationships. No matter where we are or who we are with, this truth is eternal. In the presence of the Beloved within and outside of us, we don't have to pose or perform. We don't have to be smart, funny, informed, famous, young, handsome, beautiful, or anything else. We can relax because we know we're already loved. The people we encounter may or may not know that they, too, are completely loved, but we hope that our presence will help them to experience that reality.

By contrast, when we're looking through the ego-self lens in our relationships, nothing and no one is ever quite good enough. Or someone is always better or worse than we are. We're always managing a false self-image in relation to others, and people will likely feel judged in our presence. It's as if, in our relationships, we put on and take off different styles of psychic clothing to match the pretense we're inflicting on ourselves and others. As we emerge from the it-world of the self-centered ego, we see how often we've lived in the mind-state of fear, blame, comparison, and complaint, and how often we've needlessly separated ourselves from ourselves and from others.

Practicing the inner gaze of belovedness and manifesting this affectionate gaze in our relationships is a subtle art that requires sensitivity and nuance. It's not a matter of pretending or imagining that I am an idealized version of myself or that other persons are idealized versions of themselves. Beloved is who we really are, with all our quirky ways, despite the fact that some people may not like or respect us. Trusting in the love of God, we can acknowledge our past mistakes; we can recognize that we've harmed others, and we can do our best to make amends and make things right. We don't have to become someone we're not. We can see our limitations without being attached to them. We can look affectionately on our brokenness because, as Leonard Cohen sang, "Brokenness is how the light gets in." Because we trust that Jesus sees us in this way, we are released from shame in the presence of others. But, again, we should not merely "believe" this. It's a moment-to-moment practice, every day.

We can experience relationships as holy even if we're not specifically thinking about the incarnation and if we're not Christian. As I've said, the sacred Thou is not the sole possession of any one tradition. I can only say that Jesus is the One who introduced me to this interpersonal majesty. Christian or not, what matters is our intention to be rooted in divine love in all our interactions, and to work with every feeling and thought that arises to bring our whole experience into harmony with that unconditional, inclusive love. It doesn't mean being nice, serious, or happy all the time. There will be times when love calls us to confront someone, to hold someone accountable, or to protect someone from harm; there will be times when love calls us to laugh uproariously, to weep, or to confess. Being awake in the you-world of awareness requires full presence, availability to being affected, clarity about our purpose, and readiness to take whatever action love inspires. This is a lifetime piece of work.

THIRD PERSON PRACTICE IN RELATIONSHIPS

Which turns us then, finally, to Third Person awareness, when we experience ourselves as part of a larger "we" in which we inter-are with others, participating in a dynamic choreography that is always evolving, sometimes liberating, sometimes dangerous, and always challenging. As this awareness deepens, we become ever more vigilant and sensitive to moments of separation from others, God, and nature. The "betweening" power of the Holy Spirit won't let us forget how connected we really are. The Spirit continually draws us into harmony with ourselves, with other people, and with the natural order of things. We might agree conceptually that our essence is beloved and that all beings are kin, but how do we actually practice this way of being in our daily lives? The Spirit is our resource and guide.

We need the Spirit's connective energies because in a competitive, capitalistic society we are constantly tempted to separate from the natural world and from others. If we are not mindful, we become our resumés and whatever product we must sell to survive. We know that we harbor inner voices that can separate us from our beloved core Self where everything and everyone is connected. And we know that, indeed, there are real enemies outside of us. The Spirit is always—always—inviting us into alignment with nature and others. How do we envision and act appropriately from this vision while also protecting ourselves and others and avoiding the temptation to isolation, cultism, and tribalism? First, we must claim our intention to live the life that Jesus envisioned, a life of kinship to which we ourselves feel drawn. Second, we must commit ourselves to periods of silence when we can let our attachments to the self-oriented voices within us and to our negative judgments and opinions fall away. And third, we must trust that the Holy Spirit is here to help us as we reach out to help others.

The Holy Spirit has been called our inner comforter, inspiration, and guide. We need this support because we face inner and outer destructive powers that oppose the holy Presence, and our ego-power is simply not sufficient to meet the challenge. Jesus knew that he lived in a violent society (Mt 11:12), and he predicted his own crucifixion many times. Violence seems to be embedded in the natural order, and every living being is fighting for survival. Seeking universal kinship can expose us to danger, but Jesus invites us to follow him on the path of love. The Spirit will be with us, and we know that we will be guided and protected (1 Pet 1:3–9). God doesn't say, "I will not let you suffer," but rather, "I will always be with you in your suffering."

As we allow the orb of trinitarian awareness to circulate among the three Persons, we develop a paradoxical capacity to accept reality as it is (First Person awareness), while simultaneously longing for something better, healthier, more just, compassionate, and creative in our communities (Third Person awareness). When we relax our grip on a self-centered existence and reach out to others in community, it helps to know that this effort is not merely an honorable (and exhausting) self-help project. We reach out as individuals, but we are also participating with others in the Love project that transcends us. We can feel drawn out of our isolation by the holy You in Rebbe Levi Yitzhak of Berditchev's "Song of You" (from Chapter 8). We may feel alone, but we are never alone in our aloneness. Our longing to participate in a beloved community comes from our Dear Far-Nearness, who conveys the capacity to be transformed in love. How soon will this transformation happen? An ancient Roman Catholic expression asserts that it exists *already and not yet.*

When we attend a moving liturgy, a contemplative gathering, or a public concert, and we feel a certain presence in the group that seems to transcend the individuals and knit us together into a communion of care, that's the Holy Spirit. When leadership is wise and trustworthy in such gathered events, we feel safe to experience our deep connection with the people around us. When a family gathers with an open heart to share life stories, or when we play games and are swept up in an especially vivid love for one another, that's the Holy Spirit at work. When we witness someone who has been terribly hurt come forward to forgive the perpetrator, that's the Holy Spirit at work. The desire for revenge falls away in the Spirit's Presence, as do defensiveness, cynicism, and self-consciousness. When the fullness of the Spirit is present and acknowledged, we are changed for the better. A core Third Person practice is to recognize the blessing of mutual belonging and mercy.

THE HOLY SPIRIT'S PRESENCE IN GROUPS

I have hosted both Christian and interfaith contemplative groups at the Empty Bell for nearly thirty years. My trinitarian intentions are the same in both types of groups, but in the interfaith groups I am careful not to overemphasize Christian language, and I don't imply that Christianity is the best spiritual tradition. Just because this tradition has been the best for me doesn't mean that it's the best for everyone. I listen for how a Hindu, Buddhist, or Sufi practitioner might name what I call God, the Incarnate One, or the Holy Spirit. In specifically Christian groups, we focus on the Roman Catholic or Episcopal scripture for the day, and in the interfaith groups I suggest a topic to reflect on for a couple of days before we meet. My hope is that as participants learn to listen to one another in kindly, nonreactive ways, they will take this way of being with them into their families and communities. I see all of this as the work of the Holy Spirit.

After twenty minutes of silence, I usually include opportunities for both triads (groups of three) and the whole group to share in a confidential setting. I tell participants that we are spelunking down into our bodies, memories, and emotions, and that the miner's light that we wear on our helmets is the Spirit's love. I ask that people share what is on their hearts. We assume that the ambience of our sharing is love. I ask people to take three slow breaths before responding to what someone else has shared. Together, we co-create an atmosphere where no one feels that they must rush in to speak next. We seek to listen into the silence after someone speaks, to let the speaker's words, images, and presence resonate in our psyches and souls. We assume that this kind of listening facilitates the communal knitting in love that the Spirit seeks among us. In the silence we can discern how what has been shared connects with our own experience. In this way we feel closer to the person who has spoken, and we get in touch with our basic humility, as if to say, "Oh, this is what it's like to be you and what it's like to be human!" When our meeting adjourns, we often feel that we have touched a poignant and precious unity among us, a unity that also appreciates diversity. This is what the Holy Spirit does, bringing the experience of one-in-many and many-in-one. We experience friendship as inspired by a Holy Spirit.

I ask participants to treat speaking and listening as a contemplative exploration of kinship. I say: "Notice how you are listening. Witness without judgment what memories are stirred up as you listen to others speak, and notice why you are, or are not, speaking." Our intention is not to judge ourselves or others, but rather to notice with empathy and to convey kindness toward oneself and others. Being in groups can provide a powerful nest for birthing new insights. The key is a certain neutrality—not listening for anything in particular, and not preferring pleasant and comforting experiences over troublesome ones. If I do find myself judging others—making them wrong in some way—I try to avoid self-condemnation and, rather, to examine myself: "Where is this judgment coming from? What really bothers me about this person, and what does this say about me?" As Jesus has said, "How can you say to your neighbor, 'Friend, let me take out the speck in your eye,' when you yourself do not see the log in your own eye? You hypocrite, first take the log out of your own eye, and then you will see clearly to take the speck out of your neighbor's eye" (Lk 6:42). The Spirit moves most freely when we are detached from our preferences and from rigid narratives about what's happening.

Contemplative silence is most helpful when we are resolved to make an honest assessment of ourselves. This means not taking our thoughts for granted. Sitting in silence, we not only witness our thoughts. We are grateful for them, and curious about them. Our thinking affects our feelings, our behavior, and our intentions. Witnessing our inner life is also called detachment by many spiritual teachers. Those who host contemplative groups are simultaneously witnessing their inner experience and the visages and behavior of group members. The group's leader must be aware of how group members are affecting one another and should notice when someone's comments or emotional display might trigger an atmosphere of judgment or danger. Sometimes the host will share a gentle reminder from the "Principles of Sharing," which are inspired by the Pentecost experience described in the Book of Acts.[7]

---

[7] See "Principles of Sharing," at http://www.emptybell.org/articles/principles-of-sharing.html.

Being aware of our breathing in the midst of conversations usually slows down the rapid-fire reactions of group dynamics. Going slower allows a depth of self-presence in the midst of a conversation. Knowing that the Judeo-Christian ancients identified the Holy Spirit as breath is an immediate reminder that God is continuously present as we breathe. I often emphasize that we did not create our breath and don't own our breathing. When a group first gathers, someone watches a timer and lets everyone know that about three minutes is a good maximum time to share. But over the years I have found that participants gradually learn to follow the deep listening guidelines without being reminded and without needing to use material objects like a bell or a talking stick. People begin to sense the value of a slow, respectful, and reflective time in which one can be both inwardly and outwardly present to what is happening. It's a slow dancing perichoresis of friendship.

After silence, the Christian contemplative group focuses on the Hebrew and New Testament readings currently being shared around the world in Roman Catholic and Episcopal churches, followed by triads and whole-group discussions of the scripture lessons. Our interfaith groups proceed differently. Before convening an online interfaith meeting, I email a topic and ask participants to meditate on it before we meet—topics such as trust, fear, longing, love, memory, impatience, family relations, or anxiety. Sometimes I ask an open-ended question, such as: "What spiritual practices bring you peace?" "From whom did you learn how to love?" "Do you believe in God or have an experience of God?" "How has the pandemic affected your spiritual life?" "What gives you hope?"

During the pandemic our meetings have occurred on Zoom. For me, the Holy Spirit transcends the digital divide, and I have been struck by the quality of honesty and vulnerability in our online sessions. Participants often say that although our isolation in the pandemic separates us physically, our shared predicament and our willingness to be honest and vulnerable with one another bring us together more closely than ever. Most participants enjoy looking into each other's faces, even if they are only on a screen. Some find that our virtual gatherings have helped them to see the Spirit's Presence in others' faces, while others experience Zoom gatherings as impersonal and long for a return to the in-person meetings.

Being in the Spirit zone isn't always comfortable. For instance, someone may say something we disagree with, or do something that hurts us, or perhaps we inadvertently cause hurt. Perhaps someone ignores us. When we trust the Spirit within and among us, we can let the little hurts go and resolve to address any lingering "dis-ease" later. If someone obviously hurts another person in the group, I, as host, address it in a firm but gentle way. Trusting that the Spirit is the ultimate host of a contemplative group helps me to be patient with momentary unresolved interactions. In all groups I share my belief in the Holy Spirit, and I ask for feedback. Participants understand that I trust the Spirit to be our actual host, and that the Spirit inspires us to speak our truth with empathy and care and to work out differences in ways that can blossom into mutual understanding.

In those few times when I've felt uneasy with someone's sharp tone, I've asked to meet the person privately, and we've come to an understanding. In thirty years of working with hundreds of fellow seekers, I've reluctantly asked only four people to leave a group. My sense is that some people who have been traumatized in past relationships may not be ready to benefit from contemplative listening in the Spirit. Occasionally I remind participants of the value of psychotherapy and Twelve-Step groups.

Memories of what someone said during a meeting may fade, but when participants keep returning, year after year, we are confident that something good is happening. I sometimes tell participants that the resonance of our mutual care will *always* circulate in our souls, even when we don't remember what happened. In my experience, other people are more likely to experience the Spirit's presence when I, as group leader, practice trinitarian awareness: letting go of my opinions, judgments, and stories about what's happening; opening to what is happening within me as I listen to others; being available for friendship; and trusting that God's Presence and inclusive Love permeate the ambience of the group.

PRACTICING ALL PERSONS AT ONCE

Awareness of the trinitarian Persons in our relationships is a moment-to-moment practice. The First Person (presence, self-emptying, detachment, and unknowing), the Second Person (entering into I-thou relationships as inspired and informed by our I-Thou experience of devotional and unconditional love), and the Third Person (participating in the dynamic dance of the Spirit's sacred communion making) are all valid dimensions of God's presence *and* of our own consciousness. When the Holy Trinity is merely a theological concept, it is abstract and anemic, having no direct connection to our actual experience. To understand the true meaning of the Trinity, we must *be* the Trinity and practice the Persons. At any moment we may find ourselves more in one dimension or another, and there's no way to plan or decide in advance which aspect of the Trinity might move to the foreground. It helps if we stay in touch with our desire for union with God and remain inwardly flexible, open, and resilient, always ready to respond appropriately. All three Persons are ways to *be* our True Selves in each moment, to become incarnations that reflect the incarnation of the Divine-human Person, Jesus Christ. In our Empty Bell community, misunderstandings and misjudgments are to be expected and resolved privately, or in conversation apart from the whole group. Mistakes are not considered bad, just opportunities for more learning.

Throughout this book I've described personal and relational practices that tap the three dimensions of divine awareness. In taking up these practices with a sincere intention to be available to God's grace, we become more awake and responsive. Due to differing personalities, some of us will perceive and practice our spiritual journeys more naturally from the First, the Second, or the Third Person. And some religious communities may be more fluent in one aspect of trinitarian consciousness than in another.

For example, in mainstream Christianity today, it's common for Quakers and contemplative Christians to favor silent meditation (First Person), and for other Christian communities to enjoy devotion to Jesus (Second Person) in the form of vocal prayer, song, and scripture. Still others may favor exuberant, dynamically embodied singing, dancing, and liturgies that tap the sense of belonging or the dedication to justice that comes with an emphasis on the passionate presence of the Holy Spirit (Third Person). Some Christian communities don't offer silence; some don't invite intimate devotional prayer and song; and some don't offer elaborately orchestrated and emotionally charged liturgies. As we grow in faith, we can notice whether we are particularly drawn to one of these three approaches, recognizing that we may need different kinds of support at different points in our journey, and remembering that each Person of trinitarian awareness circulates within the others. And when all three Persons are freely dancing within us, we are participating in the dance of transcendent and embodied Love.

Epilogue

Schindler's List: A Window into Trinitarian Consciousness

I have suggested that it is possible to *live* the Holy Trinity. What does this way of living look like? Seeing examples of incarnation can inspire us and nourish our hope for a better life.

In *Schindler's List*, actor Liam Neeson plays the charismatic German businessman Oskar Schindler. There's a moment in the film that exemplifies the dance of the Trinity in one person's heart and mind. In the midst of the terrible Nazi persecution of Jews, Schindler seizes upon a business opportunity, employing Jews at rock-bottom wages to make armaments for the Nazis. Schindler is a morally decrepit opportunist who treats his Jewish laborers as objects to further his greed: a clear and dramatic example of Buber's I-It world. As Schindler directs the factory's operations and witnesses the horrors of the Holocaust, his heart gradually opens. He begins to see the laborers as individuals, with names, histories, families, and hopes, and to care for them as his I-It world dissolves into the world of I-Thou. Soon his concern for individual people motivates him to bribe the Nazi generals and guards in order to save as many Jews as he can. At the end of the movie, the Jewish workers and the Nazi guards simultaneously hear a radio broadcast that the war is over. Schindler goes to a Nazi leader's office, knocks on his door, and says, "I think it's time for the guards to come into the factory."

Hundreds of workers, managers, and guards gather on the floor and in the balconies of the huge factory. Schindler stands on a skywalk and addresses everyone. He announces the end of the war and tells his workers that they are now free to go. Everyone is stunned into stillness. He confesses: "I am a member of the Nazi Party. I am a profiteer of slave labor. I am a criminal." Schindler turns to address the Nazi guards who are standing on a high platform to one side. He acknowledges that the Nazi commandant has been ordered to kill all the Jews before the guards retreat from the factory. He tells the Nazis that now is their chance to kill everyone or to leave the factory and reject the identity of murderer. After moments of tense silence, all the Nazis file out. Schindler turns back to the workers and says, "In honor of the countless victims among your people I ask that we observe three minutes of silence." The camera moves in on Schindler who, with tears in his eyes, bows and makes the sign of the cross across the Nazi pin on his lapel. He puts his hands together in prayer.

As the silence begins, one worker, who is also a rabbi, Menasha Levartov (played by Ezra Dagan), stands in the middle of the crowd and begins to recite the Kaddish, an ancient Jewish prayer of grief and blessing. Soon, hundreds of workers are responding as they stand on the concrete floor. Some are hugging and crying as their voices join and move through the air in waves of shock, anguish, and relief. This profound and touching moment crafted by director Steven Spielberg is a dynamic living icon of interspiritual reality. Schindler, with a Christian background and a Roman Catholic wife, has not shown any overt religious behavior throughout the movie, but now he has hit bottom. His passion for life, his suffering, and his open heart have blended and burned through his defenses. We witness a successful Nazi businessman and a newly reconverted Roman Catholic man bow to a sacred Hebrew prayer while crossing himself with the sign of Christ's crucifixion. In this dramatic moment Schindler's consciousness radiates a holiness that transcends religious dogma and boundaries.

I will take some liberty here to interpret a trinitarian dimension to Oskar Schindler's experience as he crosses himself. For most of the film Schindler speaks openly about his primary goal in life: to make money. His secondary goal was sexual conquest and infidelity. But now he manifests First Person awareness. He is raw and open, with nothing to prove and nothing to gain or lose. He is in completely new territory, stepping off the edge of everything he has known. He has emptied himself of his greed and his sexual addiction. During his whole adult life he was willing to manipulate people and ignore

Nazi atrocities to accomplish his self-centered goals. Now, all his addictions and his ordinary identity have dissolved. He has entered the unknown of the Jewish-Christian "I AM," Thomas Merton's ineffable True Self.

But this moment is not detached from practical reality. As Schindler stands before the Nazis and the praying Jewish workers to cross himself, viewers are mindful that he has spent everything to save these one thousand Jews from death, and mindful too that he has recently returned to his marriage with his devout wife. He is about to return to an ordinary life that has been broken open and become extraordinary. As Schindler listens to the Hebrew chant, he knows that he has given up everything to love and to protect the workers. He's not worried. He is ready to give his life for those he loves. He has emptied himself into a boundless, totally inclusive love. To see Schindler make the gesture of the cross at that moment is to see someone step into the kenosis, the self-emptying of Christ—that state of consciousness we are calling the First Person of the Holy Trinity. He is letting go of who he thought he was and becoming someone new. He doesn't know who he is becoming, and he may die for this conversion, but he is willing to accept the risk.

Schindler also manifests the Second Person because his intensifying conversion to *care* has been accomplished through his interest and commitment to specific, embodied, I-thou relationships. Schindler's friendship with his Jewish accountant, Itzhak Stern (played by Ben Kingsley), has become the portal to a depth of unselfish love and friendship that Schindler had never experienced before. At first, Schindler treats Stern as a kind of object he can manipulate, an "it," a means to Schindler's primary goal of becoming rich. But by the time that he crosses himself in prayer, Stern is a dear friend for whom Schindler would die. Likewise, Schindler has been gradually converted to the world of I-Thou as a result of his many intense encounters with his Jewish laborers and also because he gradually realizes the depth of love that his wife has for him and how much he loves her.

Throughout the film Schindler becomes awakened to the personhood of his workers and his need for friendship. Before these final moments, when Schindler knows the war will soon end, he orders Stern to make sure the munitions the factory makes for the Nazis won't work. He quietly approaches Rabbi Levartov and tells him to hold a traditional Friday night Sabbath service, and he himself will supply the wine. And one day, knowing that time is short, Schindler paces back and forth in front of Itzhak Stern's desk, dictating the names of hundreds of workers, along with many of their relatives, who he wants to save from certain death. Gradually, he has committed their names and faces to a memory that is now resplendent with grief and care. His commitment and compassion for specific people have become the gateway to a love that transcends the particular relationships. From the trinitarian perspective, Schindler's I-thou experiences lead him to the transpersonal I-Thou, the Second Person that circulates within all of these relationships.

And Schindler manifests the Third Person of the Trinity, the Holy Spirit, as he allows his strong personal boundaries to dissolve into the community of Jewish workers. When we reach the dramatic moment of the Kaddish on the factory floor, it's obvious that Schindler has surrendered himself to the holy "among and between" of the Spirit's love. He confesses his Nazi identity, his distinction from the Jewish workers, at the same time relinquishing his separateness and joining the Jews in prayer. When he crosses himself at the brink of life and death, in the presence of the Nazis, we might say he is standing within the communion of being, the perichoresis that is the Holy Trinity, simultaneously distinct and in union. Schindler is not *thinking* about the Trinity in that factory. But he is dynamically abiding within the consciousness we call trinitarian. I can't help but think of the Pentecost story in the New Testament Book of Acts:

> When the day of Pentecost had come, they were all together in one place. And suddenly from heaven there came a sound like the rush of a violent wind, and it filled the entire house where they were sitting. Divided tongues, as of fire, appeared among them, and a tongue rested on each of them. All of them were filled with the Holy Spirit and began to speak in other languages, as the Spirit gave them ability. Now there were devout Jews from every nation under heaven living in Jerusalem. And at this sound the crowd gathered and was bewildered, because

each one heard them speaking in the native language of each.
. . . All were amazed and perplexed. (Acts 2:1–12)

When Schindler crosses himself in the midst of the Kaddish, he seems transfigured, becoming holiness itself as his ego dissolves. His mind and body instinctively express the transcendent in a Roman Catholic gesture, even as the Jews are expressing holiness in their own language. This is the mark and mind of the Holy Spirit: When people gather, aware they're in a life-and-death situation, they might still be simply themselves, with their own distinctive language and symbols, but at any moment they might become one in the Divine Spirit. It is the experience described by St. Paul: "Jews or Greeks, slaves or free . . . we were all made to drink of one Spirit" (1 Cor 12:13); and "There is no longer Jew or Greek, there is no longer slave or free, there is no longer male and female; for all of you are one in Christ Jesus" (Gal 3:28).

In moments like this, when we see as Christ sees, all of our requirements for who's "in" and who's "out" fall away. Thinking, categorizing, analyzing, and judging are stilled and the mind is emptied so the fullness of Divine Presence can be realized.

We have described how each Person of the Trinity is not a separate being, a separate god. That mistake would be called Tritheism—three gods who only *appear* as one. Likewise, within the living flame of Schindler's experience, the three dimensions of his consciousness are happening simultaneously. He is not sequentially walking through the arenas of emptying, opening to the sacred I-Thou, and participating in a unity of Spirit with his workers. Rather, his awareness is dancing in and among these Three Persons. He is emptying everything he has, and has become love incarnate.

The eighteen-hundred-year-old tradition of the Holy Trinity tells us that the ultimate reality in which we are created—and which is reflected in our consciousness—is three centers of Holy Presence manifesting as one—three centers inwardly circulating or dancing as one. The mind-bending paradox is that each of the three is also circulating within each of the others. So, we can say that the Second Person is radiating from the First and Third, and so on. Let us look again, as in Chapter 2, at the paradoxical symbol in this ancient image one often sees in old Christian churches (see Figure 11.1).

Figure 11.1. Black and white photo of stained glass at St. John's Church, Ashfield, Massachusetts. Photo by author.

The Father both is and is not the Son, and Christ both is and is not the Spirit. The rational mind has reached its limit of comprehension. We are created in the image of a God who creates the very possibility of reason from a boundless love that transcends reason. Our minds and hearts must become flexible, open-ended, and resilient in order to understand how something or someone can be both and neither, one and separate, human and Divine. Reason and faith in an unseen power of love have become one.

The Hindu tradition of Advaita Vedanta suggests that all interpersonal relationships—between people or between humans and Divine figures—are way stations on the journey to the One, a One that surpasses all distinctions on the relative level of reality. But the Holy Trinity has a different view of ultimate Reality. The Trinity is not a mere relative appearance that masks the face of the One. Schindler both is and is not a Nazi, is and is not only a Christian or a Jew. His ability to live these paradoxes in his defining moment reflects the ultimate dance of the perichoresis. The three and the one are always dancing—simultaneous, creative, eternal, and dynamic. Schindler is dancing, experiencing three dimensions of his human/Divine life at once. He is emptying himself (First Person), experiencing the particularity of mutual love with specific people (Second Person), and participating in a Spirit-inspired-and-led holy oneness with his Jewish workers (Third Person). These dimensions of spiritual awareness are not the same and not different. Schindler is not experiencing these dimensions in separate compartments of his consciousness. If this were so, he might be diagnosed as having multiple personality disorder. But that is not the case. We cannot reduce the One-in-Three or the Three-in-One.

In the factory scene Schindler is manifesting his coherent, integrated, individual self (with a specific historical identity as Oskar Schindler) while inwardly his awareness is circulating in the Divine. His heart and his consciousness have become fully enfolded in the Divine Mystery of the incarnation. Schindler's three entry points of contact with the Divine are perfectly attuned, because his faith and his intention are manifesting his largest, most authentic, inclusive Self.

Everyone must leave the factory by midnight, even though most have nowhere to go. As the workers prepare for Schindler's departure, one prisoner donates the gold in his tooth and a friend melts it into a ring and inscribes it to Schindler. In the last scene Schindler stands outside the factory, ready to step into his car and leave. He knows he'll be treated as a criminal by the conquering Soviets and Americans. Hundreds of workers surround him. Itzhak Stern steps forward, hands Schindler the ring, and says, "It's Hebrew from the Talmud. It says, 'Whoever saves one life saves the world entire.'"

Schindler collapses into Stern's arms, sobbing, "I could have got more out. I could have got more out." As Schindler cries, standing near the trunk of the car that will take him and his wife away from the camp, scores of workers surround and hug him. A woman worker receives and prepares three prisoner's striped uniforms and gives them to Schindler and his wife. They are then driven away, in disguise as

Jewish prisoners wearing the flimsy uniforms featuring the Star of David on the lapel. As a Christian, I imagined that Jesus would have done the same, proud of his Jewish heritage and even on the cross wondering if he could have saved more. Even on the cross, Jesus assigned no blame—only a boundless generosity as he dies alongside two thieves and says of his murderers, "Forgive them. They don't know what they are doing" (Lk 23:34). In the dance of Schindler's consciousness, he has become transparent to Jesus Christ, who gives his life for others.[1]

We can see in this beautifully crafted and acted movie that the trinitarian consciousness is not only about one person's inner life and personal consciousness. Schindler did not go alone into the wilderness or into a monastery to realize himself as a whole person in the Spirit. He almost certainly did not spend twenty minutes a day meditating. Schindler's whole story is on a public stage in the midst of intense depravity, compassion, danger, and suffering.

Schindler's List portrays a universal drama of goodness and evil. The Nazis manifest the archetype of evil, and Oskar Schindler evolves into an archetype of goodness. Rabbi Levartov manifests the courage and true grit of a faithful person who is thrown into the pit of death yet continues to pray and to radiate God's presence. The rabbi sings for the Light that is within us all, one that is latent in the Nazis and yet beginning to shine even in them as they drop their weapons and leave the factory.

As Schindler and his wife are driven away, hundreds of workers flow around the car in silent tribute. The last scene is a Pentecost of love.

---

[1] S. Mark Heim suggests that "we might think of the single 'I' of the godhead as a kind of super-consciousness that arises from the three persons being 'of one mind.' On the other side, we could think of the three persons as distinct 'organs' within one consciousness, rather like one software program running on a network of three linked processors." S. Mark Heim, *The Depths of the Riches: A Trinitarian Theology of Religious Ends* (Grand Rapids, MI: Eerdmans, 2001), 158.

Acknowledgments

I could say that I wrote this book, but in fact a wellspring of friends and teachers are circulating through this "I." My dear grandparents, Fred and Leona Radenz, are here. Abiding in their German Lutheran tradition, they introduced me to Jesus. The Carmelite monks of The Common in Peterborough, New Hampshire, taught me how to access the timeless contemplative writings of St. John of the Cross and St. Teresa of Avila and pointed me onward to other Christian mystics such as Meister Eckhart and Thomas Merton. I am forever grateful to my friend and mentor, Fr. Henri Nouwen, who opened my heart to a new and living depth of relationship with Jesus. Thanks go to all the Buddhist teachers in the Zen, Pure Land, Vipassana, and Tibetan traditions who helped me understand the kenosis of Christ as an actual experience. I offer a bow of thanks to my shakuhachi teachers, David Duncavage and Yodo Kurahashi Sensei. I first glimpsed this pathway to trinitarian awareness through the work of Raimundo Panikkar and S. Mark Heim. Thank you for your pioneering theology. Several friends listened and gave feedback as my ideas took shape. I particularly want to thank Daniel Berlin for his insights into Jewish mysticism.

I am grateful to my agent, Arnie Kotler, and to Robert Ellsberg and Jon Sweeney at Orbis Books for honoring this vision of the Holy Trinity and for providing excellent editorial advice.

Words are not adequate to express the depth of my gratitude and love for one of my great editors, Rev. Dr. Margaret Bullitt-Jonas, who happens to be married to me. Throughout the fifteen-year process of writing this book I have tried to live the Trinity in all my relationships. Thank you, Margaret, for being my sounding board as I've

to understand trinitarian consciousness and for being so patient and discerning with me when I lost my way.

Since 1994 I have hosted contemplative groups at the Empty Bell sanctuary, located first in Watertown and now in Northampton, Massachusetts. I dedicate this book to each of the hundreds of dear fellow seekers who have come to the Empty Bell to meditate, to pray, and to share in the Holy and Eternal Presence who lives within and among us. I am blessed by your honesty, wisdom, and trust.

Glossary

Abba (Aramaic and Hebrew): Father or Daddy, the name Jesus used for God

aionios zoe (Greek): eternal life

amorphia (Latin): formlessness

amor ipse notitia est (Latin): knowing that is infused with love

anatman (Sanskrit): no-self

anaesthesia (Latin): used by Evagrius (345–99) to indicate a mind that is completely free of attachments to the material world and to self-centered thoughts and opinions

Anthropocene: the epoch that begins with the start of significant human impact on the earth's geology and ecosystems, including the anthropogenic crisis of climate change

Apollinarianism: an early Christian heresy that asserted that Jesus did not have a human soul, that his soul-place was occupied by the eternal Logos

Apophatic (Greek): without images; also called *via negativa,* the perception of the divine reality beyond the realm of ordinary perception

Arianism: an early Christian heresy that asserted Jesus was more mortal than divine

Attachment: This word is commonly used differently in psychological and spiritual discourse. Psychologically, emotional bonding, especially in infancy and childhood, is critically important. Attachment theory explains how the parent-child relationship emerges and influences subsequent development. In spiritual discourse, attachment is often used as a negative concept, describing a person's excessive bonding to ideas, thoughts, and beliefs. Unless otherwise indicated, I use the latter meaning in spiritual and religious discourse.

Begotten: not made of material substances but born directly from the Creator; in the Creed of Nicaea, Jesus Christ is said to be begotten

Big Bang: the moment of creation from nothing about fourteen billion years ago; called the Great Flaring Forth by Passionist priest Thomas Berry

capax infiniti (Latin): capable of perceiving and manifesting infinity

Ch'an: indicates Chinese pronunciation of Zen, a sect of Buddhism that focuses on meditation

Christ (from the Greek *Christos*): the eternal aspect of Jesus of Nazareth

circumincessio (Greek): mutual indwelling; the interdependent relationship of the Persons of the Trinity

Cloud of Unknowing: title of a book on Christian contemplation by an anonymous fourteenth-century Anglican

compunctio amoris (Latin): tears of pure transcendent love

compunctio timoris (Latin): sacred tears, the gift of tears

contemplatio (Latin): falling silent into the boundless open sky of nondual Christ awareness

Dear Far-Nearness: name of God used by Marguerite Porete (d. 1310)

desolación (Spanish): state of profound spiritual emptiness that amounts to a unity with God, used by St. John of the Cross

detachment: contemplative practice in which one lets go of or creates a space around objects of awareness

dilatantur (Latin): a mind that is infinitely enlarged in contemplation; word used by Gregory the Great

divinization (Greek; *theosis*): a transformative meditative process leading to union with God; a key spiritual practice in the Eastern Orthodox and Eastern Catholic Churches

Docetism: an early Christian heresy that asserted Jesus only appeared to be human but was not really human

Ein Sof (Hebrew): God prior to any material or spiritual manifestation, the Endless One (*she-en lo tiklah*), the unending, or Infinity, a direct experience of the sacred in the Jewish mystical tradition of the Kabbalah

Elohim (Hebrew): a masculine plural word used for God

Emmanuel (Hebrew): God among us

Eutychianism: an early Christian heresy that asserted Jesus was more divine than mortal

Filius (Latin): Son, the Second Person of the Trinity

Gentiles: non-Jews

Gnophos (Greek): thick darkness where God dwells

Gospels: the good news, the New Testament, along with various letters, the canon of stories about Jesus Christ

Gregory of Nazianzus: fourth-century mystical theologian of the Eastern Orthodox church

Gregory of Nyssa: fourth-century representative of the mysticism of darkness

Hagios Pneuma (Greek): Holy Spirit

heresy: belief contrary to orthodox doctrine

hypostasis (Greek): a being who is conscious, can use language, contemplate eternity, and form an I-thou relationship

I-Thou or I-You: a direct interpersonal encounter between a person and the Divine (Buber)

I-thou or I-you: a direct interpersonal encounter between a person and any other (Buber)

Ichion JuButsu (Japanese): to become a Buddha in one sound

imago Dei (Latin): image of God

imago Trinitatis (Latin): the inward image of the Trinity in which we are created

indiferencia (Spanish): used by St. John of the Cross to indicate a state of profound spiritual emptiness that amounts to a unity with God

Kaddish: Jewish mourner's prayer to express praise to God

kataphatic (Greek): with images

kenosis (Greek): self-emptying, dimension of contemplative prayer whereby the presence of God comes to a person who has detached from all that is not God; Christ's kenosis (Phil 2:6) is an actual experience of holiness that is available to all

Komuso (Japanese): Japanese mendicant monks of the Fuke school of Zen Buddhism who flourished during the Edo period of 1600–1868. They played shakuhachi as a spiritual practice.

lectio divina (Latin): sacred contemplative reading of scripture

Lichtung (German): complete clearing and opening of awareness; term used by Heidegger

Logos (Greek): Word, name for the eternal Christ who was present at the Great Flaring Forth

Mahayana (Sanskrit): Great Vehicle, branch of Buddhism whose ideal archetype is the bodhisattva, one who seeks complete enlightenment for the benefit of all beings

meditatio (Latin): silent reflection on scripture, images, memories, or music

metanoia (Greek): spiritual transformation, change of heart and perspective toward the good

methexis (Greek): participation, being transformed in Christ through grace that comes by participating in the Spirit; term used by Orthodox theologians

nada (Spanish): nothing; term used by St. John of the Cross to indicate state of profound spiritual emptiness that amounts to a unity with God

Namaste (Sanskrit): God in me addresses God in you

nondual consciousness: a quality of awareness in which subject and object are not separate

Nous (Greek): mind, the capacity for mental perception and consciousness, mind as the source and context of thinking, remembering, intending, feeling, and understanding

Pater (Latin): Father, the First Person of the Trinity

perichoresis (Greek): dance-around of Love, early Christian definition of God

phos (Greek): revelation of light

rima contemplationis (Latin): flashes of divine light received in contemplation

Ruach (Hebrew): holy breath or spirit

Sabbath: a day committed to sacred rest, prayer, meditation, and contemplation

self (small "s"): the solid ego, conditioned by human history and personal chronology

Self (capital "S"): a self that has been transformed and become transparent to divinity

Son of God: a term used in the Jewish and Christian traditions; the term "sons of God" occurs in Genesis 6:1, in Hebrew, *ben Elohim*; for Christians this name refers to Jesus Christ

Son of Man (Greek: *Anthropos*): literally, Son of Human

spiritual bypass: using spiritual practices to bypass worldly responsibilities and relationships, a term made popular by clinical psychologist John Welwood

Spiritus Sanctus (Latin): Holy Spirit, the Third Person of the Trinity

Suizen (Japanese): Blowing Zen, a Buddhist practice of playing shakuhachi flute as a means of attaining Enlightenment

superessential unity: a term applied to the One by the Platonic philosophers, especially Proclus; this is a sense of unity which transcends material reality, unity that is beyond thought.

theoria (Greek): direct vision of God, union with God not mediated by words or images, contemplation

tov (Hebrew): good; in the Genesis story of creation, God creates all things and pronounces everything as good

transparency: psycho-spiritual term for when the walls of a person's ego-self can be seen through, into the Presence of God; a person who is transparent in this way is a living truth, never having to lie

True Self: the consciousness of someone who has transcended the ego-self, the mortal/eternal awareness that Jesus exemplifies; term used by Thomas Merton

vestigia Trinitatis (Latin): the marks and images of the Trinity in all things

via negativa (Latin): journey into the darkness of God by emphasizing what God is not

Vipassana: school of Buddhist practice derived from the Theravāda tradition of Southeast Asia in which the meditator endeavors to attain insight into the three marks of existence: suffering, non-self, and impermanence. The archetypal ideal is the *arahant*, who has gained insight into the true nature of existence and achieved enlightenment.

YHWH (Hebrew): name for God

Zen sickness: attachment to emptiness

Index

About the Author

Robert A. Jonas, EdD (Harvard University) and MTS (Weston Jesuit School of Theology), is founder and director of the Empty Bell, a contemplative sanctuary in Northampton, Massachusetts, which features an emphasis on Buddhist-Christian dialogue and the arts. Jonas is an author, musician, environmental activist, and retreat leader.

A Christian in the Carmelite tradition, he has also received spiritual formation with Buddhist teachers. He is a student of Suizen, the Japanese shakuhachi bamboo flute, a member of the Society for Buddhist-Christian Studies and the Eckhart Society, and past board member of the Kestrel Land Trust and the Henri Nouwen Society. He is a visiting lecturer at the Northwind Seminary, and author of several books and articles including *The Essential Henri Nouwen* and *Rebecca: A Father's Journey from Grief to Gratitude.* One of Jonas's shakuhachi albums, "Blowing Bamboo," is available on iTunes. For more information, visit emptybell.org